ABRAHAM LINCOLN

CIVIL WAR STORIES

HEARTWARMING STORIES ABOUT OUR MOST BELOVED PRESIDENT

COMPILED AND EDITED BY

JOE WHEELER

HOWARD BOOKS
A DIVISION OF SIMON & SCHUSTER, INC.
New York • Nashville • London • Toronto • Sydney • New Delhi

Howard Books
A Division of Simon & Schuster, Inc.
1230 Avenue of the Americas
New York, NY 10020

First Howard Books hardcover edition June 2013

HOWARD and colophon are trademarks of Simon & Schuster, Inc.

For information about special discounts for bulk purchases,
please contact Simon & Schuster Special Sales at
1-866-506-1949 or business@simonandschuster.com.

The Simon & Schuster Speakers Bureau can bring authors to your live event.
For more information or to book an event, contact the Simon & Schuster Speakers
Bureau at 1-866-248-3049 or visit our website at www.simonspeakers.com.

Designed by Renato Stanisic

Manufactured in the United States of America

10   9   8   7   6   5   4

Library of Congress Cataloging-in-Publication Data
   Abraham Lincoln Civil War stories : heartwarming stories about our
most beloved president / compiled and edited by Joe Wheeler. —First
Howard Books hardcover edition.
     pages   cm
   Includes bibliographical references.
   1. Lincoln, Abraham, 1809–1865—Anecdotes.   2. Presidents—United
States—Anecdotes.   3. Lincoln, Abraham, 1809–1865—Miscellanea.
4. Presidents—United States—Miscellanea.   I. Wheeler, Joe L.
   E457.15A1525 2013
   973.7092—dc23   2013005259

ISBN 978-1-4767-0286-5
ISBN 978-1-4767-0287-2 (ebook)

CONTENTS

PART TWO

�֎

CIVIL WAR—THE EARLY YEARS

PART THREE

※

CIVIL WAR—THE LATER YEARS

PART FOUR
❋
TO LIVE ON IN HEARTS IS NOT TO DIE

EPILOGUE

NOTES

Never in my writing career has such a thing happened before—
and on the same subject to boot. Back in 2008, Denny Boultinghouse
of Howard/Simon & Schuster guided my biography,
Abraham Lincoln: A Man of Faith and Courage, through to completion.
Now, five years later, Denny's wife, Philis Boultinghouse, Senior Editor
at Howard, has made possible this monumental book,
Abraham Lincoln Civil War Stories.
Without their guiding hands,
it is doubtful these two books would ever have been born.
Thus it gives me great joy to dedicate this book to

PHILIS AND DENNY BOULTINGHOUSE

It is significant that when the great Lincoln Memorial in Washington, D.C., was dedicated in 1922, out of all the thousands of Lincoln poems that had been written, only one was deemed worthy to be the Dedicatory Piece: Edwin Markham's "Lincoln, the Man of the People." Lines from it—especially the last one—have become iconic around the world. Consequently, I felt it imperative that it should anchor this definitive book of Lincoln war stories.

From an original unretouched negative made in 1864, at the time Lincoln commissioned Ulysses S. Grant as lieutenant general and commander of all armies of the Union.

INTRODUCTION

LINCOLN, THE MAN OF THE PEOPLE

Edwin Markham (1852–1940)

When the Norn-Mother saw the Whirlwind Hour,
    Greatening and darkening as it hurried on,
She bent the strenuous heavens and came down
    To make a man to meet the mortal need.
She took the tried clay of the common road—
    Clay warm yet with the genial heat of the Earth,
Dashed through it all a strain of prophecy;
    Then mixed a laughter with the serious stuff.
    It was a stuff to wear for centuries,
A man that matched the mountains, and compelled
    The stars to look our way and honor us.

The color of the ground was in him, the red earth;
    The tang and odor of the primal things—
    The rectitude and patience of the rocks;
The gladness of the wind that shakes the corn;
    The courage of the bird that dares the sea;
    The justice of the rain that loves all leaves;
    The pity of the snow that hides all scars;

The loving-kindness of the wayside well;
The tolerance and equity of light
That gives as freely to the shrinking weed
As to the great oak flaring to the wind—
To the grove's low hill as to the Matterhorn
That shoulders out the sky.
And so he came
From prairie cabin up to Capitol,
One fair Ideal led our chieftain on.
Forevermore he burned to do his deed
With the fine stroke and gesture of a king.
He built the rail-pile as he built the State,
Pouring his splendid strength through every blow,
The conscience of him testing every stroke,
To make his deed the measure of a man.

So came the Captain with a mighty heart:
And when the step of Earthquake shook the house,
Wrenching the rafters from their ancient hold,
He held the ridgepole up, and spiked again
The rafters of the Home. He held his place—
Held the long purpose like a growing tree—
Held on through blame and faltered not at praise.
And when he fell in whirlwind, he went down
As when a kingly cedar green with boughs
Goes down with a great shout upon the hills,
And leaves a lonesome place against the sky.

IT TOOK MORE THAN 150 YEARS

Joseph Leininger Wheeler

Yes, it has taken that long for this collection of stories about Lincoln to become a reality. One hundred of it being our family contributions. My late mother, Barbara Leininger Wheeler (born in 1912), spent her entire lifetime collecting and performing (as a stage-performing elocutionist) thousands of pages of short stories, poetry, and readings. And she loved Lincoln more than all the rest of our presidents put together. In this, she is anything but unique, for it is still true today, of all age groups, that Lincoln dominates the presidential market. Just look at the rows and rows of books about Lincoln on bookstore shelves.

Most Americans don't realize that the same phenomenon remains true for short stories written *about* Lincoln. Reason being that few people know they even exist! In fact, I did an exhaustive search through generations of high school literature textbooks to see how many Lincoln stories have been picked up by textbook editors. I found only two: one, a chapter from Carl Sandburg's monumental biography of Lincoln's life, and the other, Bailey and Walworth's "He Loved Me Truly."

One reason for this is that most Lincoln stories weren't written by academics but by men and women from America's heartland, and they were kept alive by oral tradition. At virtually every school, civic, or church function, elocutionists of all ages would recite the most beloved stories, poems, and readings of the age. Sadly, today that tradition is all but extinct.

Indeed, up until the late 1800s, it was virtually a given that if a public speaker, politician, or minister alluded to any of three works (the Bible, Bunyan's *Pilgrim's Progress,* or the *McGuffey Readers*), most everyone, young or old, in the audience would catch the allusion. That is no longer true. Just watch the *Jeopardy!* programs each evening: There is no longer any cultural denominator that our culture shares. Not even the Bible. In cultural tests I've administered to various groups through the years, the only two genres that register at all on people's radar screens are sports and media trivia.

SO HOW DID THESE STORIES SURVIVE?

First of all, they survived through oral transmission. Virtually all of them are based on true incidents in Lincoln's life. During the first couple of generations after his passing, these stories thrived in the American heartland, many being passed down from one elocutionist to another. However, not until the 1880s did very many get written down.

In my own lifetime spent searching (as a story archeologist) for these precious vanishing Lincoln stories (they continue to crumble out of existence with each day that passes), I have found stories 1) still in the oral tradition, 2) handwritten, 3) carbons, 4) typewritten, 5) spirit-duplicated (if you're older you'll remember purple fingers and hands), 6) mimeographed (such a gooey mess to work with!), 7) printed, 8) computer-typed, and, of course, 9) clipped out of magazines, newspapers, and books. If you were to paw through my story archives, you'd find them all! Early magazine editors did the most to keep these stories alive. I unearthed the majority of the strongest Lincoln stories in older magazines. And now, with print increasingly on the defensive, surviving copies are increasingly harder to find.

At the very pinnacle of my personal bucket list is this: *Put together a definitive collection of the most memorable Lincoln stories ever written before I die.* And this collection is the result. I know of no other person who has ever amassed a comparable collection.

If you check the acknowledgments, you'll discover that the bulk of the surviving Lincoln stories were printed during the period I call the Golden Age of Stories (1880s through the 1950s). Ever since television and the digital age thundered in upon us, the magazines that enabled writers to earn a living by specializing in stories that internalized core values have, one after another, been forced to either close their doors or specialize in contemporary social media instead.

AND NOW?

It is my earnest hope that you will discover in these simple but moving stories answers to some of your own deeper questions about life and its meaning. In these stories—far more than in Lincoln history and biography—you will begin to understand why Lincoln continues to grow in stature around the world. And you will find virtually everything in these stories amazingly relevant to today's day-to-day problems and challenges.

You may wish to access my recent biography, *Abraham Lincoln: A Man of Faith and Courage* (New York: Howard/Simon & Schuster, 2008), so that you may better understand life and times during the bloodiest war in our history. Many years of my life went into the evolution of that biography, written not just for the academic or historian but for the average person who seeks to find in but one book the essence of our greatest American.

So welcome aboard! I would love to hear from you, and especially about your reactions to these stories. You may reach me at:

Joe L. Wheeler, Ph.D.
P.O. Box 1246
Conifer, CO 80433
www.joewheelerbooks.com

THE FRONTIER YEARS

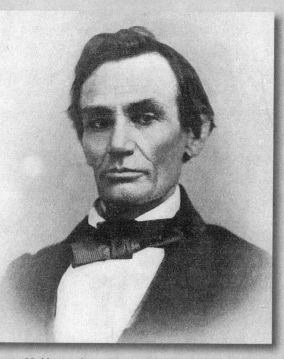

Halftone plate engraved by H. Davidson from an ambrotype made a few days after the Lincoln-Douglas debate in Galesburg, Illinois, October 7, 1858.

Of all the pre–Civil War poems that captured the turbulent times that smouldered into the raging four-year conflagration, famed poet, critic, essayist, editor, diplomat, and professor James Russell Lowell's "Once to Every Man and Nation" stands alone. Lowell, a fervent admirer of Lincoln and a deeply committed abolitionist, wrote this seminal poem (as the core of an abolitionist tract, The Present Crisis*) in 1845. Most of us know this poem only because it is in our hymnals, but if you reread it now against the backdrop of the generation preceding the Civil War, and the slave issue that refused to die, you will see why the Civil War was almost predetermined.*

ONCE TO EVERY MAN AND NATION

JAMES RUSSELL LOWELL (1819–1891)

Once to every man and nation
Comes the moment to decide,
In the strife of truth with false-hood,
For the good or evil side;
Some great cause, God's new Messiah,
Offering each the bloom or blight,
And the choice goes by forever
'Twixt that darkness and that light.

So the Evil's triumph sendeth,
With a terror and a chill,
Under continent to continent,
The sense of coming ill,
And the slave, where'er he cowers,
Feels his sympathies with God
In hot tear-drops ebbing earthward,
To be drunk up by the sod.

Then to side with truth is noble
When we share her wretched crust,
Ere her cause bring fame and profit,
And 'tis prosperous to be just;
Then it is the brave man chooses,
While the coward stands aside,
'Till the multitude make virtue
Of the faith they had denied.

By the light of burning martyrs,
Christ, Thy bleeding feet we track,
Toiling up new Calvaries ever
With the cross that turns not back;
New occasions teach new duties,
Time makes ancient good uncouth;
They must upward still and onward,
Who would keep abreast of truth.

Though the cause of evil prosper,
Yet 'tis truth alone is strong;
Though her portion be the scaffold,
And upon the throne be wrong;
Yet that scaffold sways the future,
And, behind the dim unknown,
Standeth God within the shadow,
Keeping watch above His own.

COUNTDOWN TO THE CIVIL WAR

JOSEPH LEININGER WHEELER

As, in spite of some weaknesses, Republicanism is the sole hope of a sick world, so Lincoln with all his foibles, is the greatest character since Christ.

—JOHN HAY, U.S. SECRETARY OF STATE

Lincoln was a humanitarian as broad as the world. He was bigger than his country—bigger than all the presidents put together.

We are still too near his greatness, but after a few centuries more our posterity will find him considerably bigger than we do. His genius is still too strong and powerful for common understanding, just as the sun is too hot when its light beams directly on us.

—LEO TOLSTOY

It is said that "no man is a hero to his valet," yet even after John Hay had served as Lincoln's private secretary all during the war, Lincoln remained his hero; so much so that Hay and his fellow secretary, John Nicolay, spent many years after the war writing their monumental biography, *Abraham Lincoln: A History*. After all these years, it is still the greatest Lincoln biography of them all.

I have arranged the Lincoln Civil War stories in chronological sequence, so that they mirror the times they chronicle. Consequently, there has been no conscious effort to place them according to their relative emotive power. Each author's work will speak for itself.

LINCOLN: A WORK IN PROGRESS

During the years of research that went into my Lincoln biography, I discovered that the iconic Lincoln the world so reveres today was anything but a full-blown product, but rather a roughhewn work in progress who evolved as long as he lived.

Quite candidly, my greatest fear during the years of research was that I would find significant cracks in his character, validation of the attacks of critics who even today caricature him, some portraying him as a totally secular man devoid of spiritual principles. I never found anything to substantiate such assumptions. But when I concluded my research, the monolith still towered into the sky, devoid of fissures.

I did discover that though Lincoln was steeped deeply in the Bible during his growing-up years (hence the rhythm of the King James translation rings throughout his Civil War speeches), by the time he became an adult, he'd become thoroughly disenchanted with the vicious infighting between Christian sects; so much so that though he faithfully attended Presbyterian church services with his wife, Mary, he never officially joined any church. As for his reasons for not doing so, he often declared that he was searching for a church that had as its sole creed Christ's answer to the question, "What do I have to do to make it into the kingdom?" *"You must love the Lord your God with all your heart, all your soul, and all your mind!" This is the first and greatest commandment. A second is equally important: "Love your neighbor as yourself." All the other commandments and all the demands of the prophets are based on these two commandments* (Matthew 22:37–40).

Lincoln never found such a church. Interestingly enough, during the years of research for my two biographies of St. Nicholas, I discovered that the Early Christian Church had as its sole creed what is called the

Didache, "The Way of Life," which is in essence an expansion of Christ's injunction in Matthew 22:37–40. Not until Emperor Constantine politicized the church after the Council of Nicaea did Christianity disintegrate into snarling sects, each with its own doctrines and creeds.

So it was that, in essence, Lincoln put God on hold for close to twenty years. It would not be until the untimely death of his little son Eddie, who died of consumption (tuberculosis), that Lincoln gradually clawed his way back to a deeply personal relationship with God.

Today, we have a misperception that the Civil War did not begin until the firing on Fort Sumter in Charleston Harbor, early April 1861. Not so. The Civil War began much earlier; the Fort Sumter attack was merely the culmination of treasonable acts spread out over many years.

After his ignominious defeat as a congressman, discredited by his principled stand against the Mexican-American War—he felt it was merely a power grab for more land—Lincoln retreated into his circuit-riding law practice and let the rest of the world drift by.

Then, five long years later, one morning in mid-May 1854, Lincoln was jolted out of his trance by the realization that the nation he loved was breaking apart. The two Americas (one slave and one free) were once again at each other's throats. It had happened many times before, and always the North had backed down and agreed to flimsy cut-and-paste compromises. But this time, 235 years after slavery had been introduced, Lincoln realized that something bigger than himself, a cause worth dying for, was calling him into service. The catalyst proved to be the epic debates with the so-called Little Giant, Stephen Douglas. The two friends had debated each other many times before, and Douglas had always won, so he must have felt he had little to fear by agreeing to debate Lincoln in towns all across Illinois. But the Lincoln he now faced had been reborn in the ashes of defeat. By the time the debates ended, Lincoln had become a household name across the country.

Then the dominoes began to fall, one after another, as the countdown to Fort Sumter began. In the most unlikely of all possible scenarios, Lincoln won the Republican Party's nomination for president and then won

the national election as the southern members of Congress began packing
their bags and leaving. As the awesome burden of the presidency and the
breaking apart of the republic settled upon his shoulders, Lincoln was
driven to his knees, for he now realized that only God could sustain him,
guide him, and comfort him in the awful days ahead.

In the throes of this inner anguish, the beaten-down Lincoln arose
like the proverbial phoenix and, virtually single-handedly, almost alone,
steered the ship of state through the hell of the Civil War.

And it was in the midst of this Götterdämmerung that these Lincoln
stories were born.

The boy Lincoln reading by the fireside. Painting by an unknown artist.

HOW LINCOLN PAID FOR HIS FIRST BOOK

Earle H. James

Even at the end of his life, when Lincoln sifted through the passing years, nothing he'd ever owned meant more to him than that long-ago water-soaked book.

T he shadows were creeping heavily across the meadows and woodlands when a half-timid rap at the kitchen door of neighbor Crawford's farmhouse, and the good-natured "Come in," brought over the threshold a face homelier than the Creative Artist usually lets drop from His hand; but the manliness and soul-purpose already alight, went far to make up for any lack of grace.

The boy's face was downcast and troubled, and his "good evening" so short that Mr. Crawford replied, "Why, good evening to you, Abe. What on earth ails you? Hain't lost your last friend, have you Abe?"

"No, the case is not so bad as that, Mr. Crawford."

And as Abe hesitated for a moment, silent and perplexed there was nothing in the overgrown youth other than the unquenchable light of his great, groping soul, to suggest the future greatest man of his country. Tall for his years, grotesquely awkward, his big unshod feet showing up far below his dangling overalls, he was a sorry picture, as he stood, holding a book, crumpled, discolored, well-nigh as unkempt as himself.

"I can't tell you, Mr. Crawford, how sorry I am; a mishap has befallen your book. By the light on the hearthstone I read it last night until the fire went out; then up in the loft, until my candle burned out."

"And did you drop off to sleep, readin', Abe?" asked Mr. Crawford, with a merry twinkle in his eye, "and then did the straw bed blaze up, and did you souse the book to put out the fire?"

For once there was no answering gleam of fun in Abe's clear eye, as he replied, "There wasn't a wink of sleep, Mr. Crawford, long as my candle held out to burn, for it's the most interesting book I ever read. I just devoured every word. But when my light gave out, there was nothing for me but just to lay the book on the bed close up against the logs, where I couldn't roll onto it. But a heavy rain set in after I got to sleep, and the cabin, you know, is none too tight. The rain poured through on the book and the bed, and when I woke up at daylight, both were soaked. Now I want you to tell me how much the book is worth."

"Worth! Well, I don't know. It might be worth seventy-five cents, Abe."

"I'm afraid that won't cover it, Mr. Crawford. Anyway, it's ruined, and I want to pay you every cent it's worth, some way. But you know I don't have any money. I can work it out if you are so minded. Will you be satisfied if I work for you three days?"

"That's just like you, Abe, my boy. You was always that way, not willin' to do a mean or unjust act, or a thing that you didn't think was right on the square with others, no matter how you suffered over it."

The three long days of work were at last done, in Abe's thorough way, and he was about to start for home, happy in the thought that he had fully repaid his neighbor for the damage to his book.

"You jest hold on, Abe," Mr. Crawford called out. "That ain't fair! I'm lettin' you pay for the book an' then keepin' it myself. You did as good a job as any worker on the farm, so that book belongs to you, not me."

The young backwoodsman was too much surprised and overjoyed at the thought of actually owning a book, and especially this book, for

any wordy expression of thanks, but he managed to let neighbor Crawford understand how greatly he appreciated this new turn that made him
owner of such a treasure. He, however, soon saw the justice of the trans-
action, and felt that it was fairly his.

The boy's big bare feet seemed light as he strode swiftly home through
the shadows across the Indiana prairie, holding tight to his precious book.
It was the story of the life of the great and good George Washington, and
told of the sacrifices, the unselfish patriotism and tireless devotion of the
Father of his Country. It found its way into the very depths of Abe's soul,
never to be lost until he, too, was called to greater service and sacrifice for
his country.

• • • •

When the years had gone by and Abraham Lincoln had, through the
guiding hand of Providence, become the savior of his country, this incident remained distinct in his memory. His friends often heard him say
that the possession of that book—the first he'd ever been able to call his
own—gave him more pride and joy than any other one thing in his entire
life.

Woodcut depicting Lincoln's home in Springfield, Illinois.

CHILDHOOD IN LINCOLN'S TOWN

Octavia Roberts Corneau

What would it have been like to grow up in Lincoln's hometown of Springfield, Illinois, and be able to ask neighbors, friends, and relatives about their firsthand memories of the Lincoln family?

Let's listen in!

When I was a little girl I lived in the prairie town of Springfield, Illinois, where Abraham Lincoln had made his home for the greater part of his manhood. I was born too late to know Lincoln, but the older men and women of the town, who were the friends of my grandparents, had been his friends and neighbors. From them I acquired a knowledge of our great townsman long before I ever opened a school book. It was a pleasant way to make the acquaintance of a historical figure.

Books will tell you that Lincoln first came to Springfield in 1837, after he had been admitted to the bar and was entitled to hang up a "shingle" announcing himself as a lawyer, but his first appearance among us was not as a lawyer, but as a pilot. I wish you could have heard the story as Springfield children used to hear it from an old lady we called Aunt Catherine.

Aunt Catherine was so old that she had looked on the face of La-fayette. She thought of Lincoln as having lived but yesterday. The little mirror that hung over her high-backed chair had been given to a member of her family by Washington. She made no use of the back of her chair, for she had been bred in a day when girls were not encouraged to loll. I wish you could have seen her with her bright, birdlike eyes and her straight spine and her delicate white hands as she told about Lincoln the pilot.

THE YOUNG PILOT

"You may not know," she would begin, "that we Springfield people once hoped to prove that the Sangamon River was navigable."

We would smile, for we knew the craftless river well—a shallow, muddy stream that lay a mile beyond our town.

"Yes, we actually hoped to prove that it would float a steamboat," Aunt Catherine would continue. "Capital was raised and a Captain Bogue sent to Cincinnati to purchase a steamboat, which he was to sail back through the waters of the Ohio, the Mississippi, the Illinois and finally over our own Sangamon. There was great excitement in town when we learned that the steamship *Talisman* had been bought, and that Captain Bogue had started back. All went well until the boat got as far as Beardstown; then the real difficulty lay before her, for now she must make her way through the snags of the Sangamon. Who was to pilot her?"

We waited to hear.

"At Beardstown, a young man in breeches much too short for his long legs got on board and said he knew the river. His name was known to no one; it was Abraham Lincoln. Lincoln brought the *Talisman* the rest of the way and landed it near a mill. Oh, what excitement there was in Springfield! All the people in town rode out to the river as fast as they could get there over the terrible roads. Most of us were on horseback, but some few were in fine carriages. We sang and cheered to think that a steamboat had come to us from the east. We did not know that it was the last time one was ever to make that long trip.

"Of course we could not do enough for the captain and his party. We took them all into town and gave them a fine ball. What an evening it was way back in 1832!"

"Did Lincoln dance at the ball?" some child would ask.

Aunt Catherine would stare. She was very much of an aristocrat. Her finely arched brows would go up and up. "Lincoln?" she would say in surprise. "Lincoln was only a common pilot. Naturally he was not invited; only gentlemen were bidden."

Could any story have impressed better upon us Lincoln's humble beginning?

Later, however, Lincoln was invited to Springfield balls. I knew that, for I saw an old invitation issued by the gentlemen of Springfield to the ladies, asking them to attend a dance at the American House, our best hotel in the early days. The name of the first gentleman was that of my grandfather, Nicholas Ridgely, and that of the last, Abraham Lincoln. By that time Lincoln was a practicing lawyer; moreover, he was a member of the legislature, one of what people called the "long nine."

The "long nine" were nine men who were all exceedingly tall. Old folk remembered their picking their way in single file through the mud to the church where the legislature met while the State House was being built.

Mr. Ninian Edwards was one of the "long nine" too. He lived in a fine old brick mansion. Every stick of his furniture had come from the East and had been made to order. Lincoln had been entertained in that fine house many a time. He had sat on the haircloth sofa with its embroidered back and courted Mary Todd, Mrs. Edwards's sister. He had been married to her between the folding doors of solid walnut.

How easily we Springfield children could picture the legislative parties given there, the wooing on the sofa, the wedding; for when I was a little girl the old mansion had become a private school. Every day I walked up the long path to the door that Lincoln had so often entered, recited my lessons in what had been Mrs. Edwards's fine conservatory, and when I needed correcting sometimes was spoken to by the principal in the soft gloom of the old drawing room where Lincoln and Mary Todd had been married.

From the fine old brick mansion Lincoln had led his bride to their first home: a room in the Globe Tavern. The remains of that old tavern stood across the street from the church I attended. I could look over there any Sunday morning and see where Lincoln and his bride had lived. It was easy to imagine him there, for a lady had told me a pretty story of Lincoln at the Globe. She had boarded there one winter when Lincoln was away at Congress, and she remembered his coming back at the close of the session and his progress through the tavern dining room, stopping to shake every outstretched hand. In those days the tavern rooms were heated by stoves, and the Congressman had not been above carrying up armfuls of wood for many of the ladies. How simple it all was and how easy after such stories to remember that Lincoln had been to Congress!

Of course Lincoln did not always live in a hotel. He had soon bought a modest house on the corner of Eighth and Jackson Streets. The house had belonged to the first rector of our church. I knew his granddaughter well. Once she let me see the deed conveying the house from Dr. Charles Dresser to Abraham Lincoln. Once one of Dr. Dresser's relatives, a very old woman and extremely deaf, told me how Lincoln had appeared at the rectory early one November morning in the rain and said in his homely parlance, "I want to get hitched up to Miss Todd tonight. Can you tie the knot, Doctor?"

THE LINCOLN HOUSE

I often saw Lincoln's house on Eighth and Jackson streets. It was open to the public as a memorial. Strangers could see only the lower rooms, but townsfolk, who knew the cordial custodian, could go anywhere, even up to Lincoln's own bedroom.

We all knew Mrs. Johnson, who had lived next door to the Lincoln house when she was a girl. She remembered well how Lincoln used to watch the baby for Mrs. Lincoln, pushing the child to and fro in a little buggy with one hand while he read a book, which he held in the other.

Mrs. Johnson could remember how "wild" and undisciplined Willie and Tad were and how devoted their father was to them. Once he had been seen with them in the drug store, treating the boys to soda water. As they were far from being rich, one glass had to do for both. First Willie had a long swig, then Tad!

Not until we had heard many such stories, which made Lincoln a dear and familiar figure, did any of us open a United States history; then of course we came upon Lincoln the world figure. How we glowed to think that Springfield had sent him forth as one of her own sons!

MEMORIES OF THE CANDIDATE

The first historical mention of Lincoln was likely to be as a candidate for the United States Senate. He had run against Stephen A. Douglas, the idol of the Democratic party, and, though he had been defeated, he became nationally well known owing to the seven great debates that he had held with Douglas in seven scattered towns of Illinois. To hear of the debates at first hand from men who had been to Ottawa, Freeport, Alton and the others was a wonderful experience. Nearly everybody in Illinois had managed to attend at least one of the seven. My Uncle Charles had gone as a boy to Ottawa. He had been too young to weigh the arguments for and against the extension of slavery, but was old enough to remember the occasion in great detail. How well he reproduced it all for us!

He would begin by describing the great crowd, the banners, the bands, the torches, the enormous excitement that ran through the mighty audience. Then he would picture himself as a little lad squeezing through the mob until he found a place in the front row, of his looking up into the face of Douglas as the Little Giant opened the debate. He made us see Douglas, small of stature with a head like a lion's and beautifully dressed, eloquent and polished. When Douglas finished—so my uncle would relate—there seemed to the audience nothing left for poor Abraham Lincoln to say.

At that point my uncle, being an excellent mimic, would show us how Lincoln got to his feet, and how awkwardly he faced the crowd; then my uncle would imitate Lincoln speaking in a high falsetto that carried in the open air. He said he began one address by saying, "Judge Douglas's argument is as thin as the shadow of the hen that crossed the road day before yesterday." A roar of laughter rolled up from the crowd.

Of course the greatest day in the history of Springfield was the day Lincoln was nominated for the Presidency. From then until his election Springfield was in a high state of excitement. The boys and girls bore their part during the tumult. One boy carried the telegram to Lincoln that announced the nomination. Others marched as Wide Awakes in the various parades. One of them hauled a cannon to Lincoln's door and asked him to christen it. When he left naming it to the boys they called it "Mary Lincoln" in honor of Lincoln's wife.

Many of the girls went to his farewell reception and described in years to come the beauty of Mrs. Lincoln's fine dress over hoop skirts and the cordiality of Lincoln's smile. When Lincoln left for Washington the young folk mingled with the elders to wave him farewell.

And all these memories are a much-prized heritage in the old town where I grew up.

Woodcut from 1873 depicting Sarah Bush Johnson Lincoln.

HE LOVED ME TRULY

B E R N A D I N E   B A I L E Y   A N D   D O R O T H Y   W A L W O R T H

The thirty-one-year-old bride had no idea of what she had tackled when she married her widowed childhood sweetheart, of the explosive potential of housing eight people from two different families in a room only eighteen feet square. Nor what her coming would mean to the scrawny ten-year-old boy named Abe.

T he bride rode with her husband on the high front seat of the jolting wagon. She was 31 years old. In 1819 that was middle-aged, for most pioneer women died early. It was a cold December day, and they were headed north toward forest country.

Yesterday Tom had come to her house in Elizabethtown, Kentucky, all the way from his Indiana farm. He had come straight to the point: "Miss Sally, I have no wife and you no husband. I came a-purpose to marry you. I knowed you from a girl and you knowed me from a boy. I've no time to lose. If you're willin', let it be done straight off."

That morning they had been married. The preacher wrote down that she, Sarah Bush Johnston, had been three years a widow, and that Tom's wife had died last winter. The horses and wagon Tom had borrowed waited outside. The wagon was piled high with her household goods, so that there was scarcely room for her three children. Tom had two children of his own. He hadn't told them he was bringing back a new mother. There was a shadow in Sarah's steady blue-gray eyes when she thought about that. Maybe they'd feel she didn't really belong.

A raft ferried the wagon across the half-frozen Ohio River. The air became colder; the wheels sank in the snow. After five days they came to a log cabin in a small clearing. It had no windows, and the door was only a deerskin-covered opening.

Tom called and a little boy ran out of the door. He was thin as a scarecrow and wore a ragged shirt and tattered deer-skin pants. The look in his eyes went to Sarah's heart. She got down from the wagon, opened her arms and folded him close.

"I reckon we'll be good friends," she said. "Howdy, Abe Lincoln."

She had never been in the wilderness before; she had known small-town comfort. This was a one-room cabin. Its floors were hard-packed dirt. The bedstead was crudely made of boards, with a mattress of loose cornhusks. The bedcovers were skins and cast-off clothing. Ten-year-old Abe and his 12-year-old sister slept on piles of leaves up in the loft. They climbed up to it by means of pegs fastened to the wall.

The furniture was a few three-legged stools and a table axed smooth on top. Dennis Hanks, an 18-year-old cousin of Tom's first wife, Nancy Hanks, was living with the family. He had been trying to cook with a Dutch oven, one battered pot and a couple of iron spoons.

Although she must have expected a place far better than this, all Sarah said was, "Tom, fetch me a load of firewood. I aim to heat some water."

This new stepmother with the rosy face and the bright curly hair wasted no time. As soon as the water steamed, she brought out of her own belongings a gourd full of homemade soap. Then, in front of the hot fire, she scrubbed Abe and his sister and combed their matted hair with her own shell comb.

When the wagon was unpacked, little Abe, who had not said a word, ran his bony fingers over such wonderful things as a walnut bureau, a clothes chest, a loom and real chairs. That night when he went to bed in the loft he did not find the leaves. Sarah had thrown them outdoors. In their place was a feather mattress, a feather pillow and warm blankets.

In a couple of weeks, a body wouldn't have known the place. Sarah worked hard, and she could make other people work, too—even Tom. He meant well but was likely to let things slide. She never said he must do thus and so. She was too wise and gentle. But somehow Tom found himself making a real door and window for the cabin. He laid a floor, filled the cracks between the logs, whitewashed the inside walls.

Sarah wove homespun cloth and made shirts for Abe, coloring them with dye she steeped out of roots and herbs. She made him deerskin breeches that fitted, moccasins and a coonskin cap. She held her mirror so he could see himself for the first time—and he said, "Land o' Goshen, is that *me?*"

Sometimes in the early morning when Sarah laid a new fire in the ashes, she got to thinking it was queer how things had come about. When Tom Lincoln had courted her 14 years ago, she had turned him down for Daniel Johnston. Tom had been married to Nancy Hanks, who had died. Now, after all these years, Tom and she were together again, with his children and her children to feed and care for.

The cabin was 18 feet square and there were eight people under its shabby roof. Somehow, Sarah felt, she must make them into a family that loved each other and felt as if they had always been together. There was plenty of chance for trouble, with the two sets of young 'uns who had never laid eyes on each other till now. Those first weeks, Sarah felt mighty anxious, especially about Abe.

Maybe, if it hadn't been for her, Abe wouldn't have lived to be a man. He had always grown so fast and never had enough to eat. But now, when he had eaten enough johnnycake and meat and potatoes that were cooked through, not just burned on top, he stopped looking so pinched. He wasn't so quiet anymore. Now that he had some flesh on his bones, he was fuller of fun than anybody. He learned to tell yarns, like his father.

Sometimes Sarah thought that she loved Abe more than her own children. But it was just that she knew, deep down in her heart, that Abe was somebody special who didn't belong to her but was hers to keep for a while.

When Abe was little, Tom hadn't minded his going to school. But now that the boy was older and stronger, Tom didn't see why he shouldn't stay home and chop down trees and thresh wheat or hire out to the neighbors for husking corn at 30 cents a day. Of course, he felt proud when the neighbors came to have Abe write their letters. The boy used the pen he had made from a buzzard's quill and the ink he'd made from brier-root. But Abe was "reachin' too fur" when he spent so much time reading books. Tom told Abe a man didn't need to know so almighty much to get along.

If Sarah hadn't taken Abe's part against his father, Abe wouldn't have had as much schooling as he did, though goodness knows it wasn't much. Abe would rather read than eat. He'd read in the morning, soon's it was light enough to see. He'd read in the evening when the chores were done. He walked 17 miles to borrow books from Lawyer Pitcher at Rockport: *Aesop's Fables*, *Robinson Crusoe*, *Pilgrim's Progress*, Shakespeare, *The Statutes of Indiana*.

When a book he'd borrowed was rained on, he worked three full days to pay for it. Once he gave a man 50 cents for an old barrel and found at the bottom of it Blackstone's *Commentaries*, a famous book on law. You'd think he'd found a gold mine. He began reading late at night by the fire. When Tom complained, Sarah said, "Leave the boy be." She always let him read as long as he wanted to. If he fell asleep there on the floor, she would get a quilt and wrap it gently around him.

He did his arithmetic with charcoal on a board. When the board got too black, he'd scrape it off and start again. If he read something he liked a lot, he'd write it down. He was always writing and was always running out of paper. After he wrote something, he'd read it out loud to Sarah by the fire, after Tom and the rest had gone to bed. "Did I make it plain?" he always asked her. She answered him as well as anybody could who didn't know how to read or write.

They told each other things they told nobody else. He had dark spells when he thought it was no use to hope and to plan. But Sarah knew Abe needed a lot of encouraging.

In 1830 Tom decided to look for better farm land in Illinois. Abe helped his father build the two-room cabin where Sarah and Tom were to spend the rest of their lives. The place was hardly built when the time came for Abe to leave home. He was now a grown man, 22 years old. He had a chance to clerk in Denton Offut's store over in New Salem.

At first he came home often. After he became a lawyer, he visited there twice a year. Every time Sarah saw him, it seemed as if his mind was bigger. Other folks' minds got to a place and then stopped, but Abe's kept on growing. He told her about his law cases, about his going to the state legislature and his marrying Mary Todd. After Tom died, in 1851, Abe saw to it that Sarah didn't want for anything.

When she heard Abe was going to Charleston for his fourth debate with Stephen A. Douglas, she went there, without saying a word to Abe. It would be enough—it had always been enough—just to watch him. She was one of the crowd on the street as the parade went by: oxen, carrying three men splitting rails, and a sign, "Honest Abe, the Rail Splitter."

Now here he came, riding in a shiny black carriage, and tipping his tall black hat right and left. Was that her Abe? She tried to make herself small, but he saw her and made the carriage stop. Then, right in front of everybody, he got out of the carriage, came over, put his arms around her and kissed her. Yes, that was her Abe.

She wasn't the crying kind, but alone where nobody could see her, she cried when he was elected President. In the winter of 1861, before he went to Washington, he crossed the state to see her and to say good-bye, coming by train and carriage in the mud and slush. He brought her some fine black cloth for a dress. It was really too beautiful to put the scissors into. She'd take it out and feel it once in a while.

Abe looked tired. He had a lot on his mind, but they had a fine talk. Even when they were silent, they still said things to each other, and he still had respect for what she thought. When he kissed her good-bye, he said he'd see her soon. But somehow she knew she wouldn't see him again.

Four years later, they came and told her he was dead. The newspapers wrote the longest piece about his real mother. That was as it should be. But some folks came and asked her what sort of boy Abe had been. She wanted to tell them, but it was hard to find the words. "Abe was a good boy," she said. "He never gave me a cross word or look." Then she added, "He loved me truly, I think."

Often, during the four years that remained to her, she would sit of an evening and think of Abe. She remembered him as a little boy. She was baking johnnycake for him. She was weaving him a shirt. She was covering him with a blanket when he had fallen asleep over his books.

Her death, on December 10, 1869, passed unnoticed by the nation. For many years she was not even mentioned by historians and biographers. More recently, the graves of Thomas and Sarah were marked with a suitable stone. Their home site has been made into a state park, with a reproduction of the two-room cabin that Abe had helped to build. Only in the last few years have Americans come to know that when Abraham Lincoln said, "All that I am I owe to my angel mother," he was speaking of Sarah—his beloved stepmother.

PART TWO

CIVIL WAR— THE EARLY YEARS

Drafting the Emancipation Proclamation. On September 22, 1862, he issued a preliminary proclamation, written some two months earlier. The final Proclamation of Emancipation was signed on January 1, 1863. Walter Taylor painted this depiction for Scribner's Magazine.

James Sloan Gibbons (1810–1892), a Delaware banker and abolitionist, wrote the following stirring poem on July 2, 1861, in response to Lincoln's urgent plea for three hundred thousand more recruits. The poem/song swept the North. As the hundreds of thousands of soldiers marched from battleground to battleground, drums keeping cadence and flags flying in the wind, they sang to while away the hours. So, as you read these lines, just imagine you were one of them, or a civilian listening to the tramp, tramp, tramp of hundreds of thousands of feet, literally shaking the ground (case in point, Elsie Singmaster's gripping story, "Mary Bowman of Gettysburg"), and imagine what this song must have sounded like coming from such a vast host of men! The same phenomenon was true with the armies of the South, who sang their own favorites (such as "Dixie") as they marched. It is indeed ironic that the soldiers fighting America's bloodiest war (more than 600,000 died) sang as they marched and around their campfires in the evenings.

THREE HUNDRED THOUSAND MORE

James Sloan Gibbons   July 2, 1862

We are coming, Father Abraham, three hundred thousand more,
From Mississippi's winding stream and from New England's shore;
We leave our ploughs and workshops, our wives and children dear,
With hearts too full for utterance, with but a silent tear;
We dare not look behind us, but steadfastly before:
We are coming, Father Abraham, three hundred thousand more!

If you look across the hill-tops that meet the northern sky,
Long moving lines of rising dust your vision may descry;
And now the wind, an instant, tears the cloudy veil aside,
And floats aloft our spangled flag in glory and in pride,
And bayonets in the sunlight gleam, and bands brave music pour:
We are coming, Father Abraham, three hundred thousand more!

If you look all up our valleys where the growing harvests shine,
You may see our sturdy farmer boys fast forming into line;
And children from their mother's knees are pulling at the weeds,
And learning how to reap and sow against their country's needs;

And a farewell group stands weeping at every cottage door:
We are coming, Father Abraham, three hundred thousand more!

You have called us, and we're coming, by Richmond's bloody tide
To lay us down, for Freedom's sake, our brothers' bones beside,
Or from foul treason's savage grasp to wrench the murderous blade,
And in the face of foreign foes its fragments to parade.
Six hundred thousand loyal men and true have gone before:
We are coming, Father Abraham, three hundred thousand more!

STALEMATE

JOSEPH LEININGER WHEELER

And so the war began. All assumed it would be over in no time—especially those living in the North. But it didn't work out that way. Lincoln went into the war feeling that since the North held the higher ground morally, God would grant the Union armies victory after victory, and the war would be over.

Month after month passed, and the slaughter only increased. Time after time, southern generals would miraculously snatch victory from the jaws of defeat, even when outnumbered by two- or three-to-one margins. It just didn't make sense to Lincoln. The war continued to be a stalemate, with neither side able to gain a lasting advantage over the other.

Then, the Lincolns' favorite son, little Willie, the light of their home and hope for the future (Eddie had died of consumption; Robert, always a bit distant, was away at Harvard; and Tad was, in the vernacular of the times, "slow"), came down with typhoid. Since tens of thousands of soldiers camped on both sides of the Potomac and generated a great deal of waste, uncontaminated drinking water was in increasingly short supply. What followed is so significant in terms of certain stories in this collection that I am referencing some pertinent passages from my Lincoln biography, *Abraham Lincoln: A Man of Faith and Courage*:

As the weeks passed, Willie's fever ebbed and returned. Each time it returned, it would get worse (and with it came diarrhea, painful cramps, internal hemorrhaging, vomiting, exhaustion, and delirium). His companion, Bud Taft, was constantly at his side, refusing to be parted from him. In early February, Tad came down with typhoid, too. Lincoln would come into the room, stand there drinking in the feverish face of his son, lean over to smooth the light brown hair, and go out without saying a word. Mary was up night and day with her two boys, generating dark circles under her eyes.

Newspapers were covering the story of Willie Lincoln, the little boy who had captured the city and nation's heart. Over and over people would ask, "Is there any hope?"

"Not any. So the doctors say."

Willie seemed better on Thursday morning, February 20, 1862. But that afternoon the fever worsened again, and by 5 o'clock it was all over. John Nicolay, exhausted from the pressures of the day, was dozing on his office couch when the president walked in: "Well, Nicolay," said he, choking with emotion, "my boy is gone—he is actually gone!" and bursting into tears, turned and went into his own office.

Elizabeth Keckley, Mrs. Lincoln's seamstress, would never forget the sight of Lincoln coming into that room:

> I never saw a man so bowed down with grief. He came to the bed, lifted the cover from the face of his child, gazed at it long and earnestly, murmuring, "My poor boy, he was too good for this earth. God has called him home. I know that he is much better off in heaven, but then we loved him so. It is hard, hard to have him die!" Great sobs choked his utterance. He buried his face in his hands, and his tall frame was choked with emotion. . . . I did not dream that his rugged nature

could be so moved. I shall never forget those solemn moments—genius and greatness weeping over love's idol lost.

Willie's body was embalmed, placed in a metal coffin (finished in rosewood and silver), and carried into the Green Room, adjacent to the East Room, where the services would be held. Beautiful even in death, he was dressed in evening clothes, eyes closed, hands crossed on his chest, one hand holding a small bouquet of exquisite flowers.

One look at that small beloved face sent Mrs. Lincoln into convulsions. According to Elizabeth Keckley:

Mrs. Lincoln's grief was inconsolable. . . . Around him, love's tendrils had been twined and now that he was dressed for the tomb, it was like tearing the tendrils out of the heart by their roots.

Mrs. Keckley also witnessed one sadly prophetic scene:

In one of her paroxysms of grief, the president kindly bent over his wife, took her by the arm, and gently led her to the window. With a stately solemn gesture, he pointed to the lunatic asylum: "Mother, do you see that large white building on the hill over yonder? Try and control your grief, or it will drive you mad, and we may have to send you there."

Even Congress shut down on the day of Willie's funeral. The service was conducted by the Reverend Dr. Phineas D. Gurley, pastor of the New York Avenue Presbyterian Church, which President and Mrs. Lincoln attended. Officers in uniform and all of official Washington was represented there, including Seward, with quivering lips, and McClellan, with misty eyes. More would have attended but nor'easter winds came up that morning, blowing off roofs and toppling chimneys and steeples.

After the funeral service, the casket was removed to the hearse. Behind the pallbearers followed a little group of children, the members of Willie's Sunday school class, which he'd always so faithfully attended.

LINCOLN'S DARK AND LONESOME VALLEY

I have felt His hand upon me in great trials and submitted to His guidance, and I trust that as He shall further open the way, I shall be ready to walk therein, relying on His help and trusting in His goodness and wisdom.

—ABRAHAM LINCOLN

Life would never be the same, neither in the White House nor in the Lincoln marriage. The historian Benjamin P. Thomas, author of *Abraham Lincoln: A Biography*, notes that without question, of all the multitudinous sorrows life dealt Lincoln, none could compare to the death of Willie. As for Mary:

> The defiant courage with which she had faced the gibes of society and the cruel spotlight of a hostile press wilted at the loss of a second child. She never again entered the guest room where Willie died or the Green Room, where his body had been embalmed. All except the necessary functions of the White House stopped.

Thomas notes that, for the next three years, Lincoln "would live in virtual seclusion and it became the fate of the overburdened president to walk alone, haunted by the fear that his distraught wife might go insane." Mary spent more and more time in the sanctuary of her bedroom, often weeping uncontrollably. Fewer people came to see her now, and she refused to see most of those who did.

The impact of all this on little Tad was devastating. Though he had finally recovered after a lingering illness, he never returned to his previous strength. Now he was parted from Willie—the light of his life—and his mother, who couldn't look at him without thinking of Willie. Nor did he have the consolation of Holly, Bud, and Julia Taft, the boys' close playmates, for since they, too, reminded Mary of Willie, she never invited them to the White House again.

That left him only one refuge—his father. After Willie's death, deprived of the companionship of playmates his own age, Tad could rarely stand any kind of absence from his father. Now, instead of sleeping in a bed with his brother, he insisted on sleeping with his father. Government officials, staff, and visitors found themselves saddled with the presence of Tad whether they wanted him or not.

(*Abraham Lincoln: Man of Faith and Courage*, pp. 180–83)

Since a number of the Lincoln stories feature Tad, too, I've included these passages so readers will be forewarned about the long-term repercussions of Willie's passing on the Lincoln family as well as on all those who interacted with Lincoln from that time on.

So it was that Lincoln, in spite of sorrow and emotional separation from his wife at home, was forced to add those to the crushing burdens of the presidency, and the military defeats that just kept coming.

By mid-1862, Lincoln became convicted that a key reason why northern armies continued to lose battle after battle was that the North had failed to address the cancer of slavery: if the war continued to be fought just to preserve the status quo—which included slavery—then there was no moral high ground for the North at all!

On July 22, Lincoln brought his plan to issue an emancipation proclamation to his Cabinet. Secretary of State William Seward objected on
the grounds that issuing such a document without either an amendment
or a military victory to give it strength would make the United States a
laughingstock. So it was put on hold.

By September 16, Generals Robert E. Lee and Thomas "Stonewall"
Jackson had come perilously close at Antietam Creek, in Maryland, to
threatening Washington itself. General McClellan, although commanding almost twice as many men as Lee, managed only a standoff in the
battle. More than 26,000 men fell at Antietam.

Nevertheless, the Union forces had fought the Confederate invasion
to a standstill and had turned the army away. Five days later, Lincoln
called his Cabinet together and announced that after wrestling with God
over the issue of slavery and the continued casualties in battle after battle,
he had come to a conclusion. "I made a solemn vow before God," he said,
"that if General Lee were driven back from Pennsylvania, I would crown
the result with the declaration of freedom for the slaves." Since he already
knew of the division in the Cabinet, he did not even take a vote, as had
been his custom.

On January 1, 1863, Lincoln signed the Emancipation Proclamation—
as he had vowed to God he would.

In this section, we include only those stories set in time prior to January 1, 1863.

Depiction of one of the Lincoln-Douglas debates by an unknown artist.

WHEN LINCOLN PASSED

MABLE McKEE

Young Richard Trowbridge, kin to the queen of England, vowed that someday this suspicious innkeeper would pay for doubting his word.

But then, sitting on top a stagecoach with a tall, ungainly stranger— who kept him laughing at his stories—his own slights began to dim. And he watched as this strangely attractive ugly stranger went out of his way to serve two judges who had gone out of their way to be rude to him.

Young Trowbridge had no way of knowing that this humble man, this serving man, would someday be considered the greatest man of his age.

When Richard Trowbridge walked across the dining room of the Eagle and Lion Inn that morning, Ezra Ross, the merchant, thought of a young prince. The youth carried his head like one. His dark eyes flashed as if giving a challenge to A. Beste, the innkeeper, who gave him some terse orders about directing the service in the room.

But Ezra Ross didn't dream that the lad who was serving him was related to a king. The flash in the boy's eyes merely accompanied a bitter surging in his heart because he had to take orders from the innkeeper. Though no one knew it, the surging promised a time of reckoning with the man who had refused the boy credit at his inn until his uncle could arrive. Instead, the innkeeper had told him that he would have to work for his room and board or find other lodgings.

A woman called Cindy came in from the kitchen to gather up the empty dishes on the table. Then Ezra Ross left the room, Richard Trowbridge following a little later. His work was over until dinner time. He wandered out to sit on a bench in front of the tavern and watch the stagecoaches come in.

Two judges walked up and down in front of the inn, discussing politics. They talked of the Kansas-Nebraska bill and the new party— Republicans, its supporters called it. Often both of them quoted Col. Richard Thompson's opinion of different leaders in those turbulent times.

Mention of Col. Richard Thompson brought a smile to Richard's lips. When his uncle or the colonel arrived, it would become known who he was. He imagined these men, who had called him "Boy" and ordered him to do their most menial tasks, would then treat him with honor. His heart beat exultantly. *I, who am related to a king, will then come into my own*, he thought proudly.

His uncle wanted Richard to read law in Colonel Thompson's office when they had become settled. He himself was to buy one of the packing houses on the other side of the river. An advertisement that it was for sale had been inserted in a Philadelphia newspaper, and this it was that had interested John Seymour in the little town on the Wabash. Long before his nephew had come from England, his uncle had wanted to leave New York City and Philadelphia and journey to the Northwest Territory, reported by western settlers to be the garden spot of the world.

Suddenly there was a commotion among the men in front of the inn. A cloud of dust from down the street, the scattering of small boys playing in the road, and the rushing around of the Negro boys who carried the luggage of travelers into the inn, told one story—the coach from the West had been sighted.

A few minutes later it was in front of the inn. A wave of disappointment went through the crowd of watchers. There was only one occupant, a man asleep on the back seat. Scant attention was given him by the young dandies who were watching for the return of the town's two belles. Immediately they scattered, and the two Negro boys ran around the tavern to play in the back yard. Richard Trowbridge, the habitual "loafers," and the judges were the only watchers left. Richard turned toward Charles Lesser, the driver of the coach, who had started to climb down from his high seat to get water for his horses.

He slumped into a heap when his feet touched the ground. One of the men and Richard ran to him. The boy who was related to a king liked the kindly stage driver. He had brought him on the last lap of his journey to the Wabash and allowed him to drive his horses much of the way. His illness now distressed Richard.

The blueness of the driver's face and trembling of his hands told the story. He had contracted that deadly disease of early settlers along the river—the ague. His teeth chattered so much they could hardly understand his request for a driver to take the coach on to Indianapolis. Finally he managed to ask, "Will you drive it, young mister?"

Unconsciously Richard threw up his shoulder. "Young Mister" was a title the old driver had given him on their trip over as the boy drove and the old man pointed out different trails along the way. Now he answered in a sturdy fashion, "I'll be glad to drive for you." His dark eyes flashed with pride. "You know I can manage the horses, sir. I'll see that they have food and water and care exactly as you do."

The old man was helped into the inn, and Richard made ready to mount the driver's seat. But just then he became aware of some commotion at the coach itself. The two judges who were going to Indianapolis had opened the door and were surveying a great, long, lanky Westerner who was asleep, sprawled on the back seat. Another traveler had climbed on the front seat. Their intention of talking politics on their way to the capital city could not be carried out if they were required to occupy different seats.

One of them prodded the sleeping man—prodded him until he awoke with a jump. He yawned, and it seemed to Richard that his mouth was at least a yard wide. Then he smiled sleepily, and instantly his homely face became beautiful to the boy.

He drawled out in nasal tones that grated on one's nerves, "Howdy, friends? What can I do for you?"

Rather imperiously, Judge Hammond stated their request for the back seat of the coach, so their talk would not be interrupted. He suggested that the stranger sit on the front seat with the other passenger. His request brought a still broader smile to the Westerner's lips. Slowly and with difficulty he managed to move his long legs and then the rest of his body from the coach. He reached under the seat and brought out a stove-pipe hat which he fitted on his head.

Tall, lanky, with ill-fitting clothes, the man stood then. His rugged features were crooked and angular and indescribably homely. His shoes were ill-fitting. So was the collar of his shirt. His neck was extremely long and reached far above it. His hands hung from his sleeves and dangled like those of a scarecrow. Many of the people who were coming out of the candy store across the street stopped in front of it to stare at the strange-looking person.

Richard was sure he would never forget this man so long as he lived. He had seen no other that looked like him. He visualized the word "Yankee," which he had heard applied contemptuously in New York to the pioneers of the Middle West.

The tall man, who had started to climb into the coach's front seat, suddenly stopped. "Why, here's a new driver," he exclaimed, and smiled his rare smile again. "He doubtless will need some instruction about the road. I'll ride with you, young man, if you don't object."

He swung himself onto the high seat beside Richard, and soon they were driving down the dusty road, past children who shouted at them, and women who stared and waved. The beautiful bay horses pranced as if on parade. Richard lifted his head with the same pride he had shown back in England when he and his mother had driven with their cousins to Buckingham Palace to see their relative, the queen.

Soon they were out of the town and passing through a woods of sycamore and poplar trees. Thick underbrush grew all around. Wild vines covered the trunks of the trees nearest the road, which was so rough that Richard on the high driver's seat had a terrible time keeping his balance. After a time they reached a district in which it had rained the night before. Soon they were in a region where the road was muddy and water stood in the deep ruts.

Once Richard gave a terrific lurch, and just then the tall, ungainly man reached out his strong hand and clutched him. "Sit closer to me, son," he said kindly. "It takes more than a jolt to unseat a backwoodsman. That made me think of Tom Harden and the time he tried to ride the oxen. Never heard that story, I reckon?"

He himself laughed at the story of disaster and fun he told. His voice was squeaky at times; deep and soft again. His laugh was still stranger than his voice. But his story was good and told so well that Richard laughed uproariously and forgot all his former troubles. Ahead of them lay a stretch of corduroy road. The tall man told Richard that it had been built by laying logs crosswise in the road where swampy land prevented filling in. He told of cutting down the trunks of such trees and of splitting rails for all the fences on his father's farm.

"Pretty nice little village—that Terry Hut," he said after a time. "Reckon you're going to live there. I went through there when I was a boy, moving a family from Boonville over to Illinois. I made three dollars that way. I stayed all night in the Spencer wagon yard. I reckon it's still there?"

Richard was interested in this man in spite of himself. The expression "wagon yard" had caught his fancy back at the inn when he first heard it. He had gone down to the place they called wagon yards, watched the farmers drive their loads of corn and other produce into them for the night, and make their beds in the wagons filled with straw. It was always amusing to see them crawl into this straw, drawing heavy covers around them, ready to sleep all night.

He could imagine the tall stranger crawling into such a wagon bed, folding up his legs for the night, and then sleeping soundly the sleep of the just.

On and on the stranger talked, telling stories about the people who had lived in the Hoosier county which had been his boyhood home and about the men who kept store or were attorneys in Springfield, Illinois, which was then his home. When he mentioned the fact that he, too, was a lawyer, Richard sat up straight. "Do you know Col. Richard Thompson?" he asked excitedly. "He's a lawyer back there where we came from."

"Dick Thompson!" chuckled the stranger. "Reckon I do know him. He's the brightest, keenest lawyer in the whole Middle West. He's up at Indianapolis now lookin' after the legislature there, I should say."

"I'm going to read law in his office," Richard raised his head proudly. "My uncle, who met him while he was in Washington, arranged for that."

"You are!" the tall Yankee seemed delighted. "Reckon you'll know all the rudiments of law then. Up at Indianapolis they say what law Dick don't know ain't ever been written. That reminds me of a story Abner Williams told about his school-teacher. Don't suppose you ever heard that?"

Dick shook his head. When it was finished and the boy had laughed many hearty laughs, he in turn began to talk. He went back in time to England, told of his royal relations there, of the death of his parents, and the urge for adventure which had brought him to America. He told of his journey across the prairies to Indiana and of the innkeeper who had made him work when his money gave out. He admitted that he was too proud to ask for credit in his uncle's name at the packing establishment. Almost vindictively he added the information that his uncle would see that this innkeeper was properly humiliated for his treatment of him.

"Reckon I wouldn't do that, son," the tall man spoke slowly, persuasively, sweetly. A beautiful smile came over his rugged face. "He didn't mean to be rude to you. He's often been cheated that way. When people have been cheated, they can't be blamed for doing as he did. Guess he didn't know the story about the man who went to a feast and took a high seat only to be sent down lower, and about the one who took a low seat and was sent higher. That's in the Bible, son. Think you'd better read it someday."

At his own suggestion, Richard allowed the man to take the lines. He drove like an experienced horseman, not talking much, but watching the rough, muddy road ahead of him. When he did speak he told of how the national highway over which they were driving had been built and improved during the last twenty years.

Once they stopped the coach at a little gully to get a drink. The tall driver told Richard the spring was the finest in that district. He led the way through a thicket where tall ferns grew, and to the rocks from which trickled a stream of cold water. They drank from their hands like boys. When they came back to the coach, Judge Hammond had his head out of the window, frowning impatiently. "We want to get to Indianapolis before dark," he said. "Will we have time to stop at the Half-Way House for dinner, do you think?"

Richard hesitated. He had almost forgotten there was a hostelry by this name on the road. The tall stranger who was studying the position of the sun, finally answered. "Reckon we shall, judge. They'll have dinner ready any time they see us." He added to Richard: "We'd better eat there, too. I'm as hungry as Enoch Rent's bear. Now I must tell you that story."

After they had climbed back onto the top of the coach, they heard Judge Hammond's stentorian voice talking about "Whigs" and "Butter-nuts" and "slaves."

"*Slaves!* Men and women and children sold like cattle!" And the man who was driving grew stern. "The judge says they should be allowed in Indiana to work in the fields. Slaves here! The ordinance of the North-west Territory fixed that."

Richard was fascinated by his new friend's talk. He would have to know about Indiana's laws and ordinances if he became an attorney like the famous Colonel Thompson, as his uncle desired.

Finally they were at the Half-Way Inn—a long low frame and log building, set back in a big yard. Here all coaches that traveled along the

national road stopped for meals or to stay overnight. A fat, jolly-looking
host ran out to ring a dinner bell. He waved his hand at the coach, calling
a greeting to the old driver who he thought was driving. The tall stranger
waved back, cordially, cheerfully, kindly.

Richard had driven the coach as near the side of the yard as he could,
but still a muddy space intervened between it and some boards that were
laid to the inn door. Before he could descend from the high seat to open
the door of the coach for his passengers, the tall man was out of the seat,
onto the ground. He jumped across the mud puddle, spattering his long
coat, and was in the yard where some loose boards lay. He picked up
two or three, carried them to the end of the board walk, and made an
extension to the coach door so the passengers were able to walk to the inn
without getting their feet muddy.

When Judge Hammond complained of a touch of ague and said that
the drizzling rain would make him bedfast, the tall man ran back to the
inn and came back carrying a heavy coat to him.

Who is he, anyway? Richard asked himself. *He acts like a servant, but
speaks like an educated person. I wonder if it would be rude to ask his name. I
told him mine, but he didn't offer to tell me his. I'll wait a little while longer.
Perhaps he'll tell me later.*

Surmising that the boy had no money, the tall man graciously asked
him to be his guest for dinner, and together they went into the dining
room.

The rest of the trip was a quieter one for the man and the youth. The
drizzle became a slow, pronounced rain, which seemed to sadden the tall
man still more. He dropped into a silence, broken suddenly when his
voice seemed fairly to wail, "I can't bear to think of the rain falling on the
lonely graves of the people you love."

Richard's eyes filled with quick tears as he thought of the two new
graves in England which held his father and mother. He drove on and
on, through mud puddles and water at times. Trees loomed tall on each
side of the road. Sometimes the woods were so dense that it seemed like

night as they passed through them. The coach jolted from one side of the road to the other. A feeling of elation rose in the boy's heart as he thought of the two pompous men inside the coach, still talking politics. He hoped they were jolting from one side of the seat to the other.

Just before they reached Indianapolis the stranger talked again. Richard, according to his advice, was not to worry if his uncle didn't arrive soon. The work at the hotel was not hard. Indiana was a democratic State; and when he did get started in law, people would give him extra praise for having worked his way in time of emergency. "Remember this, son," he added with a kindly smile, "if you try always to serve like a king, you can't go wrong."

Richard noticed the man's awkward hands, showing by their calloused spots and their roughness that their owner had worked at the hardest manual labor. He listened with more interest then as the stranger spoke of honest labor scars.

Soon they were at the little hostelry in the capital city at which the coach stopped. Richard noticed that the tall man remained in his seat while he sprang to the ground and opened the coach door for his passengers. They hurried toward a distinguished-looking little man whom every one seemed to know.

While he was watching the three talk together, Richard noticed that his tall, ungainly friend was unfolding his legs and coming to the ground with a single jump. The noise of his landing drew the attention of other people in front of the inn, particularly that of the distinguished-looking man who was talking to the judges. Hurriedly he came toward Richard's friend. "Why, Mr. Lincoln," he began, "I had no notion you were coming stagecoach."

"Dick Thompson!" the tall man clutched his hand, and his face was wreathed with a hundred smiles. "I'm glad to meet you so soon. And here," his other hand reached out for Richard's, "is my young friend who has come all the way from England to see you. Since I've come only from Illinois, I reckon that gives him the first chance to talk to you."

Richard Thompson, who had heard that the young Britisher was coming and who knew all his sad history since the death of his parents, at once gave the boy a cordial handclasp. "Abraham Lincoln," he said, turning to the tall stranger, "is the best lawyer and the most intelligent man in the country. You'll always be glad to have him for a friend."

Judge Hammond and his companion were staring at the Westerner with open mouths. Abraham Lincoln, the lawyer who was then stirring the country through his debates with Stephen Douglas, had given them his seat in the coach at their request. He had carried boards and made a walk so they would not step in the mud. They could not speak, so great were their amazement and confusion.

Richard stood speechless, too. But through his heart went one sentence: *He served like a king.*

• • • •

Some years later Richard Trowbridge stood in Indianapolis again. This time he was a man, with a pretty young woman, dressed in long, hooped skirts, tight basque, and tiny hat, clinging to one arm as they waited at the station. The sleeve which should have held his other arm hung empty. He had left that at Gettysburg.

It was raining as it had been that day back in the long ago when Richard had driven the coach along the National Road. Crowds thronged the station—crowds which were tragically silent and restless. Women sobbed and men were grief-stricken.

Abraham Lincoln was passing—on his last journey from Washington to his home town, Springfield, Illinois. He was coming more quietly than he had ever traveled before, coming in a casket wrapped in flags, for he had been killed by an assassin's deadly bullet.

Richard Trowbridge turned to his wife. "I shall never forget how he carried that board to the coach," he said softly. "I shall never forget that he told me always to serve like a king."

A sound of weeping rose, mingled with the noise of an engine. Slowly it came—the dark, snorting steel creature back of which Abraham Lincoln lay. Richard Trowbridge saw it through the mourning people around him and the station building, draped in black. And he said softly to himself more than to the woman by him, "Years from now they'll know that the greatest American of them all is now passing."

Illustration created by Ralph Nelson for St. Nicholas Magazine.

THE STRENGTH CONQUERED

T. Morris Longstreth

Frank had had enough. This time he'd get even—even if the means to that end weren't—quite—straight.

Then he overheard voices. . . .

T he Widow Hoplin lived with her one son Frank on the outskirts of Springfield, Illinois. This meant that it was a walk, in those days, of about ten minutes to the center of town and Billy Logan's store, where the boy worked. For five years, now, Frank had been taking that walk through frying sun and freezing wind; and every morning of that time his mother had seen him off with a kiss of encouragement, had welcomed him with another at night. He was the embodiment of all her secret hopes.

One July evening he returned tired and crestfallen. His greeting was languid, and as his mother looked into his brown, steady eyes she fancied that for the first time they were trying to avoid her gaze. A cold mist seemed to fill her heart. Frank was seventeen now, and it was natural, she thought, that his troubles, his friendships, his pleasures might sometime come between them and the companionship they had always had. But not yet, she had hoped.

"It's been hot today, hasn't it, son?"

"Um-n," he growled, drawing some cold water into a basin and sousing his thick brown hair in it.

"And so I suppose McAnan chose this day to slip off and let you finish his work." She said it very quietly, very sympathetically.

"*Jehosaphat*, he did!" said Frank; "and I'm tired of it. I'll get even with him."

"There's the towel, Frankie, and there's some ice-tea in the cold cellar all ready."

Not too dry, but already mollified, the boy put his strong arms about her and gave her the kiss she had wanted at the door. *It pays to wait; it pays*, she thought, her warmth of love dispelling quickly that mist of doubt. And that was why she did not protest at once about Frank's "getting even" with McAnan. Only, just before he went to bed, she said, "If I were you, dear, I'd wait just a little before doing anything about McAnan."

"I've waited good and long," he said.

"Providence manages these things pretty well, I've found, if one doesn't interfere, but goes right on doing his duty."

"Providence must have gone to sleep, then." He laughed dryly, not at all convinced. "I haven't much confidence in—"

She held up her finger to her lip, then said: "You remind me of a story I heard Abe Lincoln tell today. I was going by the telegraph-office and he was there with a lot of men, and I stopped to inquire whether he'd received any favorable news from the Republican Convention in Chicago—"

"I know," interrupted Frank, "that's another thing I've got against McAnan. He says they'll never nominate a man who buys a ten-cent beefsteak for his breakfast and carries it home himself—just as though that made a difference!"

"As I was saying, Frank," and she rebuked his interruption with an added gentleness, "I asked Abe what hope he had of the nomination. 'Every hope, ma'am,' he said, with that low laugh of his; 'but I seem to be a minority of one in these parts. My friends here don't seem to have much more confidence in my pulling through this scrape than the old lady did in the accident. You heard of her, didn't you? The horse had run away with her in the buggy. She said she "trusted in providence till the britchin' broke, and then she didn't know what on airth to do!"

Frank laughed. "Well, Mother, I'll give providence the reins for a little while longer. Do you think Abe'll be President?"

"Yes," she said quietly, "Abraham Lincoln is straight, and he goes straight for what he wants, and the straight way is the shortest way. I'll join his minority of one."

"You're a brick, Mother," said Frank. "If I get anywhere, which doesn't seem likely, but if I do, it'll be because you have pointed out the straight line." He sighed inaudibly, for he was thinking of the long way to go. He was still working for four dollars a week, and had been for two years.

"Sweet dreams," she called after him as he started upstairs. Then she sighed, too.

• • • •

By the next afternoon, Frank's reliance on providence had again diminished almost to zero, at the same time that the temperature had reached a hundred. He was arranging canned goods on the shelves of the Logan store, and listening to the serpent, in the guise of Jude Graham, an older man, who was tossing the cans to Hoplin.

"But I reckon you wouldn't actively object to a dollar raise," said Jude.

"Not actively, if it could come a straight way," said Frank.

"I don't see as how that's so very crooked. You could put the money back, of course. McAnan's cheatin' Billy, ain't he? Of course he is. Well then, you cheat McAnan and it rids us of him, gets you his place, and don't cheat Billy in the end. What do you say?"

The boy pondered. It was a clever sort of revenge for a long-continued injustice on the part of McAnan. But it was the sort of thing that Frank could never even have mentioned to his mother. "Why don't *you* do it, Jude?" he murmured.

"If I had a lot to gain, like you, I would. Besides, if things didn't turn out just right, I've got two kids and a wife and I couldn't afford to lose the job."

"Well I've a mother," said Frank; and he might have added another reason, his own self-respect, had not a shout of laughter from a group of men in the front of the store drowned all talk for the moment.

"Abe's feeling pretty good today," said Hoplin, when he could be heard.

"I reckon you would, too, if you thought you was goin' to be President of the United States; though I reckon he's the only one that's so sure about it."

"Don't you think he'll be nominated?" asked Hoplin, quickly.

"Dug says not. Dug says that Abe's too blamed honest to treat politicians in the way they'll understand. Just like what I was sayin' about you. You're too honest to—"

"And yet," said Hoplin, "Abe's either going to be President or mighty close to it, which ain't bad for a fellow grown up in this town."

"Bein' mighty close wouldn't be such an awful big consolation to me," sneered Jude, "any more than stayin' on four per would seem an awful big occasion for bein' cheerful when I could just as well have five."

Another roar of laughter interrupted. Both workers looked at the group silhouetted against the front windows, and both saw a tall, lanky man gesticulating with long, skinny arms, like a shadow-picture of a scarecrow. Each time he made a point, it was emphasized by a roar of laughter, and sometimes he would bend and laugh, too.

"I'm goin' up to hear Abe's latest," said Jude. "I reckon you can finish them two shelves without me. But think over what I was a-tellin' you."

Hoplin paused and thought. It was very hot. Ambition was in the air, particularly in the air of that store where Lincoln came daily to talk over things with his friends. If he got McAnan fired and himself installed in McAnan's place, as both deserved, he would at last have some good news to tell that waiting mother of his. Hoplin stooped to pick up some more cans, and a nausea of his job came over him. A cheer for Lincoln came from the street. The boy straightened up. "By Abraham, I'll do it!" he said; "old Abe won't be the only one to get ahead."

Jude came back. Hoplin told him that he had made up his mind to take the step suggested. The older man slapped him on the back. "Good for you, Hoppy, and put it through tonight. Glad you've taken the short cut to success at last."

"What was going on up front?" asked Frank, glad to change the subject.

"Oh, Abe is on one of his high horses, refusin' to give in a point or two about promisin' a couple of delegations something. They say it'd make the nomination sure, too. Abe thinks he's smart, too, throwin' these stories of his into your eyes, like dust, to keep you from seein' things. He just got off one about Cy and the schoolmaster."

"What was it?" asked Hoplin.

"Oh, I can't tell it the way Abe does. It went something like this: It was locking-up time and Cy says to the Schoolmaster, 'Can I go now, teacher? The sun's going down.'

" 'Reckon not,' says the schoolmaster; 'we're comin' up, that's all.'

" 'Don't you s'pose I've got eyes?' says Cy, who's a big hulking feller and not afraid of any schoolmaster.

" 'Reckon so, Cy, but it's the earth that goes round. The sun keeps as still as a tree. When we're swung around so we can't see him any more, all the shine's cut off and we call it night.'

"Cy looks at the schoolmaster a moment and then says, 'Gosh, what a fool you are!' "

Jude paused. Hoplin said nothing. Jude said, "Abe thinks that settles the whole question, whatever it is. But if he stays on being so set about them delegations, I reckon he'll be still practicin' law next week."

Frank still said nothing. He had a secret envy of the character which could resist temptation while it was being shown kingdoms. It was a pity that Hoplin could not have remembered just then that it was also in a grocery store that Abe Lincoln had resisted and found strength.

• • • •

By the next afternoon many things had happened. In Chicago, the bal-
loting had begun. Seward led. There was not a great deal of hope in the
streets of Springfield for their townsman. An occasional telegram kept
the prairie town in touch with the events. Many men clustered around
the telegraph-office, but Lincoln himself was lounging with the same old
cronies about the fireless stove in Logan's store. He was having an argument nearly as hot as the afternoon with his friends.

Frank Hoplin this afternoon was not arranging cans. He had been
moved up a peg, for the little plot had worked, and McAnan, suppos-
ing some past indiscretions had been discovered which might lead to
still greater undiscovered ones, had withdrawn without much to-do and
without suspecting Hoplin's part in his dismissal. Frank had spent the
morning going briskly about his new work, trying to suppress the uncom-
fortable feeling connected with it. But trouble made his eyes—usually so
steady—restless, and he dreaded going home. He would have to tell his
good news to his mother; she would guess that it was not all good. To
keep his mind off of his own troubles, he edged nearer the group and
heard Lincoln say: "No, Dug, you sha'n't get me to look at myself through
a magnifying-glass. For I'm still just the man, I reckon, that I always was;
and in this particular case I'm nothing and the truth is everything."

Dug hitched his chair and said: "You're too all-fired honest, Abe.
You're so danged innercent that they'll side-track you."

"Dug's right," interjected a third; "if you don't get the votes of them
two delegations as suggested, Abe, you'll sure be side-tracked."

"That's not quite accurate," said Lincoln, earnestly; "they can hold
me up, maybe; but only I can do the side-tracking. The fatal thing is to
get switched from the truth. It's when a man begins taking those pleasant
little detours that he finds he's run up into a stall, or got derailed, on his
lie. No, sir, I'm going to stick by the main line."

"But. Abe—" began another.

"I won't do it." And Lincoln waved his hands humorously about to fan himself. "Dug, how many legs has a sheep?"

"Four."

"And how many legs will your sheep have if you call his tail a leg?"

"Five."

Lincoln looked inquiringly at Nathan Andrews. "Five," said Andrews. All nodded.

"You're all mistaken," said Lincoln, "for calling a tail a leg doesn't make it one."

They laughed, and so did Lincoln, for he had won his point with them. But Hoplin did not so much as grin. He was thinking of what this strange strong man who had always been hanging around, so much like them and yet so different, had just been saying about getting side-tracked on a lie. Would the lie of which he had just been guilty side-track *him*? It was certainly making him feel separated from his usual contented self.

Presently the men began to leave. But Lincoln did not, for Billy Logan, the store-keeper, had entered, and the Presidential possibility, sprawling out and wiping the perspiration from his lean face, called out, "Heard any new stories, Billy?"

"Not any funny ones," said the store-keeper. "There's one not so funny, though, Abe. They say that unless you humor them two delegations a mite, you're a dead man."

"Who says that?"

"Ashton and the rest."

"Then Ashton and the rest will soon experience the novelty of seeing a dead man rise up and go home to his supper." Just at that moment a boy entered with a telegram. Lincoln read it, and the lines on his furrowy face deepened.

"Not a death in the family?" asked Billy, to whom a wire could mean not less than that.

"No, that pesky manager is still trying to get me to feed promises out of an empty bin."

"But be you going to refuse, Abe?" solicitously.

"Those two delegations demand places in the cabinet, places that the biggest men in this country won't know enough to fill, and they want me to promise them to a pair of clothes-pins."

"You—you couldn't just let 'em down a bit easy, Abe?" persisted Billy, who was terribly afraid that his townsman would lose.

Lincoln looked up at him almost sorrowfully, and said quietly. "Don't you know me better than that, Billy, after all these years? If nominated, I shall be thankful; if not, it will be all the same. But come what will, I'll bait no hook with a lie."

Billy felt the rebuke, and averting his eyes, caught sight of Hoplin still hanging around. He could not understand the reason for the haggard look on Hoplin's face—the outward expression of Frank's inner desire to right himself at any cost. The store-keeper called out, "Hey, Hoplin, ain't you gone yet? Tryin' to live up to your new job, eh?" And Billy nudged Lincoln, adding, "How long will a new broom sweep so all-fired clean, Abe?"

But Lincoln didn't hear. "Got a piece of paper, Billy?" he asked. "I'll fix these fellows right off." And spreading the paper across his knee, he wrote the reply telegram.

Hoplin was drawn to this big man as moth to flame. The longing to be clean of his lie, the admiration for this honest, great man, had wrung a decision from him. He would confess. He opened his mouth to speak, to right himself, when Billy said, "Can I see what you wrote, Abe?"

Lincoln shoved the paper to the store-keeper who read slowly:

"I authorize—no—bargains—and—will—be—bound—by—none.

—A. LINCOLN."

It was a moving moment. The storekeeper shook his head slowly, and from Hoplin's sight the familiar boxes and barrels faded. He saw only one thing, the gaunt, kindly face of this self-made Lincoln, and suddenly, without effort, he blurted out: "Listen here, Mr. Logan; I've done what ain't right and I want to tell you. I reckon if Mr. Lincoln can throw over being President as easy as this, I can be honest, too. I've got to get it off my conscience—can I?"

The two men, amazed by this outburst, listened while Frank Hoplin told about his juggling of the money to discredit Mr. McAnan, of his desire to advance, as much for his mother's sake as for his own, and of his intention now to tell McAnan.

"But Mac ain't the sort who'll forgive you and make it any too comfortable here," said Billy, at the end.

"I know, I know!" exclaimed Hoplin, shaking with relief; "but I couldn't go on feeling the way I did. If it wasn't for Mother, I'd be the happiest fellow in the world at this moment." And he did draw a breath of huge relief. "But I can hunt around."

Lincoln had been studying the boy. "What sort of a job do you hanker after, Hoplin?" he asked.

"I want to learn to be a telegrapher," said Hoplin.

"Which reminds me," said Lincoln; "I'd better get this message to the office before it closes."

"I'll take it," said Hoplin, at once; "I go that way, anyhow."

"Then we'll go together. I want to ask you a question or two. And Billy," and here Lincoln winked discreetly at the storekeeper, "don't say anything about Hoplin's affairs or mine."

Three minutes saw the strange couple, the tall man with his admirer pacing to keep step, nearing the telegraph-office. A shout went up from the distant crowd about it. Immediately, a youngster extricated himself from the group and, seeing Lincoln approaching, ran to him, shouting, "Mr. Lincoln, Mr. Lincoln! You're nominated!"

A thrill warmed Hoplin's chest. He shot out a hand and said, "May I have the first shake with the next President?"

"You can have more than that, Hoplin. Maybe the day will come when I can offer you a job in Washington? How'd you like that?"

Hoplin's eyes misted with gladness. A twinkle came into Lincoln's as he waved the telegram in his face and said, "You won't insist on being in the Cabinet—right at first?"

His answer was not heard. The crowd was upon them, shouting, wild with enthusiasm. Some were laughing, some were half crying, all were exulting. But Hoplin, standing back a little, was happier than they. He had something to tell his mother now.

• • • •

It was the dusk of another July day, but two years later. Those years had left their mark on everybody. Telegrapher Hoplin, sitting by his instrument in an alcove of the White House, was no longer the callow store-boy, but an experienced and reliable young man, stalwart and with a firmness of jaw which had developed in these years of strain and responsibility. Even more heavily had the time set its seal on Lincoln, who was standing beside Hoplin and saying, "If that is all their news, I shall start directly."

"I wish you wouldn't ride out there by yourself, Mr. Lincoln," said Hoplin.

A rare smile crossed the President's care-worn cheeks. "Don't you join that crowd of fussers, too, Hoplin. Stanton and Lamon never will be happy until I go out surrounded by a cordon of nurses."

"But those threats—" began the youth.

The smile disappeared, but the tired voice was just as firm as it said: "I long ago made up my mind, Hoplin, that if anybody wants to kill me, he will do it. If I wore a shirt of mail and kept myself surrounded by a bodyguard, it would be all the same. There are a thousand ways of getting at a man, if it is desired that he should be killed. And now, to leave that subject, how is your mother?"

"She is better, sir. Today's her birthday."

"In that case, get this message through to McClellan, and then close up shop for tonight. You stick too close to things."

"It's your example—again," said Hoplin, softly, recollecting that scene in Logan's store. "I reproach myself for not being down there with the fighters."

"Everybody can't be the carving-knife," said Lincoln, quickly. "Please give my regards to your mother, *soon*." And the President left the room.

Shortly after that, Hoplin saw him riding off, unaccompanied, on his favorite horse, "Old Abe," bound for the Soldiers' Home, where Lincoln was living during the hot weather. Hoplin wiped his brow, which was very hot and aching. His hours had been long, the summer's strain had been intolerable, his mother, who had come East to keep house for him, was not well, and his sympathetic nature cried out against the criticism of the man whom he loved and saw laboring beneath the staggering burden of his office. A bond had grown up between the telegrapher and the man who had made his progress possible, and Hoplin could not see him so near the breaking-point without a personal sorrow. Also, threats of assassination had been rife recently. Lincoln was the only one who laughed at them.

Hoplin had difficulty in getting his message through to headquarters, and had to wait for the repeat. It came and he was locking a desk when the *tap-tap* began again. It was from the Soldiers' Home and said, *"Good reason for President to require escort tonight if taking his usual course."* There was no signature. All the dormant suspicions of the past few days swam to life in Hoplin's brain. The President had been gone for some time, but he rode slowly, and the escort could catch up, perhaps. Yet Lincoln hated fuss, could, indeed, become indignant if someone assumed the right of interference. Often on these long rides he thought out his great problems. Hoplin wondered what to do. "I'll go myself," he said aloud. He got his revolver from the desk, and went down to the stables, where a horse, which was his to use, waited. But a difficulty had arisen: there were two roads the President might have taken, a long and a short. Hoplin decided to send an armed guard of four on the long way, and he would take the short himself. For an instant he wavered. He was tired, his mother was waiting, it was her birthday, he was not required to go on this errand. Yet something within impelled him; he swung on his horse, and, after giving the necessary directions, trotted westward.

It was a sultry evening. A three-quarter moon made a dim glow over everything. Fireflies careered like little comets over the fields outside the city. Hoplin trotted on and on, between hedges, through a patch of woods, along wide fields. Soon he would reach the junction of his road and the main one along which the armed escort would have passed, if they had hurried. Hoplin dimly wondered whether they had passed, or whether he should wait a while. He was mortally weary. He slowed down his horse to a walk. There was a crossing a hundred yards ahead, bathed in the furnace-like glow of the hazy moon.

Suddenly he stopped. He heard the hooves of a horse trotting on the hard road. A shiver, as of some presentiment coming from that hovering mystery of moonlight, shook him. He forced himself to smile, saying aloud, "What a scared cat you are!" and urged his horse on. At the same moment, a shot struck the still night as startlingly as a fire-gong. Hoplin's horse reared. A man rose from the bushes at the right. Hoplin dismounted. The man, as he could see, was undecided as to whether to take aim again at a horseman dimly seen on the main road, or to escape from Hoplin. The boy, letting go his horse, approached the man without flinching. He must divert the shot from that tall figure in the gloom. He spoke. The man yelled for him to keep back. Hoplin sprang, the other fired blindly at him, then dashed past, mounted Hoplin's horse and rode off in desperate haste, leaving a boy with a shattered arm kneeling in the dust. But the President was spared that second bullet.

A strange confusion appeared from nowhere. Hoplin had staggered to his feet. He must find out whether Lincoln had been harmed. The confusion materialized. Horses galloping, men shouting, a light showing, two figures nearing, appeared beside him. "Cut the miscreant down!" cried one. But the other held out his saber to protect Hoplin, who cried, "Is Mr. Lincoln safe?"

Two other horsemen appeared. "Is the fellow disarmed?" cried one, adding, "Keep back, Mr. President, please."

"I heard Hoplin's voice" said Lincoln, in agitated tones.

"You must not risk yourself," cried the trooper. "We have the man."

"Is it likely—" but pain cut short Hoplin's cry of protest, and for an instant the strange tableau stood motionless beneath the moon, an injured boy trying not to faint into a trooper's arms, two others, still unconvinced that he was not the attempting assassin, poised with weapons drawn, the ungainly head of a great nation pushing back the soldier detailed to protect him.

Lincoln rested on one knee there in the dust. "Frank," he said, "Frank, is there any place but your arm that's hit?"

Hoplin, with an effort, smiled and said, "No."

"Thank God!" said the President, "for it is my fault. But don't any of you tell Ward Lamon, the marshal of this district."

There was something so whimsical in this that Hoplin smiled again, and said, "But he didn't hit you?"

"Only through the hat," said Lincoln, "but the one you took in my stead might have hit the mark. I suppose it takes some practice to hit a thin fellow like me where it matters. Now let's see—" And still on one knee, Lincoln arranged a sling for the wounded arm out of his handkerchief and then gave instructions for two of the guard to take Hoplin home.

"Then I'll look in and take the blame tomorrow," he said, in his grave, kindly voice. "A nice birthday gift I'm sending to your mother, a son shot in my service!"

"If you knew Mother better, you'd know she'd like me to be—that is," and he colored, "I mean, she'll be the happiest woman in Washington tonight."

"And we'll try to keep her so," said Lincoln, taking Hoplin's good hand with a grip whose pressure both men understood.

• • • •

Twenty-four hours, nearly, had passed. Frank Hoplin pale, but keen with an undefined expectancy, sat up in bed, his arm bandaged, his mother beside him. There was a quick step on the porch, a knock on the door. Mrs. Hoplin hastened to it. Frank heard a voice faintly inquiring, "Is this where Captain Frank Hoplin lives?"

"Why—Mr. President, won't you—can you come in?"

Then he heard that familiar chuckle, "Mr. President—nonsense! You used to call me Abe Lincoln, Sarah Hoplin."

"Well, you startled me calling Frank 'captain,'" she said, regaining her composure instantly.

"That's been his name since noon. Stanton'll send around the commission as soon as it can be made out. How is he?"

"Come in and see for yourself. He'll be terribly set up by seeing you."

"I reckon it's a good thing for the inhabitants of Springfield to get together every so often." Lincoln bent under a curtain and appeared before Frank. "Hello, Captain!"

Hoplin flushed with surprise, delight, affection, and admiration pent up within him. For half an hour they talked, the mother listening with shining eyes. With the commission went a saddle-horse, they learned. When he had recovered would they be able to come to dinner at the White House, "with Mary and the children"? Gossip of Springfield followed. When Abraham Lincoln rose to go, Mrs. Hoplin tried to express her gratitude. He stopped her, saying, "I came not only to thank Frank, but to congratulate you."

"Me," she said in surprise.

"His mother," said Lincoln, softly. "His mother's influence is the red line running through a man's life—for good or evil. Look closely at a fine man and you will see a good mother. Frank is the living witness of your secret hopes, and that is why I congratulate you."

To Frank he said but little, and if his mother had heard, she would not have understood. It was only: "Don't thank me, Boy, thank yourself and then McAnan. It's the strength we conquer that becomes our own." And the giant left the room, left a lad of nineteen pondering his slow and gracious words.

Illustration by an unknown artist.

MORE THAN HIS SHARE

Author Unknown

Little Blossom's brother was to be shot for sleeping at his post on sentry duty. Was there nothing in the world anyone could do to save him?

Like so many memorable Lincoln stories, this short but moving story has been kept alive by people who love it, for a century and a half. No one knows who wrote it. Most likely someone once told the story— perhaps Blossom herself—someone wrote it down, and it somehow survived, one battered handwritten copy to another, until typewriters were invented; then the cycle of typewritten, then photocopied, stories began.

B ennie Owen was a farmer boy in the state of Vermont. When Abraham Lincoln sent out a call for volunteer soldiers to help put down the rebellion, called the Civil War, Bennie Owen begged permission of his father to enlist. After much pleading Farmer Owen gave his consent, and Bennie went to war. With him went Jemmie Carr, a neighbor's son, and from then on these two homes were always filled with anxiety fearing some evil tidings might come that one or both of these boys had been killed in battle.

One morning a telegram was received by farmer Owen, and this is how it read: "Private Benjamin Owen, found asleep at his post while on picket duty last night. The court martial has sentenced him to be shot in twenty-four hours as the offense occurred at a critical time."

Mr. Allen, the village minister, had heard of the sad news, and hurried to the home of the Owen family to give them counsel and comfort.

"I thought, Mr. Allen, when I gave my Bennie to his country, that not a father in all this broad land made so precious a gift—no, not one. The dear boy only slept a minute, just one little minute, at his post; I know that was all for Bennie never dozed over a duty. How prompt and reliable he was! I know he only fell asleep one little second; he was so young and not strong, that boy of mine! Why, he was as tall as I and only 18! And now they shoot him because he was asleep when doing sentinel duty. Twenty-four hours, the telegram said—only twenty-four hours. Where is Bennie now?"

"We will hope with his heavenly father," said Mr. Allen, soothingly.

"Yes, yes; let us hope; God is very merciful."

" 'I should be ashamed, Father,' Bennie said to me, 'when I am a man, to think I never used this great right arm,' and he held it out so proudly before me—'for my country when it needed it. Palsy it rather than keep it at the plow.'

" 'Go, then my boy,' I said, 'and God keep you!'

"God has kept him, I think, Mr. Allen!" and the farmer repeated these last words slowly, as if, in spite of his reason, his heart doubted them.

"Like the apple of His eyes; Mr. Owen; doubt it not."

Blossom sat near them listening with blanched cheek. She had not shed a tear. Her anxiety had been so concealed that no one had noticed it. She had occupied herself mechanically in the household cares. Now she answered a gentle tap at the kitchen door, opening it to receive from a neighbor's hand a letter. "It is from him," was all she said.

It was like a message from the dead! Mr. Owen took the letter, but could not break the envelope on account of his trembling fingers, and held it toward Mr. Allen with the helplessness of a child. The minister opened it, and read as follows:

"Dear Father: When this reaches you I shall be in eternity. At first it seemed awful to me, but I have thought about it so much now that it has no terror. They say they will not bind me, nor blind me; but that I may meet my death like a man. I thought, Father, it might have been on the battlefield, for my country, and that when I fell, it would be fighting gloriously; but to be shot down like a dog for nearly betraying it—to die for neglect of duty! Oh, Father, I wonder the very thought does not kill me. But I shall not disgrace you. I am going to write you all about it; and when I am gone, you may tell my comrades. I cannot now.

"You know I promised Jemmie Carr's mother I would look after her boy, and when he fell sick, I did all I could for him. He was not strong when he was ordered back into the ranks, and the day before that night I carried all his luggage, besides my own, on our march. Toward night we went in on the double-quick, and though the luggage began to feel very heavy everybody else was tired too; and as for Jemmie, if I had not lent him an arm now and then he would have dropped by the way. I was all tired out when we went into camp, and when it was Jemmie's turn to be sentry, and I agreed to take his place; but I was too tired, Father. I could not have kept awake if a gun had been pointed at my head; but I did not know it until—well, until it was too late."

"God be thanked!" interrupted Mr. Owen, reverently. "I knew Bennie was not the boy to sleep carelessly at his post."

"They tell me today that I have a short reprieve given to me by circumstances—'time to write to you,' our good colonel says. Forgive him, Father, he only does his duty; he would gladly save me if he could; and not lay my death up against Jemmie. The poor boy is broken-hearted, and does nothing but beg and entreat them to let him die in my stead.

"I can't bear to think of Mother and Blossom. Comfort them, Father! Tell them I die as a brave boy should and that, when the war is over, they will not be ashamed of me, as they must be now. God help me; it is very hard to bear! Good-by, Father! God seems near and dear to me; not at all as if He wished me to perish forever, but as if He felt sorry for His poor, sinful, broken-hearted child, and would take me to be with Him and my Saviour in a better—better life."

A deep sigh burst from Mr. Owen's heart, "Amen," he said solemnly. "Amen."

"Tonight, in the early twilight, I shall see the cows all coming home from pasture and precious little Blossom standing on the back-stoop waiting for me; but I shall never, never come! God bless you all. Forgive your poor Bennie."

• • • •

Late that night the door of the "back-stoop" opened softly and a little figure glided out and down the footpath that led to the road by the mill. She seemed rather flying than walking, turning her head neither to the right nor to the left, looking only now and then to heaven, and folding her hands as if in prayer. Two hours later the same young girl stood at the Mill depot watching the coming of the night train; and the conductor as he reached down to lift her into the car, wondered at the tear-stained face that was up-turned toward the dim lantern he held in his hand. A few questions, and ready answers told him all; and no father could have cared more tenderly for his only child than for little Blossom. She was on her way to Washington to ask President Lincoln for her brother's life. She had stolen away, leaving only a note to tell where and why she had gone. She had brought Bennie's letter with her; no good, kind heart like the President's could refuse to be melted by it. The next morning they reached New York and the conductor hurried her on to Washington. Each minute now might be the means of saving her brother's life. And so, in an incredibly short time, Blossom reached the Capitol and hastened immediately to the White House.

The President had just seated himself for his morning's task of looking over and signing important papers, when, without one word of announcement, the door softly opened and Blossom, with downcast eyes and folded hands, stood before him.

"Well, my child," he said, in his pleasant, cheerful tones, "what do you want, so bright and early in the morning?"

"Bennie's life, please, sir," faltered Blossom.

"Bennie? Who is Bennie?"

"My brother, sir. They are going to shoot him for sleeping at his post."

"Oh, yes," and Mr. Lincoln ran his eye over the papers before him. "I remember. It was a fatal sleep. You see, Child, it was a time of special danger. Thousands of lives might have been lost for his culpable negligence."

"So my father said, sir," replied Blossom, gravely. "But poor Bennie was so tired, sir, and Jemmie so weak. He did the work of two, and it was Jemmie's night, not his; but Jemmie was too tired, and Bennie never thought about himself, that he was tired, too."

"What is this you say, Child? Come here, I do not understand," and the kind man caught eagerly at what seemed to be a justification for the offense.

Blossom went to him; he put his hand tenderly on her shoulder, and turned her pale, anxious face toward his. How tall he seemed! And he was President of the United States, too. A dim thought of this kind passed for a moment through Blossom's mind; but she told her simple and straightforward story and handed Mr. Lincoln Bennie's letter to read.

He read it carefully; then, taking up his pen, wrote a few hasty lines and rang his bell.

Blossom heard this order given: "Send this dispatch at once!"

The President then turned to the girl and said, "Go home my child, and tell that father of yours, who could approve his country's sentence, even when it took the life of a child like that, that Abraham Lincoln thinks his life far too precious to be lost. Go back, or wait until tomorrow; Bennie will need a change after he has so bravely faced death; he shall go with you."

"God bless you, sir," said Blossom; and who shall doubt that God heard and registered the request?

• • • •

Two days after this interview, the young soldier came to the White House with his little sister. He was called to the President's private room, and an honorary strap fastened upon his shoulder. Mr. Lincoln then said: "the soldier that could carry a sick comrade's luggage and die so uncomplainingly deserves well of his country." Then Bennie and Blossom made their way to their Green Mountain Home. A crowd gathered at the Mill depot to welcome them back, and as Farmer Owen's hand grasped that of his boy, tears flowed down his cheeks, and he was heard to say fervently, "The Lord be praised."

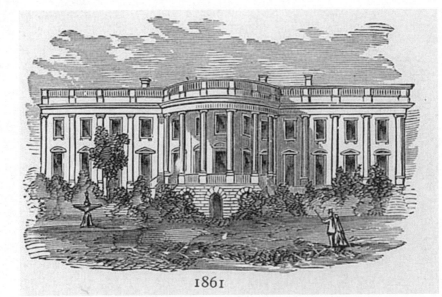

A woodcut of the White House as it appeared in 1861.

BOYS IN THE WHITE HOUSE

Ruth Painter Randall and Joseph Leininger Wheeler

Our early presidents were all older men, thus the Lincolns were the first to bring children with them to the White House. Needless to say, the nation was fascinated by them.

To Mary Lincoln, 1861 was a happy year. She had achieved her heart's desire: being mistress of the White House. Congress had entrusted her with $20,000 to refurbish the White House, and thus the Executive Mansion was now beautiful inside. Having always loved entertaining, she now had enough money to put on dinners that were the talk of the city. Last and foremost, her two boys were happy.

When the Lincolns moved into the executive mansion, they'd been almost overwhelmed. Thirty-one rooms—not counting stables, outbuildings, and conservatory! Their entire Springfield house could have fit in the East Room alone. Once they settled in, though, they realized that all that space was anything but theirs. It belonged to the people. In the entire first floor, only the family dining room was off-limits to the public. Even on the second floor, half the rooms were public. Though the aged doorkeeper, Edward McManus, was supposed to screen the public, in reality anyone who wanted to come in could come in—and did.

America had never before had children in the White House, and the nation took to the boys warmly. Though the Lincoln lads were already thoroughly spoiled by their indulgent parents, now they became more so, as they were showered with toys, pets, and other presents.

Of the three Lincoln children still living, Robert (now eighteen years old) had been shortchanged the most in fatherly interaction. His father had been away half the time on the court circuit when he was young, and when Robert had gotten older, he was away at college. Robert would always feel he'd never gotten to know his father the way his brothers had. Now a student at Harvard, Robert would be dubbed by his classmates "the Prince of Rails." And for good reason, for Robert was the mirror image of his aristocratic Todd forebearers and "to the manor born." Robert's preference for the trappings of wealth may have been another reason he and his father were always a little distant from each other.

Willie (who turned eleven that December) was everyone's favorite. He was good-looking, always cheerful, and mature for his age. He had light-brown hair, fair skin, and blue eyes. Perhaps because he mirrored his father in so many ways, his mother adored him and called him "my comfort." In fact, both parents instinctively felt that with Eddie dead, Robert a bit distant, and Tad afflicted by slowness of mental growth, Willie would be their mainstay when they got old.

Willie Lincoln was obsessed with the wonder of the age: railroads. By the age of ten, being fascinated by mathematical figures and machines, he'd constructed a virtual railroad from Chicago to New York, keeping his timetables to the minute. Willie would always beg his father to take him along on all railroad trips. He also loved hotels and theaters.

Willie was also the most deeply spiritual of the Lincoln boys. He loved to play church with Tad and declared that he would be a preacher when he grew up. And, like his father, he loved poetry.

Willie and Tad were inseparable and together turned the White House upside down. Not until Teddy Roosevelt's rambunctious family came along would the executive mansion be subjected to this many indignities.

Thomas, known as Tad (eight when they moved into the White

House), was happy, lovable, and exasperating. Ruth Painter Randall noted that Taddie would burst into the room where his father was sitting, looking for something, and having found it, throw himself on his father "like a small thunderbolt," give him a wild, fierce hug, and then rush from the room before his father could put out a hand to detain him.

Tad had always been slow at his lessons. His parents, recognizing his limitations, had wisely permitted him to grow at his own pace. His speech impediment made the boy extremely frustrated because most people couldn't understand him. But his father *always* did. As had been true with little Eddie, Tad had a tender heart and was intuitively sympathetic to those who suffered. Each of the four Lincoln sons had absolute integrity as a bedrock of his character.

Upon arriving at the White House, Willie and Tad investigated every room, alcove, and closet. Once settled in, they moved from one prank to another. Shortly after moving in, the boys were strongly attracted to three visitors: Bud, Julia, and Holly Taft. Mary, knowing how lonely her boys were for child companionship, invited the Taft children back the next day. They soon became inseparable.

Julia came with instructions: "Don't let those young rascals tear down the White House." The four boys paired off: Bud and Willie being thoughtful and usually showing restraint, Tad and Holly completely irresponsible. One day Tad and Holly thought it would be a great idea to take Tad's toy cannon and bombard the room where the president was meeting with his Cabinet—and did so.

Holly and Tad threw the White House into an uproar one morning when they mysteriously disappeared. They were brought back in a carriage after dark, having spent the day investigating the Capitol. Deciding to find out just how deep a certain stairwell was, they "went down steps pretty near to China." There were rats and it was "awful dark."

On one of their expeditions, Willie and Tad discovered the White House bell system. Tad, like his father, loved to investigate inner workings of things. He found out how the bells worked, and bedlam resulted, as Lincoln's secretaries, John Nicolay and John Hay were rushing to the

President's office with visions of a sudden national emergency or presidential ire; old Edward, the doorkeeper, was hurrying up the stairs; everyone was running somewhere to answer the violent ringing. The boys, of course, had a wonderful time.

Once, when Tad ate up all the strawberries the cook had been preparing for a state dinner, he was dubbed "the madam's wildcat."

The Lincoln boys also graciously gave measles to Colonel Elmer Ellsworth, a guest and dear friend. This magnetic and intense young leader of the Zouaves (named for French infantry drawn from the Berbers in Algeria), with his North African–looking uniform, would be one of the first casualties of the war. His funeral was held in the East Room.

Both of the Lincoln boys living at the White House loved attending Sunday School and church: Willie because of his plans to be a preacher and Tad because he refused to be separated from his brother.

Once, while their mother was in New York buying furnishings for the White House, the four boys and some friends put on a circus. When Julia Taft came over to see if they were behaving, she found the servants and White House staff grinning broadly. Admission charge was five cents. She discovered Bud and Willie were to be lovely Victorian ladies in the show. She saw each one was struggling into Mrs. Lincoln's dresses. Julia pinned up the train of Willie's dress, the surplus folds of Bud's, and also straightened up his bonnet. In Julia's words:

> The show opened patriotically with a rousing rendition of "Hail Columbia" by the entire "troupe." Billy Sanders and Tad Lincoln then sang "The Star-Spangled Banner." Loyal Unionism having thus been demonstrated, there followed a duet of "Dixie Land" by Joe Corkhead and Bud Taft, Bud doubtless an irresistible Southern belle in Mrs. Lincoln's white morning gown and a stylish bonnet. Willie, in a voluminous lilac silk of his mother's, cut very décolleté, probably stirred deep emotions in the audience when he joined in a duet of "Home Sweet Home."

In later years, Julia also remembered later once coming in and finding the president sitting in a big chair telling the boys exciting stories of hunters, settlers, and Indians. Willie sat on one of his knees, Bud on the other, Holly on the arm of the chair, and Tad perched on the back. A long arm then reached out and drew Julia into the circle.

Another time, hearing a terrific racket in a nearby room, Julia raced in to find the president flat on the floor with the four boys doing their best to hold him down. Seeing her come in, Tad shouted, "Julia, come quick and sit on his stomach." Mr. Lincoln's twinkle and wide grin showed he was enjoying every minute of it.

When Washington had been cut off from the world and tensions had been so high, the boys had had to lay low. But when that terrible scare was over, the boys built a protective fort on the White House roof and searched the Potomac for "enemy cruisers" with an old spyglass.

Lincoln enjoyed taking his sons with him when he visited military camps, though some frowned on it. One time he did leave the boys behind because it was a cold day and both boys had colds. But the boys tapped into that Lincoln resourcefulness and found a way to get there after all. They called the Taft children together and pulled out the money they'd made on their circus. Then off they went into the city:

As the President and dignitaries passed solemnly and ceremoniously down the line of soldiers, just after them came a rickety, mule-driven cart driven by a small, grinning coachman, and containing Willie, Bud, Holly, and Tad, each stiffly holding a battered sword at salute.

On one occasion, the Sanitary Commission in New York sent Tad a soldier doll, which he named "Jack." The doll was dressed in Zouave uniform. Sadly, Jack had unfortunate character traits, causing the boys to have to frequently court-martial him—for sleeping at his post, or desertion, or some other crime—always sentencing him to be shot at sunrise. Tad, with his toy cannon, would act as firing squad. Afterward, the dishonored Jack would be buried, undeservedly with full military honors, in the White House rose garden.

One day, Julia was in Mrs. Lincoln's room when a strange and dreadful sound came through the window.

"What is that noise, Julia?" Mrs. Lincoln asked her.

"It's probably the 'dead march,'" Julia answered. "I suppose the boys are burying Jack again.

Mrs. Lincoln told Julia to hurry out and tell the boys to cease, as it would kill the roses. She obeyed, even though she knew that previous warnings hadn't worked. Outside, Julia found a band of a broken-down fiddle, a dented horn, a paper over a comb, and Tad's drum. The irate gardener, Major Watt, arrived on the scene. Desperate for the survival of his precious roses, inspiration came to him: "Why don't you boys get Jack pardoned?"

The boys felt this was a capital idea and ran upstairs, Julia vainly trying to keep them from interrupting the president. John Hay had no better luck stopping them. Hearing all the commotion outside his office, Lincoln came out to see what the trouble was. After hearing Tad's request, the president told Tad that pardons weren't granted without a hearing, and it was up to them to tell him why Jack deserved a pardon.

Tad characteristically delivered his argument in a rush of words. Almost every day, he said, they tried Jack for being a spy or deserter or something and then they shot him and buried him and Julia said it spoiled his clothes and Major Watt said it dug up his roses so they thought they should get Pa to fix up a pardon.

The president considered these facts with due gravity and then told Tad he thought he'd made a case. It was a good law, he said, that no man shall twice be put in jeopardy of his life for the same offense. Since Jack had been shot and buried a dozen times, he was entitled to a pardon. He turned to his desk, on which so many pardons were to be signed, he wrote on his official paper: "The Doll Jack is pardoned by order of the President. A. Lincoln."

And so poor Jack was saved from execution. However, it is sad to relate that even the presidential pardon failed to reform the incorrigible Jack. In less than a week, he was again convicted of being a spy. This time, however, they decided he should be hanged from a tree in the Taft garden.

"A beautiful St. Bernard—like the one Jim loved so much."

THE TALL STRANGER

Arthur Somerset

Father was away at war, and mother was gravely ill, so there was not enough money for food—and certainly not enough to feed Jim's huge St. Bernard. So it was that poor Jim sat on the sidewalk of the Washington street, next to his dog—with a crudely lettered For Sale sign hanging from his neck.

Suddenly a very tall man was standing before him.

T oday at a family reunion of my seventy-fifth birthday, I was begged to tell again the story of the tall stranger who bought my dog.

It is a story of long, long ago. But it has been such a favorite with my sons and daughters and, later, with their own children, that I am moved to offer it to a larger public.

I was born in the city of Washington. My earliest recollections date back to the dark years of the Civil War. Perhaps the first distinct memory I have is of the day my father went away to war. I remember it, not so much because I understood at the time the significance of his going away, as because he made me a farewell present of a great, awkward, overgrown puppy.

"The poor pup followed me home from the recruiting station," he said. "I guess some fellow must have abandoned him there. But he'll make a good guardian for you and Mother while I'm gone." I remember that I cried. But Mother merely smiled. Then he kissed us goodbye.

It was not till an hour or so later, when I dashed gleefully into Mother's room with that romping puppy, that I found her on her knees beside the bed, sobbing into her pillow. "What is it, Jim?" she asked, looking up.

"Mother, I—I only wanted to know if you don't think 'Yankee' would be a good name for the puppy?" She hugged me very tight then, and pressed her wet cheek against mine. "Yes, dear," she told me. "I think that name will do very well."

Later I came to understand more clearly what war meant. I can remember lying in bed at night, with Yankee snuggled up against me, and listening to the tramp, tramp, tramp of marching men. For days it never stopped. I would fall asleep with that sound in my ears and awake to hear it in the morning. I can remember the endless pies and pans of hot biscuits my mother used to bake for the soldiers. For in those days there were no YMCA huts or Red Cross tents.

Later, I can remember the women who used to meet in our house to scrape lint for surgical dressings. Hour after hour they would sit there scraping—sometimes far into the night, after I had gone to bed. Only in the morning I could always tell when they had been there, because everything in the house would be covered with a fine white dust.

But more than any specific incident, I think, I remember the feeling of those terrible war years—the steadily increasing tension and the atmosphere of anxiety that even a child could not help sensing.

I suppose I was aware of it chiefly in my mother. Heaven knows she had enough to make her anxious. For as the war dragged into its third year she was hardly able to feed us. Yet many a time I saw her surrender her own plate of food to Yankee, watching vigilantly from the floor beside her. As he wolfed up and polished off the plate, a worried look would come over my mother's face.

"Jim," she would say, "I don't know how we can keep that dog. He's getting so big that he eats as much as both of us!" He had indeed got to be a huge dog. He had grown so fast that he was almost larger than I was myself. I never knew exactly what breed he was. St. Bernard, I think, with maybe a little mastiff blood in him or Great Dane. But I was devoted to him. So, whenever my mother threatened to get rid of him, I pleaded with her to keep him just a little longer.

There came a time, though, when my mother was really ill.

One day as she lay in her bed she told me to take fifty cents from her desk and go out and buy food. I went to the drawer in which she kept her money—it was empty. It never occurred to me that she might have put her money somewhere else. I knew so well that we were poor that just one train of thought went through my mind. The money had given out. Mother was sick. So, somehow or other, it was up to me to see that we got food.

I looked at Yankee. He looked at me out of his great mournful eyes. Then and there I made my one and only sacrifice to the Civil War—I resolved to sell my dog.

Oh, you may smile if you want. But to me, I can tell you, it was no smiling matter! My father had given me Yankee before he went away, and that dog had become the best friend I had in the world. My school teachers might punish me. Older boys might jeer at me for being poorly dressed. Even my mother might misunderstand me. But Yankee was the one friend who never went back on me and who always seemed to understand.

Nothing that I did to him ever made the slightest difference. He would lick my hand when we had no food to offer. In winter, when icy drafts blew through my room, he would sleep faithfully on the bare floor beside my bed. If I had had to go out into the world a homeless little vagabond, I know he would have asked no higher privilege than to go with me, to share whatever came to me and to guard me against enemies.

But now I felt there was nothing I could do but sell him. From the lid of an empty cracker box I made a crude sign which read: "For Sale." This I tied around his neck. Then, with burning eyes and a lump in my throat, I knotted a cord to his collar and led him forth.

I remember it was late in the winter afternoon. It must have been the winter of 1864–65. I took up my post on a street corner near the old Treasury Building in Washington where there was sure to be lots of people passing. But for a long time nothing happened.

Most of the pedestrians who went by were engrossed in conversation and did not even notice me. Those who did merely smiled and passed by. At last I got so tired that I sat down on the cold pavement beside Yankee. He was squatting on his haunches with his front legs erect. I put my arms about his neck and pressed up close against his shaggy coat to keep warm. I was not even aware of the tall stranger until he stopped in front of me.

Then my eyes took in successively his huge shoes, the length of his baggy trouser legs, the black coat that hung in loose folds from his drooping shoulders, and his gaunt, homely, furrowed face with its deep-set gray eyes and jut of black beard.

Although he wore the stove-pipe hat which gentlemen affected in those days, I cannot remember that a thing about him gave me the impression that he was rich. I had been waiting for a customer. But now, at the prospect of having one, my clasp tightened on Yankee's neck and tears began to run down along the sides of my nose.

"Do you want to—buy him, mister?" I sniffled. For a moment the tall man did not answer. His eyes seemed to be taking in the huge melancholy dog, the scrawled sign about his neck, and my patched, frayed pantaloons supported by a single gallus [suspenders] that went over my shirt.

"Why do you want to sell him, son?" he asked gently. I told him the best I could, explaining that my mother was sick and that we were poor because my father was away in the Union Army. "I see," he said thoughtfully. He put out one hand to pat the dog's head. "His name's Yankee," I volunteered. "He'll shake hands with you, sir, if you want."

The big man stooped down until the bottom of his long coat brushed the sidewalk. Very solemnly, he took the paw that my dog offered. "How much do you want for him, son?" he inquired.

I hesitated. "Do you think," I asked apprehensively, "that a—dollar would be too much?"

It seemed to me a twinkle came into his deep-set gray eyes. But he considered judiciously. "No," he decided gravely. "I don't think that's too much. But I don't quite know where I could put him if I bought him. You see, we have a lot of company at our house."

"He's hardly any trouble, sir," I put in. "He'll just sleep on the floor beside your bed or anywhere at all."

"Yes," the big man answered. "But I have an idea you could take better care of him than anyone else. So suppose I buy him and just leave him in your charge until I find out whether there is room for him in my house?"

"All right, sir," I said, overjoyed. "But any time you want him, of course—"

"Perhaps," he interrupted kindly, "I won't have room for him after all. In that case he's yours. All I'm really buying is an option on him, which means that you mustn't sell him to anybody else." His big hand reached down into his trouser pocket and drew out a roll of bills we knew as "shin plasters." But when he handed one to me I saw that it was for ten dollars. That was a lot of money in those days and my eyes must have almost popped out of my head.

"You've made a mistake, sir."

"No." He looked at Yankee and again that kindly twinkle came into his eyes. "I figure that the dog is worth a dollar," he said, "but that his board will cost at least that much each month. At the end of nine months, if I haven't called for him, perhaps the war will be over and your father will be back." Without another word or even a smile, he turned away.

Too surprised to even thank him, I just stood there and watched him stride off with his strange, shambling, loose-kneed gait. A few minutes later, with Yankee tugging madly at his leash, I dashed breathlessly into the house to show the money to my mother.

When she understood what I had done and saw the sign still fastened to Yankee's collar, her lips quivered and little puckers came into her chin. "But who was the man, Jim?" she asked anxiously. "He must be some-body we know. He must have recognized you, for a stranger doesn't hand out money like that."

"I can't remember ever seeing him before, Mother."

"It wasn't Dr. Johnson?"

"No, I don't think so."

For days she puzzled over the tall man's identity, suggesting different persons whom she thought he might have been. She was a little annoyed that I should have taken money from a man without knowing who he was, and I think she wanted to pay it back. But I was so happy at being able to keep Yankee that I hardly cared who the man was. When a week passed without my seeing him again, I began to hope that he would never come for the dog.

It was the following spring that Lee evacuated Richmond; and, a few days later came the news that he had been overtaken by General Grant and forced to surrender his whole Army.

One afternoon after that I entered the house to find my father home again. He shouted to me and I let out a whoop. It seemed as if even Yankee went wild with delight, for he raced about us and filled the house with his excited barking. Only my mother, who had smiled and laughed when father went away, was unaccountably weeping now that he had come back.

When my father had kissed me and swung me up to the ceiling, he took Yankee's big head between his hands.

"Well, Old Dog," he asked, "did you take care of them while I was gone?"

Then Mother told him the story of my trying to sell Yankee and asked who he thought had given me the ten dollars. But Father couldn't think, any more than my mother, of anyone who answered to my description of the tall stranger. So for a while that little family mystery was forgotten in our rejoicing over Father's return and in the general victory jubilation.

Then, with terrible suddenness, came the news that plunged the whole nation into mourning. I remember coming down to breakfast on that fatal morning of April 15, 1865 to find my father with the newspaper spread out on the table before him. From his face and my mother's I knew that some calamity had happened.

"What is it?" I asked. "Has there been another battle?"

My father looked up soberly. "The President was shot last night," he said, "in his box at the Ford Theatre. He is very seriously wounded."

When I went out after breakfast the word was already being passed around across from the theatre where they had carried him. I can remember still the hush of grief that seemed to settle upon the city that day. When I came into the house at dinner time, my father was driving a nail into the wall in order to hang a new picture he had bought. Photography had not been perfected in those days, and this picture was a daguerreotype portrait of some man which had been reproduced in steel engraving.

As I caught sight of the face, I suddenly recognized it. "Why, Father," I exclaimed. *"That's the tall stranger*—the man who told me to keep Yankee for him!"

My father turned, still holding the picture up against the wall with one hand. "You must be mistaken, Jim," he said.

"No!" I insisted. "That's him, all right. Why there's even the little mole he had down near the corner of his mouth!"

I shall never forget the expression that came over my father's face then, nor the way he looked at Mother. She was standing stock still in the middle of the dining room with a dish of potatoes in her hand. Suddenly tears started into her eyes.

Very deliberately, my father fastened the picture on the wall and straightened it. He came up to me and placed his hand on my shoulder. "Jim," he asked politely, "do you know who that man is?"

"I don't know his name," I replied impatiently. "But I tell you he's the man—"

My father's hands tightened on my shoulder. All at once a suspicion of who he meant grazed my mind. "Son," his words came gravely, "that man was—Abraham Lincoln!"

It seemed suddenly very still in the room. None of us moved, but just stood there looking at the picture on the wall. Then I heard Mother crying softly. I heard the rattle of Yankee's toe nails on the floor as he got up and came over to thrust his nose into her palm.

Illustrated by Charles M. Relyea for
St. Nicholas Magazine *in 1918.*

THE MISSIONARY MONEY

Olive Vincent Marsh

"Oh, no, I can't take that, Uncle Abe," she said earnestly. "I have to earn all the money I put in this box."

And that appeared to settle that.

Once upon a time, as all the good fairy-stories begin—only I must warn you that the fairy in this story was a very big fairy indeed, and very real—there lived a little girl in a little town in New York State. I know that she was a bright and happy and altogether delightful little girl, because now that she is growing old she is bright and happy and altogether delightful still.

She lived with her father and her mother and her brothers in a real, old-fashioned, homey home, where guests liked to come. One of the guests who liked to come was the great Abraham Lincoln, President of the United States. The little girl was always very happy when he came, and she used to like to sit on his lap and talk to him. She called him "Uncle Abe," and he often called her "Sissy," though her real name was Julia.

One time when the President was visiting at Julia's home and the family was all gathered in the sitting-room in the evening, Julia was counting the money in her missionary box, at one end of the table. Mr. Lincoln watched her for a moment and then asked:

"What are you doing over there?"

"I'm counting my missionary money, Uncle Abe," replied Julia.

Mr. Lincoln put his hand in his pocket and pulled out something and held it toward Julia. Julia drew back her box.

"Oh, no, I can't take that, Uncle Abe," she said earnestly; "I have to *earn* all the money I put in this box."

"That so?" said Mr. Lincoln, thoughtfully, and, making no further comment, he put his hand back into his pocket again.

The next day, when he was ready to start for the train, he said to Julia:

"I wonder if you couldn't walk down to the depot with me, Julia?"

"Oh, yes, I'd love to!" cried Julia, and she ran for her hat.

As they started down the street together, Abraham Lincoln shifted his valise to the other hand. It was an old-fashioned valise with two handles. He looked down from his great height at his little companion.

"Do you suppose," he said, "that you could help me carry my valise? It's pretty heavy."

Julia was a little surprised, for Mr. Lincoln had never asked her to help him carry his valise before; but she took hold of one of the handles, and they carried it between them all the way to the depot, talking gaily as they went. At the depot the President took the valise and pulled a shining coin out of his pocket, holding it out to the little girl.

"There, Julia," he said, "now you've earned your missionary money."

Julia was very much surprised, for she had not thought of such a thing as earning money while she was helping her friend carry his valise, but she saw that she really had earned it. Mr. Lincoln had found a way. Her face lighted up as she exclaimed joyfully:

"Oh, *thank* you, Uncle Abe!"

And then he went away on the train, and Julia ran home with the shining coin clutched tight in her hand. She thought it was the very brightest penny she had ever seen, and she hurried to put it into the missionary box, where it would be safe and sound.

The next Sunday at Sunday-school, when the missionary boxes were opened, Julia was called out into another room. There sat the superintendent and there were her father and one of her brothers, and there on the table was her missionary box. Everybody looked very serious.

"How much money did you have in your missionary box, Julia?" asked the superintendent.

"Eighty-two cents," answered the little girl, without any hesitation.

"I knew it was a mistake. It's not her box," said her father.

"Are you sure that was all you had? Where did *this* come from?" she was asked, and she saw the bright penny that the President had given her.

"Oh, that's the money Uncle Abe gave me!" she answered eagerly. "I earned it helping him carry his valise."

The shining coin was a five-dollar gold-piece, and this is a true story of how Abraham Lincoln helped a little girl to earn her missionary money. I know that it is true because the little girl, who is a little girl no longer, told me the story herself.

Illustration drawn by John Wolcott Adams in 1921.

JUST FOLKS

Mary Wells

The boy ran away from home to enlist. In Washington, the recruiter rejected him, declaring him "too young." Exhausted, the boy fell asleep in a park. When he awoke it was to the sound of a man reading—strange verses that didn't make sense then.

Did you ever see Lincoln, Mr. Warren?"

A wonderful smile lighted up the fine old face of the veteran. "Yes," he replied, "I saw him twice and talked with him once."

Mr. Warren rose and went to a little mahogany desk from which he took an old-fashioned daguerreotype case and a small brown book. He opened the daguerreotype case and handed it to me.

It was evidently a family group, two girls and a boy in the costume of the early sixties. One of the girls was beautiful, but it was the boy that held my gaze. He sat with his left hand grasping his right wrist. The attitude was stiffly conventional, but above the high black stock* the boyish face rose youthfully winning. It had at the same time a certain serious steadfastness. I looked at Mr. Warren.

A collar or a neckcloth fitting like a band around the neck.

"My sisters Mary and Harriet, and I. It was taken in 1862 shortly before I enlisted."

"Enlisted! A boy like that! Why, you couldn't have been more than fifteen! How did your parents ever consent?"

"I was just sixteen," said Mr. Warren calmly, "and my parents didn't consent." His eyes twinkled. "I ran away."

He settled back comfortably in the big chair and began:

"I was wild to go. Father had been in the service from the first, a captain of the 145th New York. He was colonel when the war ended. Grandfather Warren was looking after things at home. Every time I broached the subject of enlistment, however, either tentatively or directly, I met with a prompt and decided refusal, quite properly of course from a common-sense point of view.

"The war went on, and what with Father's letters, the war news, the different regiments going out and all there came a time when I couldn't stand it any longer. Besides, there was an indefinable, inexorable something drawing me on, though I could not have put the feeling into words. I had to go.

"Having definitely made up my mind, I laid my plans accordingly. Circumstances favored me. At that time I was attending the old academy a mile and a half from home, so that I was obliged to take my lunch. The night before I left I packed an old carpetbag that I found in the attic, stole out of the back door and hid the bag in a fence corner round the bend. Early the next morning I asked permission to spend the night with my friend Joe Brainerd. I believe a rabbit hunt was mentioned." The old man chuckled. "That would give me till the next night before anybody learned that I was gone, and by that time I hoped to be a member of Uncle Sam's army.

"I had just about enough money to get me to Washington, and I figured that, once I got there, all would be plain sailing. I was a little mistaken in my calculations," he added dryly, "but I'll come to that presently.

"It was a beautiful morning in early fall, with the leaves just beginning to turn. I stopped at the bend to look back at the old house among the trees. It was the last time I was to see it for nearly three years.

"I found the carpetbag where I had left it, and I was soon hurrying cross-lots to the junction to get a southbound train. I met nobody whom I knew, but I was pretty uneasy until I was on board and felt the grinding of the wheels as the train pulled out of the little station. Then I settled back into the hard seat, with a sigh of relief. I was off to war!

"I won't tell the details of the journey. It was the middle of the forenoon when I reached Washington; and by that time I was beginning to feel that I was a long way from home.

"As I walked through the capital I had a confused sense of heat and mud and milling people. Blue uniforms were everywhere, military vehicles were coming and going, and there was an occasional blare of music.

"I walked along with my eye out for a recruiting station, and I was not long in coming to one. They were plentiful enough in those days. Inside the tent a short, stocky man sat behind a table with a lot of papers spread before him. There was a younger man with him, evidently his assistant, and both men were busy writing. There were no other applicants at the moment.

"I entered the tent, with my heart going like a trip hammer. The officer looked up; transfixing me with a glance of steel-gray eyes; then he waited without saying a word.

" 'I want to enlist,' I said. I did not recognize my own voice.

"The man dipped his pen into a bottle of ink and held it poised over the paper.

" 'Name?' he said briefly.

" 'James Redfield Warren,' I replied.

" 'Age?' the officer at once asked me.

"At the curt question I felt the blood surging to my face and had the miserable awareness that I looked younger than ever.

" 'Going on seventeen,' I faltered.

"The corners of his mouth twitched slightly.

" 'Date of birth?'

"I gave it reluctantly.

" 'You will be going on for some time,' he said dryly; 'I suppose you know you will have to have your papers signed by your parents or guardian?'

"My heart sank. 'I thought in Washington—' I stammered.

"He shook his head. 'Eighteen is the minimum. Can't take you, my boy, unless your papers are signed.'

"His tone was kindly enough, but firmer than the Rock of Gibraltar.

" 'Next,' he added, for by that time several men were in line behind me. My case was definitely dismissed.

"I picked up my valise and went out into the street. Scarcely seeing where I went, I walked along till I came to a park, though it was not much of a park, either. In those days Washington was still rather unfinished around the edges. I sat down on a wooden bench under a big elm and faced the situation.

"There I was—miles from home and no nearer enlistment than I had been at home. I was in a strange city with only a few dollars in my pocket. Chagrin and disappointment and poignant homesickness filled my heart."

The old man paused.

"But the strange thing about it all was that I never thought of giving up."

From the daguerreotype the young face looked at me with its serious steadfastness, and I thought I understood.

"I racked my brain for some solution of the problem," Mr. Warren continued, "and all of a sudden the thought came to me that, if I could only see the President, everything would be all right. How that feat was to be accomplished I did not ask myself. I somehow took it for granted.

"With so much settled, I leaned back against the bench, conscious suddenly of an overwhelming drowsiness. The excitement and the fatigue of the last two days were beginning to tell on me. I shut my eyes for a moment.

"The moment must have lengthened itself into many. When at last I opened my eyes I found that I was not alone under the elm. At the other end of the bench a man sat reading. So absorbed was he in the book that he was totally oblivious of my presence and, indeed, of everything else round him. As I sat there half-way between waking and sleeping he closed the book and, keeping his finger between the leaves, began to recite in a low voice, with his gaze fixed on the distant horizon:

> "Fear no more the heat o' th' sun,
> Nor the furious winter's rages;
>
> Thou thy earthly task has done,
> Home art gone and ta'en thy wages.
>
> Fear no more the frown o' th' great,
> Thou art past the tyrant's stroke;
>
> Care no more to clothe and eat;
> To thee the reed is as the oak;
>
> The scepter, learning, physic, must
> All follow this and come to dust.
>
> Fear no more the lightning flash,
> Nor th' all-dreaded thunder stone;
>
> Fear not slander, censure rash;
> Thou hast finish'd joy and moan."

"He repeated slowly: 'Fear not slander, censure rash'; then, 'Home art gone and ta'en thy wages.'

"'I reckon there are always the wages,' he said thoughtfully; then again, 'always the wages.'

"He was a homely man with a lined face and awkwardly drooping shoulders, but for a moment there was a light in his plain countenance that made it radiant.

"I forgot myself and my trouble momentarily in watching this strange man who sat on a bench in a public park reading poetry and talking to himself. The contemplative look died out of his eyes. It was almost as if he were coming back from another world. He turned to find me staring at him. There was a glint of humor in the deep-set eyes.

"'Didn't know I had an audience, sonny,' he said. "Thought you were in the Land of Nod.'

"'I woke up,' I said inanely.

"'Plenty of food for thought in what I was reading.' He lifted the little book, pausing as if for my corroboration.

"'I'm afraid I didn't get the sense,' I confessed.

"'Later I, too, was to learn those lines from *Cymbeline* and to cherish them all my life.

"'Not much given to reading poetry yet?'

"I shook my head by way of answer.

"He looked at my carpetbag, which I had thrust part way under the bench.

"'Traveling?'

"'I came to Washington to enlist,' I said with what dignity I could muster.

"'How have you made out?'

"There was a sort of whimsical drollery in the slightly drawling tone.

"'I haven't made out very well so far,' I admitted reluctantly.

"Something in the friendly quizzical glance gave me confidence, and before I knew it I found myself telling him the whole story. He listened quietly. When I came to my conversation with the recruiting officer he smiled. Indeed, he had smiled more than once during my narrative.

"'Why didn't you tell him you were eighteen?' he queried. His glance fixed itself keenly on my face.

"'I didn't think of it,' I blurted out, and my companion laughed delightedly, 'But,' I said after a moment's reflection, 'I guess I wouldn't have said so anyway.'

"He surveyed me soberly.

"'No, I reckon you wouldn't,' he said. 'What are you calculating to do now?'

"'I'm going to see the President.'

"Again that queer glint of humor came into his eyes.

"'Reckon he can fix it up for you?'

"'Why, yes,' I said confidently. 'They would *have* to let me enlist if he told them to.'

"'How do you expect to see him?' my companion asked. 'He's a pretty busy man, and, besides, there's considerable red tape to go through, getting an interview.'

"My heart sank.

"'Don't you think you might as well give up the idea of enlisting, sonny?'

"That kindly earnest gaze seemed to penetrate the innermost depths of my boyish heart. I looked at him dumbly a moment; then, 'I can't give it up,' I said. It was almost as if the words were saying themselves. 'I've *got* to enlist. You see—'

"Then something queer happened. It was borne in upon me that I had no need of further words. The gaunt, plain-featured man *understood*.

"He laid his hand on my shoulder. 'I do see, my boy,' he said simply.

"Then he smiled quietly as if at an amusing thought. 'I tell you what we'll do, sonny. I'll go along with you to the recruiting station, and perhaps I can say a word or two that will help you. I know a number of the officers. Then if that fails, we'll have to make a try for the President.'

"He rose or rather seemed to unfold, for he was the tallest man I had ever seen. I felt like a pygmy beside him. He made me think of Si Adams, our hired man, only he was bigger and bonier. Indeed, all the time we had been talking he had seemed oddly familiar, and subconsciously I had been trying to think whom he resembled. I decided that I had been thinking of Si.

"We walked along, silent for the most part, for my companion was evidently busy with his own thoughts. People who passed looked at us curiously, and I suppose we made an odd picture—the tall man and the young country boy carrying the old carpetbag. I was astonished to see how many people my friend knew, especially among the soldiers. He responded absently to the various salutations.

"At the recruiting station I entered without trepidation. I had a feeling that my new friend would be a match for any recruiting officer.

"The short, stocky man gazed at us for a moment in the most open astonishment; then he sprang to his feet and gave the military salute.

"My friend returned it; then he said quietly, 'Purvis, here's a young friend of mine that wants to enlist. I'll go bail for him. Make out his papers, and I'll sign them. I reckon you'll accept me as sponsor?'

"It was really more of a command than a question, and, indeed, there was an air of quiet authority about the tall man.

"'I reckon I will, Mr. President,' said the officer.

"'Mr. President!' Comprehension flashed upon me. The resemblance that had been puzzling me, the curious glances of the people whom we had met, the saluting soldiers—it was all clear now. I stood dumfounded, abashed. But my companion was not looking at me. He had adjusted a pair of spectacles on his nose and was running his forefinger down the printed draft form till it rested on the line labeled 'Parent or Guardian.' Then slowly and painstakingly he wrote: Abraham Lincoln.

"He laid down the pen, took off his spectacles and put them back into the case; then he turned to me with twinkling eyes.

"'There, my son, I reckon that will do the business.'

"I stood before him, speechless, overwhelmed by the simple kindliness of the man. As I looked up into his face the thought that was in my mind rose involuntarily to my lips.

"'Why,' I stammered, 'you're just—'

"Mr. Lincoln interrupted me, interpreting my thought as if by magic.

"'Yes—just folks, sonny,' he said, 'just folks.'

"He turned to the recruiting officer. 'I reckon we needn't despair, Purvis, when "sixteen going on seventeen" has faith in our cause.'

"There was a strange solemnity in his tone.

"He drew from his pocket the little brown book he had been reading and handed it to me.

" 'Take it along. It's mighty good reading, and you'll understand those lines some day.'

"Then he laid his hand on my shoulder and looked down into my upturned face.

" 'Better get a letter off home right away.

" 'The folks will be getting anxious.'

"I wanted to thank him, to pour out my heart, but somehow I could not find a word; but it was not necessary. He understood.

" 'Good luck, and God bless you,' he said cheerfully.

"There was a last pressure of the big hand, and then I stood in the tent door, watching the tall form as it went slowly up the street. Only then I noticed that two soldiers were following him at a respectful distance.

"And that," said Mr. Warren, "is how I came to see and talk with Abraham Lincoln."

He handed me the worn copy of *Cymbeline*, which opened of itself to the lines so often read. I turned back reverently to the flyleaf where Lincoln's signature was penned in ink now faded.

"You said you saw Lincoln a second time," I ventured.

A look of pain came into the old man's face. "When I saw Lincoln the second time," he said, "he was lying dead in the Capitol at Washington, with a nation mourning for him."

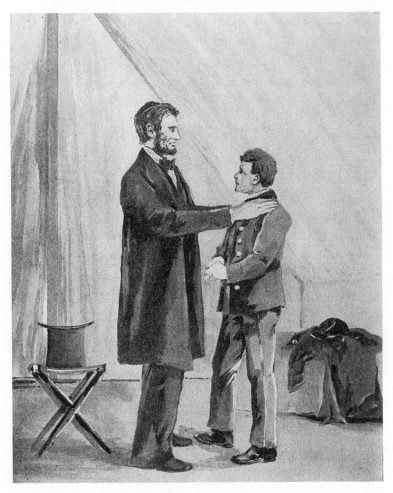

Woodcut drawn in 1892.

THE SLEEPING SENTINEL

L. E. CHITTENDEN

Since so many story writers have depicted Lincoln's reluctance to permit soldiers to die who fell asleep on guard duty, this account written by the President's Register of the Treasury reveals how true to life these other stories are.

The truth is always and everywhere attractive. The child loves, and never outgrows its love, for a real true story. The story of this young soldier, as it was presented to me, so touchingly reveals some of the kindlier qualities of the President's character that it seldom fails to charm those to whom it is related. I shall give its facts as I understood them, and I think I can guarantee their general accuracy.

On a dark September morning, in 1861, when I reached my office, I found waiting there a party of soldiers, none of whom I personally knew. They were greatly excited, all speaking at the same time, and consequently unintelligible. One of them wore the bars of a captain. I said to them, pleasantly, "Boys, I cannot understand you. Pray, let your captain say what you want, and what I can do for you." They complied, and the captain put me in possession of the following facts:

They belonged to the Third Vermont Regiment, raised, with the exception of one company, on the eastern slope of the Green Mountains, and mustered into service while the battle of Bull Run was progressing. They were immediately sent to Washington, and since their arrival, during the last days of July, had been stationed at the Chain Bridge, some three miles above Georgetown. Company K, to which most of them belonged, was largely made up of farmer-boys, many of them still in their minority.

The story which I extracted from the "boys" was, in substance, this: William Scott, one of these mountain-boys, just of age, had enlisted in Company K. Accustomed to his regular sound and healthy sleep, not yet inured to the life of the camp, he had volunteered to take the place of a sick comrade who had been detailed for picket duty, and had passed the night as a sentinel on guard. The next day he was himself detailed for the same duty, and undertook its performance. But he found it impossible to keep awake for two nights in succession, and had been found by the relief sound asleep on his post. For this offence he had been tried by a court-martial, found guilty, and sentenced to be shot within twenty-four hours after his trial, and on the second morning after his offence was committed.

Scott's comrades had set about saving him in a characteristic way. They had called a meeting, appointed a committee, with power to use all the resources of the regiment in his behalf. Strangers in Washington, the committee had resolved to call on me for advice, because I was a Vermonter, and they had already marched from the camp to my office since daylight that morning.

The captain took all the blame from Scott upon himself. Scott's mother opposed his enlistment on the ground of his inexperience, and had only consented on the captain's promise to look after him as if he were his own son. This he had wholly failed to do. He must have been asleep or stupid himself, he said, when he paid no attention to the boy's statement that he had fallen asleep during the day, and feared he could not keep awake the second night on picket. Instead of sending some one, or going himself in Scott's place, as he should have, he had let him go to his death. He alone was guilty—"if anyone ought to be shot, I am the fellow, and everybody at home would have the right to say so." "There must be some way to save him, Judge!" (They all called me judge.) "He is as good a boy as there is in the Army, and he ain't to blame. You will help us, now, won't you?" he said, almost in tears.

The other members of the committee had a definite, if not a practical plan. They insisted that Scott had not been tried, and gave this account of the proceeding. He was asked what he had to say to the charge, and said he would tell them just how it all happened. He had never been up all night that he remembered. He was "all beat out" by the night before, and knew he should have a hard fight to keep awake; he thought of hiring one of the boys to go in his place, but they might think he was afraid to do his duty, and he decided to "chance it." Twice he went to sleep and woke himself while he was marching, and then—he could not tell anything about it—all he knew was that he was sound asleep when the guard came. It was very wrong, he knew. He wanted to be a good soldier, and do all his duty. What else did he enlist for? They could shoot him, and perhaps they ought to, but he could not have tried harder; and if he was in the same place again, he could no more help going to sleep than he could fly.

One must have been made of sterner stuff than I was not to be touched by the earnest manner with which these men offered to mortgage even their farms to the aid of their comrade. The captain and the others had no need of words to express their emotions. I saw that the situation was surrounded by difficulties of which they knew nothing. They had sub-scribed a sum of money to pay counsel, and offered to pledge their credit to any amount necessary to secure him a fair trial.

"Put up your money," I said. "It will be long after this when one of my name takes money for helping a Vermont soldier. I know facts which touch this case of which you know nothing. I fear that nothing effectual can be done for your comrade. The courts and lawyers can do nothing. I fear that we can do no more; but we can try."

I must digress here to say that the Chain Bridge across the Potomac was one of the positions upon which the safety of Washington depended. The Confederates had fortified the approach to it on the Virginia side, and the Federals on the hills of Maryland opposite. Here, for months, the opposing forces had confronted each other. There had been no fighting; the men, and even the officers, had gradually contracted an intimacy, and, having nothing better to do, had swapped stories and other property until they had come to live upon the footing of good neighbors rather than mortal enemies. This relation was equally inconsistent with the safety of Washington and the stern discipline of war. Its discovery had excited alarm, and immediate measures were taken to break it up. General W. F. Smith, better known as "Baldy" Smith, had been appointed colonel of the Third Vermont Regiment, placed in command of the post, and undertook to correct the irregularity.

General Smith, a Vermonter by birth, a West-Pointer by education, was a soldier from spur to crown. Possibly he had natural sympathies, but they were so subordinated to the demands of his profession that they might as well not have existed. He regarded a soldier as so much valuable material, to be used with economy, like powder and lead, to the best advantage. The soldier was not worth much to him until his individuality was suppressed and converted into the unit of an Army. He must be taught obedience; discipline must never be relaxed. In the demoralization which existed at the Chain Bridge, in his opinion, the occasional execution of a soldier would tend to enforce discipline, and in the end promote economy of life. He had issued orders declaring the penalty of death for military offences, among others that of a sentinel sleeping upon his post. His orders were made to be obeyed. Scott was, apparently, their first victim. It went without saying that any appeal in his behalf to General Smith would lead to nothing but loss of time.

The more I reflected upon what I was to do, the more hopeless the case appeared. Thought was useless. I must act upon impulse, or I should not act at all.

"Come," I said, "there is only one man on earth who can save your comrade. Fortunately, he is the best man on the continent. We will go to President Lincoln."

I went swiftly out of the Treasury over to the White House, and up the stairway to the little office where the President was writing. The boys followed in a procession. I did not give the thought time to get any hold on me that I, an officer of the government, was committing an impropriety in thus rushing a matter upon the President's attention. The President was the first to speak.

"What is this?" he asked. "An expedition to kidnap somebody, or to get another brigadier appointed, or for a furlough to go home to vote? I cannot do it, gentlemen. Brigadiers are thicker than drum-majors, and I couldn't get a furlough for myself if I asked it from the War Department."

There was hope in the tone in which he spoke. I went straight to my point. "Mr. President," I said, "these men want nothing for themselves. They are Green Mountain boys of the Third Vermont, who have come to stay as long as you need good soldiers. They don't want promotion until they earn it. But they do want something that you alone can give them— the life of a comrade."

"What has he done?" asked the President. "You Vermonters are not a bad lot, generally. Has he committed murder or mutiny, or what other felony?"

"Tell him," I whispered to the captain.

"I cannot! I cannot! I should stammer like a fool! You can do it better!"

"Captain," I said, pushing him forward, "Scott's life depends on you. You must tell the President the story. I only know it by hearsay."

He commenced like the man by the Sea of Galilee, who had an impediment in his speech; but very soon the string of his tongue was loosened, and he spoke plain. He began to word-paint a picture with the hand of a master. As the words burst from his lips they stirred my own blood. He gave a graphic account of the whole story, and ended by saying, "He is as brave a boy as there is in your Army, sir. Scott is no coward. Our mountains breed no cowards. They are the homes of thirty thousand men who voted for Abraham Lincoln. They will not be able to see that the best thing to be done with William Scott will be to shoot him like a traitor and bury him like a dog! Oh, Mr. Lincoln, can you?"

"No, I can't!" exclaimed the President. It was one of the moments when his countenance became such a remarkable study. It had become very earnest as the captain rose with his subject; then it took on that melancholy expression which, later in his life, became so infinitely touching. I thought I could detect a mist in the deep cavities of his eyes. Then, in a flash, there was a total change. He smiled, and finally broke into a hearty laugh, as he asked me,

"Do your Green Mountain boys fight as well as they talk? If they do, I don't wonder at the legends about Ethan Allen." Then his face softened as he said, "But what can I do? What do you expect me to do? As you know, I have not much influence with the departments?"

"I have not thought the matter out," I said. "I feel a deep interest in saving young Scott's life. I think I knew the boy's father. It is useless to apply to General Smith. An application to Secretary Stanton would only be referred to General Smith. The only thing to be done was to apply to you. It seems to me that, if you would sign an order suspending Scott's execution until his friends can have his case examined, I might carry it to the War Department, and so insure the delivery of the order to General Smith today, through the regular channels of the War Office."

"No! I do not think that course would be safe. You do not know these officers of the regular army. They are a law unto themselves. They sincerely think that it is good policy occasionally to shoot a soldier. I can see it, where a soldier deserts or commits a crime, but I cannot in such a case as Scott's. They say that I am always interfering with the discipline of the Army, and being cruel to the soldiers. Well, I can't help it, so I shall have to go right on doing wrong. I do not think an honest, brave soldier, conscious of no crime but sleeping when he was weary, ought to be shot or hung. The country has better uses for him."

"Captain," continued the President, "your boy shall not be shot—that is, not tomorrow, nor until I know more about his case." To me he said, "I will have to attend to this matter myself. I have for some time intended to go up to the Chain Bridge. I will do so today. I shall then know that there is no mistake in suspending the execution."

I remarked that he was undertaking a burden which we had no right to impose; that it was asking too much of the President in behalf of a private soldier.

"Scott's life is as valuable to him as that of any person in the land," he said. "You remember the remark of a Scotchman about the head of a nobleman who was decapitated. 'It was a small matter of a head, but it was valuable to him, poor fellow, for it was the only one he had.'"

I saw that remonstrance was in vain. I suppressed the rising gratitude of the soldiers, and we took our leave. Two members of "the committee" remained to watch events in the city, while the others returned to carry the news of their success to Scott and to the camp. Later in the day the two members reported that the President had started in the direction of the camp; that their work here was ended, and they proposed to return to their quarters.

Within a day or two the newspapers reported that a soldier, sentenced to be shot for sleeping on his post, had been pardoned by the President and returned to his regiment. Other duties pressed me, and it was December before I heard anything further from Scott. Then another elderly soldier of the same company, whose health had failed, and who was arranging for his own discharge, called upon me, and I made inquiry about Scott. The soldier gave an enthusiastic account of him. He was in splendid health, was very athletic, popular with everybody, and had the reputation of being the best all-around soldier in the company, if not in the regiment. His mate was the elderly soldier who had visited me with the party in September, who would be able to tell me all about him. To him I sent a message, asking him to see me when he was next in the city. His name was Ellis or Evans.

Not long afterwards he called at my office, and, as his leave permitted, I kept him overnight at my house, and gathered from him the following facts about Scott. He said that, as we supposed, the President went to the camp, had a long conversation with Scott, at the end of which he was sent back to his company a free man. The President had given him a paper, which he preserved very carefully, which was supposed to be his discharge from the sentence. A regular order for his pardon had been read in the presence of the regiment, signed by General McClellan, but everyone knew that his life had been saved by the President.

From that day Scott was the most industrious man in the company. He was always at work, generally helping some other soldier. His arms and his dress were neat and cleanly; he took charge of policing the company's quarters; was never absent at roll-call, unless he was sent away, and always on hand if there was any work to be done. He was very strong, and practiced feats of strength until he could pick up a man lying on the ground and carry him away on his shoulders. He was of great use in the hospital, and in all the serious cases sought employment as a nurse, because it trained him in night-work and keeping awake at night. He soon attracted attention. He was offered promotion, which, for some reason, he declined.

It was a long time before he would speak of his interview with Mr. Lincoln. One night, when he had received a long letter from home, Scott opened his heart, and told Evans the story.

Scott said: "The President was the kindest man I had ever seen; I knew him at once, by a Lincoln medal I had long worn. I was scared at first, for I had never before talked with a great man. But Mr. Lincoln was so easy with me, so gentle, that I soon forgot my fright. He asked me all about the people at home, the neighbors, the farm, and where I went to school, and who my schoolmates were. Then he asked me about Mother, and how she looked, and I was glad I could take her photograph from my chest and show it to him. He said how thankful I ought to be that my mother still lived, and how, if he was in my place, he would try to make her a proud mother, and never cause her a sorrow or a tear. I cannot remember it all, but every word was so kind.

"He had said nothing yet about that dreadful next morning. I thought it must be that he was so kindhearted that he didn't like to speak of it. But why did he say so much about my mother, and my not causing her a sorrow or a tear when I knew that I must die the next morning? But I supposed that was something that would have to go unexplained, and so

I determined to brace up, and tell him that I did not feel a bit guilty, and ask him wouldn't he fix it so that the firing-party would not be from our regiment! That was going to be the hardest of all—to die by the hands of my comrades. Just as I was going to ask him this favor, he stood up, and he says to me, 'My boy, stand up here and look me in the face.' I did as he bade me. 'My boy,' he said, 'you are not going to be shot tomorrow, I believe you when you tell me that you could not keep awake. I am going to trust you, and send you back to your regiment. But I have been put to a good deal of trouble on your account. I have had to come up here from Washington when I have got a great deal to do; and what I want to know is, how you are going to pay my bill?' There was a big lump in my throat; I could scarcely speak. I had expected to die, you see, and had kind of got used to thinking that way. To have it all changed in a minute! But I got it crowded down, and managed to say, I am grateful, Mr. Lincoln! I hope I am as grateful as ever a man can be to you for saving my life. But it comes upon me sudden and unexpected like. I didn't lay out for it at all. But there is some way to pay you, and I will find it after a little. There is the bounty in the savings-bank. I guess we could borrow some money on the mortgage of the farm. There was my pay, and if he would wait until pay-day I was sure the boys would help, so I thought we could make it up, if it wasn't more than five or six hundred dollars. 'But it is a great deal more than that,' he said. Then I said I didn't just see how, but I was sure I would find some way—if I lived.

"Then Mr. Lincoln put his hands on my shoulders and looked into my face as if he was sorry, and said, 'My boy, my bill is a very large one. Your friends cannot pay it, nor your bounty, nor the farm, nor all your comrades! There is only one man in all the world who can pay it, and his name is William Scott! If from this day William Scott does his duty, so that, if I was there when he comes to die, he can look me in the face as he does now, and say, I have kept my promise, and I have done my duty as a soldier, then my debt will be paid. Will you make that promise and try to keep it?'"

"I said I would make the promise, and, with God's help, I would keep it. I could not say any more. I wanted to tell him how hard I would try to do all he wanted; but the words would not come, so I had to let it all go unsaid. He went away, out of my sight forever. I know I shall never see him again; but may God forget me if I ever forget his kind words or my promise."

This was the end of the story of Evans, who got his discharge, and went home at the close of the year. I heard from Scott occasionally afterwards. He was gaining a wonderful reputation as an athlete. He was the strongest man in the regiment. The regiment was engaged in two or three reconnaissances in force, in which he performed the most exposed service with singular bravery. If any man was in trouble, Scott was his good Samaritan; if any soldier was sick, Scott was his nurse. He was ready to volunteer for any extra service or labor—he had done some difficult and useful scouting. He still refused promotion, saying that he had done nothing worthy of it. The final result was that he was the general favorite of all his comrades, the most popular man in the regiment, and modest, unassuming, and unspoiled by his success.

The next scene in this drama opens on the Peninsula, between the York and the James rivers, in March, 1862. The sluggish Warwick River runs from its source, near Yorktown, across the Peninsula to its discharge. It formed at that time a line of defense, which had been fortified by General Magruder, and was held by him with a force of some twelve thousand Confederates. Yorktown was an important position to the Confederates.

On the 15th of April the division of General Smith was ordered to stop the enemy's work on the entrenchments at Lee's Mills, the strongest position on the Warwick River. His force consisted of the Vermont brigade of five regiments, and three batteries of artillery. After a lively skirmish, which occupied the greater part of the forenoon, this order was executed, and should have ended the movement.

But about noon General McClellan with his staff, including the French princes, came upon the scene, and ordered General Smith to assault and capture the rebel works on the opposite bank. Some discretion was given to General Smith, who was directed not to bring on a general engagement, but to withdraw his men if he found the defense too strong to be overcome. This discretion cost many lives when the moment came for its exercise.

General Smith disposed his forces for the assault, which was made by Companies D, E, F, and K of the Third Vermont Regiment, covered by the artillery, with the Vermont brigade in reserve. About four o'clock in the afternoon the charge was ordered. Unclasping their belts, and holding their guns and cartridge-boxes above their heads, the Vermonters dashed into and across the stream at Dam Number One, the strongest position in the Confederate line, and cleared out the rifle-pits. But the earthworks were held by an overwhelming force of rebels, and proved impregnable. After a dashing attack upon them the Vermonters were repulsed, and were ordered to retire across the river. They retreated under a heavy fire, leaving nearly half their number dead or wounded in the river and on the opposite shore.

Every member of these four companies was a brave man. But all the eye-witnesses agreed that among those who in this, their first hard battle, faced death without blanching, there was none braver or more efficient than William Scott, of Company K, debtor for his own life to President Lincoln. He was almost the first to reach the south bank of the river, the first in the rifle-pits, and the last to retreat. He recrossed the river with a wounded officer on his back—he carried him to a place of safety, and returned to assist his comrades, who did not agree on the number of wounded men saved by him from drowning or capture, but all agreed that he had carried the last wounded man from the south bank, and was nearly across the stream, when the fire of the rebels was concentrated upon him; he staggered with his living burden to the shore and fell.

An account of the closing scene in the life of William Scott was given me by a wounded comrade, as he lay upon his cot in a hospital tent, near Columbia College, in Washington, after the retreat of the army from the Peninsula. "He was shot all to pieces," said private H. "We carried him back, out of the line of fire and laid him on the grass to die. His body was shot through and through, and the blood was pouring from his many wounds. But his strength was great, and such a powerful man was hard to kill. The surgeons checked the flow of blood—they said he had rallied from the shock; we laid him on a cot in a hospital tent, and the boys crowded around him, until the doctors said they must leave if he was to have any chance at all. We all knew he must die. We dropped onto the ground wherever we could, and fell into a broken slumber—wounded and well side by side. Just at daylight the word was passed that Scott wanted to see us all. We went into his tent and stood around his cot. His face was bright and his voice cheerful. 'Boys,' he said, 'I shall never see another battle. I supposed this would be my last. I haven't much to say. You all know what you can tell them at home about me. I have *tried* to do the right thing! I am almost certain you will all say *that*.' Then while his strength was failing, his life ebbing away, and we looked to see his voice sink into a whisper, his face lighted up and his voice came out natural and clear as he said: 'If any of you ever have the chance, I wish you would tell President Lincoln that I have never forgotten the kind words he said to me at the Chain Bridge—that I have tried to be a good soldier and true to the flag—that I should have paid my whole debt to him if I had lived; and that now, when I know that I am dying, I think of his kind face and thank him again, because he gave me the chance to fall like a soldier in battle, and not like a coward by the hands of my comrades.'

"His face, as he uttered these words, was that of a happy man. Not a groan or an expression of pain, not a word of complaint or regret came from his lips. 'Goodbye, boys,' he said, cheerily. Then he closed his own eyes, crossed his hands on his breast, and—and—that was all. His face was at rest, and we all said it was beautiful. Strong men stood around his bed; they had seen their comrades fall, and had been very near to death themselves: such men are accustomed to control their feelings; but now they wept like children. One only spoke, as if to himself, 'Thank God, I know now how a brave man dies.'

"Scott would have been satisfied to rest in the same grave with his comrades," the wounded soldier continued. 'But we wanted to know where he lay. There was a small grove of cherry-trees just in the rear of the camp, with a noble oak in its center. At the foot of this oak we dug his grave. There we laid him, with his empty rifle and accouterments by his side. Deep into the oak we cut the initials, W. S., and under it the words, 'A brave soldier.' Our chaplain said a short prayer. We fired a volley over his grave. Will you carry his last message to the President?" I answered, "Yes."

Some days passed before I again met the President. When I saw him I asked if he remembered William Scott?

"Of Company K, Third Vermont Volunteers?" he answered. "Certainly I do. He was the boy that Baldy Smith wanted to shoot at the Chain Bridge. What about William Scott?"

"He is dead. He was killed on the Peninsula," I answered. "I have a message from him for you, which I have promised one of his comrades to deliver."

A look of tenderness swept over his face as he exclaimed, "Poor boy! Poor boy! And so he is dead. And he sent me a message! Well, I think I will not have it now. I will come and see you."

He kept his promise. Before many days he made one of his welcome visits to my office. He said he had come to hear Scott's message. I gave it as nearly as possible in Scott's own words. Mr. Lincoln had perfect control of his own countenance: when he chose, he could make it a blank; when he did not care to control it, his was the most readable of speaking human faces. He drew out from me all I knew about Scott and about the people among whom he lived. When I spoke of the intensity of their sympathies, especially in sorrow and trouble, as a characteristic trait of mountaineers, he interrupted me and said, "It is equally common on the prairies. It is the privilege of the poor. I know all about it from experience, and I hope I have my full share of it. Yes, I can sympathize with sorrow."

"Mr. President," I said, "I have never ceased to reproach myself for thrusting Scott's case so unceremoniously before you—for causing you to take so much trouble for a private soldier. But I gave way to an impulse— I could not endure the thought that Scott should be shot. He was a fellow-Vermonter—and I knew there was no other way to save his life."

"I advise you always to yield to such impulses," he said. "You did me as great a favor as the boy. It was a new experience for me—a study that was interesting, though I have had more to do with people of his class than any other. Did you know that Scott and I had a long visit? I was much interested in the boy. I am truly sorry that he is dead, for he was a good boy—too good a boy to be shot for obeying nature. I am glad I interfered."

Illustration by an unknown artist.

LINCOLN AND THE
LITTLE DRUMMER BOY

Roe L. Hendrick

The tiny little drummer boy wanted to meet the President—but how could he—Lincoln being so tall and he so small?

Not to worry.

P robably there is not, among all the villages of the North that sent soldiers to the Civil War, one from which narratives of Lincoln might not be gleaned. Among the rank and file of the great Union armies he made ten thousand acquaintances, greeting them one and all with a hearty friendliness that left no doubt of his sincerity. By soldiers who had met him, the incident was cherished as the brightest in their memory.

On one occasion a little drummer boy, securing leave of absence, accompanied a sergeant to a public levee that the President was holding at the White House. They went early, and when President Lincoln appeared and the hand-shaking began they were not long in reaching him.

The tall man, almost a giant in physical proportions, looked down with an amused smile at the tiny drummer boy, who appeared hardly ten years of age. Grasping the little fellow's right hand, the President suddenly reached out his left, swung the boy off his feet and set him gently down on a small table beside him.

"Aha, my little soldier," he said, laughing, "you shall help 'Uncle Abe' review this line today, and if your superior officer objects, why, I'll prolong your leave of absence!"

Lincoln asked the boy his age, place of residence, regiment, and where he was on duty. Then, as some of the more important officers of the Army or Navy, members of Congress or of the executive departments chanced to pass in the line, the President would gravely introduce his young assistant, with whom they were required to shake hands as well as with himself.

When the reception was over, President Lincoln took the boy into his private apartments and introduced him to Mrs. Lincoln. After entertaining him at luncheon, he dismissed him with a brief note to the commanding officer of the hospital where he was then stationed, telling why the boy's leave of absence had been extended.

Woodcut depicting Lincoln's study,
from the Keyes Lincoln Memorial Collection.

ONLY A MOTHER

AUTHOR UNKNOWN

It was November of '62 when a young surgeon was notified that he was under arrest on unspecified charges, and was to be taken to Washington by an armed guard. What could the young surgeon have done to merit such a summons?

I n November of the second year of the Civil War, a young surgeon was stationed in a hospital near Washington. One rainy morning, as he made his way to the cot of a man who was dying, an orderly stopped him.

"This is Dr. Jason Wilkins?"

"Yes."

"Sorry, Doctor, but I've got to arrest you and take you to Washington."

Jason looked the orderly over incredulously. "You've got the wrong man, friend."

The soldier drew a heavy envelope carefully from his breast pocket and handed it to Jason. Jason opened it uneasily, and gasped. This is what he read:

"Show this to Surgeon Jason Wilkins—Regiment. Arrest him. Bring him to me immediately. A. Lincoln."

Jason whitened. "What's up?" he asked the orderly.

"I didn't ask the President," replied the orderly dryly. "We'll start at once if you please, Doctor."

In a daze, Jason left for Washington. He thought of all the minor offenses he might have committed.

Jason was locked in a room in a Washington boarding house for one night. The next day at noon the orderly took him to the White House. An hour of waiting, then a man came out of a door.

"Surgeon Jason Wilkins?" said the sentry.

"Here!" answered Jason.

"This way," and Jason found himself in the inner room, with the door closed behind him. There was but one man in it besides Jason, but that man was Mr. Lincoln. He sat at a desk, with his somber eyes on Jason's face—still a cool young man, despite trembling knees.

"You are Jason Wilkins?" asked Mr. Lincoln.

"Yes, Mr. Lincoln," replied the young surgeon.

"Where are you from?"

"High Hill, Ohio."

"Have you any relatives?"

"Only my mother is living."

"Yes, only a mother! Well, young man, how is your mother?"

Jason stammered, "Why—why—I don't know."

"You don't know!" thundered Lincoln. "And why don't you know? Is she living or is she dead?"

"I don't know," said Jason. "To tell the truth, I've neglected to write, and I don't suppose she knows where I am."

Mr. Lincoln clenched a great fist on his desk and his eyes searched Jason. "I received a letter from her. She supposes you dead, and asked me to trace your grave. What was the matter with her? No good? Like most mothers, a poor sort? Eh? Answer me, sir!"

Jason bristled a little. "The best woman that ever lived, Mr. President."

"Ah!" breathed Mr. Lincoln. "Still you have no reason to be grateful to her! How'd you get your training as a surgeon? Your father?"

Jason reddened. "Well, no; father was a poor Methodist preacher. Mother raised the money, though I worked for my board mostly."

"So how did she raise the money?"

Jason's lips were stiff. "Selling things, Mr. President."

"What did she sell?"

"Old things mostly; beyond use except in museums."

"You poor fool!" said Lincoln. "You poor worm! Her household treasures—one by one—for you."

Suddenly the President rose and pointed a long bony finger at his desk. "Come here and sit down and write a letter to your mother!"

Jason stalked obediently over, and sat down in the President's seat. He seized a pen and wrote his mother a formal note.

"Address it and give it to me," said the President. "I'll see that it gets to her." Then his stern voice rising a little: "And now, Jason Wilkins, as long as you are in the Army you write to your mother once a week. If I have reason to correct you on the matter again, I'll have you court-martialed."

Jason rose and handed the letter to the President, then stood awaiting further orders. Finally Lincoln turned to Jason.

"My boy," he said gently. "There's no finer quality in the world than gratitude. There is nothing a man can have in his heart so mean, so low, as ingratitude. Even a dog appreciates a kindness, never forgets a soft word or a bone."

Needless to add, the doctor recognized the justice of the President's hot words, and at once began making atonement to his mother for his apparent forgetfulness.

Engraving made of Lincoln statue in
Chicago's Lincoln Park by J. H. E. Whitney.

A SCHOOLBOY'S INTERVIEW WITH ABRAHAM LINCOLN

William Agnew Paton

He was only a boy of fourteen when he dared to walk in on the President of the United States. But what he saw and what he heard, he'd never forget.

O ne of the most vivid and inspiring memories of my boyhood is of my interview with Abraham Lincoln in October, 1862.

I, a lad going on fourteen years of age, called at the Executive Mansion in Washington and handed to the doorkeeper a card which I had caused to be written especially for use on what was for me a very great occasion by the expert "calligraphist," as he called himself, of Willard's Hotel. Beneath my name, which the card-writer had inscribed with elaborate if not altogether appropriate flourishes, I had appended in my own schoolboy hand-writing, "Nephew of Dr. Cornelius Rea Agnew." My uncle was well known to Mr. Lincoln and this use of his name doubtless facilitated my admission to the office of the private secretary to the President, where I found the chief magistrate of my country at a desk in conversation with a gentleman, the only other occupant of the room, who was, as I afterward learned, the Minister of France.

When I entered the office the President was seated in a curiously constructed armchair made after a design suggested by himself. The left arm of this unique piece of furniture began low and, rising in a spiral to form the back, terminated on the right side of the seat at the height of the shoulders of the person seated thereon. Mr. Lincoln had placed himself crosswise in this chair with his long legs hanging over its lower arm, his back supported by the higher side. When the attendant who had presented my card to the President, and had then ushered me into the secretary's office, closed the door behind me and I found myself actually in the presence of Abraham Lincoln, I had the grace to feel embarrassed, for I then realized that I, a mere schoolboy, was intruding upon the patience and good-nature of a very busy overwrought man, the great and honored President of a country in the agony of a civil war. Noting my hesitation, Mr. Lincoln very gently said: "Come in, my Son." Then he arose, disentangling himself, as it were, from the chair, advanced to meet me, and it seemed to me that I had never beheld so tall a man, so dignified and impressive a personage, and certainly I had never felt so small, so insignificant, "so unpardonably young." As we met, the President gave me his hand, smiled down upon me, and, playing upon the similarity in the sound of my name with that of the person to whom he was about to refer, lightly asked: "Are you Bailey Peyton, the rebel guerilla we captured the other day?" I stammered an incoherent disclaimer of any relationship with the famous Confederate free-lance, of whose exploits and recent capture the newspapers had had much to say. Mr. Lincoln asked me if my uncle was well and charged me to deliver a kind message to my kinsman when I returned home to New York. Then, laying his hand upon my head, he said (how well I remember his words!) "You come of good people, you will soon be a grown man. Be a good man. Be a good American. Our country may have need of your services some day."

I had thought up a little speech to deliver when I met the President whom I had been taught to love and revere, but when I stood before him, felt his hand on my head, heard his voice, looked up into his wonderfully expressive, kindly eyes, my emotions were so deeply stirred that I could but smile through tears, and dared only to take his hand, which had dropped from my head, and press it. I looked down, abashed, not knowing what to say or do. Mr. Lincoln, evidently noting my confusion, placed his hand on my shoulders and drew me to him, saying, "What can I do for you, sonny?" Encouraged and heartened by his kindly manner, his sympathetic tone of voice, my eyes sought his again and I managed to blurt out: "Mr. Lincoln, all the boys in my school are for you." His smile broadened, he seemed much amused. Then I remember very distinctly the troubled, weary, careworn expression that passed over his face as he replied: "I wish everybody, Congress, all the people, were like you boys." I could say nothing, could only gaze into his benevolent eyes that seemed to look into my very heart. Presently he asked me how old I was, where I went to school, and a few other questions of like familiar sort. And then again, giving me his hand he said: "Now, you must excuse me; I have important business with this gentleman," indicating the personage with whom he had been conversing when I entered the room. I shook hands with the President, turned and walked to the door, then turned around for one last look, as he, reseating himself in the curious armchair, resumed his interview with the Minister of France.

I passed from the room and never again saw that wonderful, kindly face until as one of thousands upon thousands of grief-stricken, almost heart-broken fellow countrymen, I passed by his open coffin and beheld for a moment the body of "the murdered President" as it lay in state in the rotunda of the city hall of my native New York.

Through all the years that have passed since I stood in the living presence of the great leader of my people and he laid his hand gently on my head my memory has held an undimmed, imperishable picture of the good and kindly man, the war-worn, overwrought President, who, in the unbounded goodness of his heart, turned from his work, his crowding duties, forgetting for a few brief moments his cruel anxieties, to treat with sweet patience and speak gently to a schoolboy who had no claim on his attention and courtesy save that the boy was growing up to be an American citizen, one of the multitude of "the plain people" of whom Lincoln himself quaintly said: "the good Lord must love them, he made so many of them." This incident of my boyhood, this great event in my life, of all events the most memorable and inspiring, this meeting with Abraham Lincoln, was altogether unforgettable. The memory of it is to me inexpressibly sacred.

When I recall vividly, as I do, the form and face of Lincoln as it appeared to my young eyes, I can appreciate the significance of a remark made to me by Augustus Saint-Gaudens, as he stood modeling "the Chicago Lincoln": "When I began this work I despaired of making a worthy or satisfactory statue. So many, almost all, of the likenesses of Lincoln represent him as ungainly, uncouth, homely, unpicturesque; but when I had made a study of his life, had learned more and more of his character, of his natural nobility and lovableness, his deep and true human sympathy, had read of him, talked of him with men who knew him and loved him, I became more and more convinced that his face must have been the most truly beautiful of all I have tried to model." As my good friend the great sculptor created his mind-picture of Abraham Lincoln which he realized in his masterpiece, so I recall to mind his face and form after all the years that have passed since I, a small boy, stood in the living presence of the greatest of Americans. As I think of him now, his greatness of spirit, his worth, integrity, honesty of purpose, his kindliness, his wit and wisdom, his patience—all shown in his countenance and through his wonderful eyes and, as the man was altogether lovable and admirable in the highest sense, I believe that the face that smiled down upon me years ago was in the highest sense beautiful. That I am justified in my belief there is the testimony of his private secretary and co-biographer, Honorable J. G. Nicolay, who says of him: "There was neither oddity, eccentricity, awkwardness, or grotesqueness in his face, figure, or movement"; and men and women who knew Lincoln remember his "soft, tender, dreamy, patient, loving eyes—the kindest eyes ever placed in mortal head." As to his wisdom, his genius, his inestimable greatness of spirit, "his nobly humane simplicity of character," there is no need to speak.

When Edwin M. Stanton, who was standing by the death-bed of his revered chieftain, closed the eyes of the sacred dead, the great war secretary uttered what seems to me the most fitting and enduring epitaph on Abraham Lincoln:

"Now he belongs to the ages."

PART THREE

CIVIL WAR— THE LATER YEARS

Drawn by George T. Tobin from a Gardiner halftone photograph engraved by H. Davidson.

According to Kenneth W. Osbeck, Julia Ward Howe (1819–1910) was deeply anguished at the conflict between the two sections of her country. One day, as she watched troops marching off to war singing "John Brown's Body" to an old Appalachian camp meeting tune, she felt the music deserved better words. Without knowing what she was doing, she wrote the verses as they came to her, almost without looking at the paper. They first appeared in an 1863 issue of the Atlantic Monthly *as a battle song for the republic, and almost overnight, the entire nation was singing "The Battle-Hymn of the Republic."*

And not just the troops were singing it. At one patriotic rally attended by Lincoln, the song was sung as a solo. After the loud and enthusiastic applause, the president, with tears in his eyes, cried out, "Sing it again!"

—FROM *ABRAHAM LINCOLN: A MAN OF FAITH AND COURAGE,*
BY JOE WHEELER (NEW YORK: HOWARD/SIMON & SCHUSTER, 2008), P. 204

BATTLE-HYMN OF THE REPUBLIC

JULIA WARD HOWE (1819–1910)

Mine eyes have seen the glory of the coming of the Lord:
He is trampling out the vintage where the grapes of wrath are stored;
He hath loosed the fateful lightning of his terrible swift sword:
His truth is marching on.

I have seen Him in the watch-fires of a hundred circling camps;
They have builded Him an altar in the evening dews and damps;
I can read his righteous sentence by the dim and flaring lamps.
His day is marching on.

I have read a fiery gospel, writ in burnished rows of steel:
"As ye deal with my contemners, so with you my grace shall deal;
Let the Hero, born of woman, crush the serpent with his heel,
Since God is marching on."

He has sounded forth the trumpet that shall never call retreat;
He is sifting out the hearts of men before his judgment-seat:

Oh! be swift, my soul, to answer Him! be jubilant, my feet!
Our God is marching on.

In the beauty of the lilies Christ was born across the sea,
With a glory in his bosom that transfigures you and me:
As He died to make men holy, let us die to make men free,
While God is marching on.

HIGH TIDE AT GETTYSBURG

Joseph Leininger Wheeler

After Lincoln signed the Emancipation Proclamation on January 1, 1863, he had no way of knowing how the great drama would play out. All he knew was that somehow, even though he must have felt like a flimsy little boat in the vortex of a maelstrom, with no way of escape, that God was still in control.

One reality struck me as I researched this period of his life, and that was this: from the very moment that Lincoln struck off the shackles of the inhuman institution of slavery, which had lasted almost a quarter of a millennium in America, God appears to have at last taken sides. From this moment on, little would go right for Robert E. Lee and the South. All through the war, Stonewall Jackson, one of the greatest military tacticians the world has ever known, had somehow, in battle after battle, found a way to turn the tide in the South's favor. Now, in the Battle of Chancellorsville, inexplicably, Jackson was killed by his own men— "friendly fire," today's term for such a thing. One thing was for sure: Lee would feel his absence every day thereafter.

At the crucial Battle of Gettysburg, Lee desperately needed Jackson, for in spite of some of the most deadly fighting in the entire war, he was forced to retreat across the Potomac. Had he won, nothing would have stood in his way to marching on and taking Washington. Instead, Gettysburg proved to be high tide for the South, and eventually the battle grew into the stature of myth.

But Gettysburg would not have been immortalized in story had it not been for what is generally considered today to be one of the ten—perhaps five—greatest speeches in world history. It would be memorized by untold thousands of children and teenagers in generation after generation. As for stories, you'll be reading several of them. I doubt you'll ever be able to forget them once you do.

As the war waged on, hundreds of thousands of men continued to die. A shockingly high percentage were caused by disease and primitive medical help. Since there was then no accepted method to prevent infection, about the only known way to prevent a soldier from dying from his wounds was to chop off the infected part of his body, hence the staggering number of surviving veterans without feet or arms—many died anyway; the rest incapacitated for life.

All this the kindest man in the nation was forced to endure. And contemporaries all agree that this anguish seeped into his face; so much so that people who saw him up close could never erase that impression from their minds in the years that followed.

Drawing by R. Farrington Elwell, 1906.

ACROSS THE GREAT PLAINS JUST TO SEE LINCOLN

Caroline B. Parker

Since most Civil War battles were fought in the East, one would assume Lincoln paid little attention to the vast and sparsely populated West. But the West had problems, too, that could not wait. One was so pressing that the chief justice of the Montana and Idaho territories was designated as the proper emissary to the President, but that would be a long and dangerous journey by stagecoach, and eventually by train, before they should reach the westward end of the railroad line. Dangerous because of the gold they'd be carrying. Fortunately for our story, the chief justice's ten-year-old son, Wright Edgerton, was permitted to accompany his father. Many years later, he wrote down the story of his epic journey for the editors of St. Nicholas (*a magazine just for young people*).

I f you had lived in the time when Abraham Lincoln was President of the United States and your home had been out among the Rocky Mountains, a visit to Washington would have been a real event. It might be just as thrilling today, but it would be very different. If you were fortunate, and courageous, you might step into an airplane and fly over the mountains—over the clouds, even—and land down in Langley Field, or somewhere near the capital city, in a very short space of time. But the boy of whose trip I want to tell you had to travel a long way in a stage coach drawn by six horses before he reached the railway, and then he was carried by what would look to us like a toy train over plains and mountains and at a snail's pace. I am sure that the sight of our great airships would excite much less interest today than would the old-fashioned train if it should take a notion to creep across the country today.

Wright Edgerton was a boy of those pioneer days. His father had been one of the first men who had gone to the Rockies with their families more or less safely tucked away in the covered wagons which are now so popular in the movies. He was, at the time of which I am writing, the chief-justice of the great territory which comprised the present states of Idaho and Montana, and its interests lay close to his heart. When the mountains began to reveal the vast mineral wealth which they had hidden for centuries and centuries, all kinds of people who were seeking their fortunes were drawn to them.

As always happens when rich new country is opened up, quite as many lawless people as law-respecting ones were attracted to it, and the mine owners and miners began to feel that they must ask for more protection from Washington. They wanted the territory divided, so that it might be more easily governed. The early settlers knew they had a friend in the President, and that, if they could just present their problems to him, they would be sure of a sympathetic hearing, for he, too, had been brought up in the midst of pioneer hardships and difficulties.

It was decided that one of their number should be sent to present their claims to the President, and Chief-Justice Edgerton was the unanimous choice, for he had the confidence of every one who had the real interests of the territory at heart. He was not anxious to take this long journey, for it meant leaving his family and his own affairs for a number of weeks—no little sacrifice on his part.

And then the most unexpected thing happened. The men who were sending the Chief-Justice decided that his son Wright, who, although only ten years old, was a very manly little chap, should go with his father, because he really could be of considerable help to him. You may be sure that the boy saw no objection to this arrangement, and I think that, but for his stout buckskin jacket, his heart might have been in danger of bursting with joy.

The days that followed were busy ones for everybody, for there were many preparations to make. Wright's mother had no time to worry about possible loneliness, for a call on the President demanded something besides buckskin clothes, and there were no ready-made suits in that town.

The question of financing the trip was an important one, for the currency of the far West at that time was gold-dust, carried in little bags. If one went to the store for a pound of tea, along went the bag of dust, and the storekeeper weighed out enough of it to make the equivalent of the number of cents demanded for the tea. And you had to watch sharply, too, for sometimes the dust sifted through the scales to the counter, and that was your change and you must be sure and ask for it, or Mother would think you hadn't done your errand properly. When we hear our elders talking about the good old days, we may well wonder how they would like to go back forty or fifty years, when life was much more complicated, in some ways, than it is now. If you take a journey nowadays, you just tuck a checkbook into your bag; it takes up no room at all, and your money problem is solved, provided you have enough cash in the bank back home.

But Mrs. Edgerton knew how to meet almost any emergency, and so she proceeded to make sure that her two travelers had plenty of currency. She made little bags for the gold-dust, and then, as a sort of letter of credit, she sewed long narrow pockets on the seams inside of their coats and filled them with gold-dust as well.

At last, everything was ready, and all of the days which Wright thought would never pass were now behind him, excepting the last one before they were to start. And on that last evening there was to be the "jamboree," without which no one could respectably leave the country. The settlers came from miles and miles around, all laden with good things to eat and drink. You may be sure that the party given for the chief-justice was a very special one. The chief promoter and grand mogul of the event was the sheriff; and next in importance to him was old Jed the fiddler, who could loosen up the stiffest party. His voice and his fingers worked in perfect accord as he played "Money Musk," the "Virginia Reel," and other favorites, and gave his instructions: "All hands 'round; balance to your partner; swing your partner; grand right and left," and all the lively things one did in those days of strenuous dance.

In the midst of the festivities the sheriff called for quiet, and, after a most impressive speech of good will and best wishes for a successful journey and a safe return, delivered to the chief-justice a wonderful gold nugget, which was to be presented to the President as "Exhibit A" to show the riches of the country.

Wright and his father were to start early the next morning, but old Jed had got wind of a plan to hold up the stage on which they were to go, and to relieve them of everything of value, including the President's nugget. He said that the leader of the gang was, if you please, that old rascal of a sheriff who had been so loud in his expressions of good will the night before. Jed had a lot of trouble persuading the chief-justice to change his plans, for the latter thought the older man had merely picked up some malicious gossip. But he finally agreed to wait one day, because, I think, he did not want to take his boy into possible danger.

Sure enough, Jed was right. The stage was held up, and, to the great surprise of the outlaws, of whom the sheriff was one, the passengers were old Jed and four able-bodied men, all of them prepared for any emergency. The sheriff was a sheriff no longer, and was never seen in that part of the country again.

The next morning bright and early, the boy and his father went out safely on the stage, and it was not for a long time afterward that Wright knew why he had had to wait another long day before starting on that eventful journey. And as they left the little town, some of the highest mountains were still sleeping, wearing their nightcaps of clouds: but when the sun touched them, they turned all rosy, and took off their caps, and stood bareheaded as they bade the travelers good-by. And so began the long long journey to the nation's capital city.

• • • •

Wright was somewhat awed by the big city of Washington, for it was far beyond anything of which he had ever dreamed; but even the wonders of the city were dimmed by the prospect of seeing the President. But his heart did not beat much faster than his father's as the day for the interview drew near, for a President is something different, no matter how simple and friendly he may be, and you don't talk to one every day.

When the pair was ushered into the presence of this tall grave man, Wright looked past his father, as the two men stood with clasped hands, and met the very gentlest eyes he had ever seen in all his life. He sat very quietly while Mr. Lincoln listened to the chief-justice's story of his territory's prospects and needs, often interrupting with questions and statements which showed that he knew much more of what was going on out there than the frontiersmen suspected.

"I will think over all of the matters you have brought to my attention and will write you," said Mr. Lincoln. And this he did, and promised the people a separation of the territory, so that they might have two governors appointed, and Chief-Justice Edgerton to rule over the section that is now known as Montana.

When the interview was over and Wright and his father were leaving, Mr. Lincoln put his hands on the boy's shoulder, and said as though he really cared, "And you, my lad, what are you going to be when you are a man?"

Wright had thought that out long before and had his answer ready: "I want to be a soldier, sir."

"I am sure you will serve your country well," said Mr. Lincoln.

• • • •

Sometime when you visit our Military Academy at West Point, if you will look up the record of Wright P. Edgerton's service to his country, you will find that Mr. Lincoln made no mistake in his prophecy. It was in 1870 that Wright, a lad of seventeen, entered West Point. At the close of his four years as a cadet, he was for a time assigned to duty with a regiment stationed in the South. He was next chosen as one of the two artillery officers first detailed to develop high explosives.

In 1882, eight years after his graduation, he was recalled to West Point as an instructor; then, after distinguished service in the Spanish American War, was made professor of mathematics, and died at his post in 1904. His portrait now hangs in the library at West Point, an honor bestowed only upon the graduates who have won distinction.

O. F. Schmidt illustration created for
St. Nicholas Magazine *in 1922.*

A LESSON IN FORGIVENESS

T. MORRIS LONGSTRETH

T. Morris Longstreth wrote several stories about Lincoln during his long writing career, but none are more moving than this one; the time, July 7, 1863, four days after the Battle of Gettysburg. Two people—a man and a boy—are faced with a terrible decision on the same hot summer night.

In America's terrible Civil War, the punishment for desertion or sleeping on guard duty . . . was death. No officer or court, no matter how high, could stop the firing squad. Only one person had the power: the President himself—the loneliest man in the country, it often seemed.

T he Ripley brothers were as different in nearly every way as are the rapids and still pools of a mountain stream. Perhaps that is why they loved each other in a way not usually meant by "brotherly love."

Will Ripley was the "still pool." He was thoughtful to the point of appearing drowsy, honest as daylight, mild-tempered, and twenty. He was up north in Pennsylvania somewhere, either alive or dead, for the date of this story is July 7, 1863, which means, as you can read in the dispatches of the time, that the terrible Battle of Gettysburg was just over. The Ripleys, on their farm near Washington, had not heard from him for some time.

Although Will was no soldier at heart, he had responded to Lincoln's call for more men two years before, leaving his young brother, Dan, at home to help his father and mother. Dan was now fourteen, a high-strung, impetuous, outspoken lad of quick actions and hasty decisions. He was the "laughing rapid." But for all his hastiness, he had a head and a heart that could be appealed to, usually.

The only thing to which he could not reconcile himself was the separation from Will. Even Will's weekly letters—which had seldom missed coming until recently, and which always sent messages of love to Dan, coupled with encouragement to stay on the farm as the best way to aid the cause—scarcely kept him from running away and hunting up his brother. Dan knew that he and his collie, Jack, were needed to look after the sheep; he knew that his father, who was little more than an invalid, must have help. But to see the soldiers marching set him wild to be off with them. In fact, Jack seemed to be the anchor which held him. Dan sometimes even thought that he loved Jack next to Will.

The summer of '63 had been unbearably hot. There had been an increasingly ominous list of military disasters. Even the loyal were beginning to murmur against Lincoln's management of the war. Then Will's letters had ceased, and Mr. Ripley could get no satisfaction from headquarters.

Dan was irritable with fatigue and his secret worry; his family nearly sick with the heat and the tension.

The climax to this state came from an unforeseen event. Jack, crazed either by the heat or by some secret taste for blood, ran amuck one night, stampeded the sheep, and did grievous damage. Farmer Ripley doubtless acted on what he considered the most merciful course, by having Jack done away with and buried before Dan got back from an errand to the city. But to Dan it seemed, in the first agony of his broken heart, an unforgivable thing. Weariness, worry, and now this knife-sharp woe changed the boy into a heartsick being who flung himself on the fresh mound behind the barn and stayed there the whole day, despite the entreaties of his mother and the commands of his father.

That evening his mother carried some food out to him. He did not touch it; he would not talk to her.

Some time later, as the night wore on, he stole into the house, tied up some clothes into a bundle, took the food at hand, and crept out of his home. Once more he went to the grave of his slain pal. What he said there, aloud but quietly, need not be told. Sufficient it is to know that a burning resentment toward his father filled him, coupled with a sickening longing to be with his brother Will. Ill with his hasty anger, he thought that Will was the only one in the world who loved or understood him.

In the wee hours of morning he left the farm, forever, as he thought, and turned down the road which led to the Soldiers' Home, not far away, where he hoped to find someone who could tell him how to get to Will's regiment. The sultry, starless heat of a Washington midsummer enclosed him; the wood was very dark and breathless; his head throbbed. But he pushed on, high-tempered, unforgiving; he would show them all!

Suddenly he remembered that he had not said the Lord's Prayer that night. Dan had been reared strictly. He tried saying it, walking. But that seemed sacrilegious. He knelt in the dark and tried. But when he got to "as we forgive our debtors," he stopped, for he was an honest lad. This new gulf of mental distress was too much for him; it brought the tears. There in the dark by the roadside, Dan lay and bitterly cried himself into an exhausted sleep.

At the same hour another worn person, a tall, lean-faced man with eyes full of unspeakable sorrow, was pacing the chamber of the White House in the near-by city. The rebellion had reached its flood tide at Gettysburg three days before. The President had stayed the flood, bearing in tireless sympathy the weight of countless responsibilities. Now, all day long, decisions had borne down upon him—decisions that concerned not only armies, but races; not only races, but principles of human welfare. He was grief stricken still from his son Willie's death, and his secretary in the room downstairs, listening unconsciously to the steady march of steps overhead, read into them the pulse beats of human progress. Lincoln had given instructions that no one was to interrupt him. He was having one of his great heart battles.

Finally, shortly before dawn, the footsteps stopped, the secretary's door opened, and the gaunt, gray face looked in. "Stoddard, do you want anything more from me tonight?"

The secretary rose. "I want you in bed, Sir. Mrs. Lincoln should not have gone away; you are not fair with her or us."

"Don't reproach me, Stoddard," said Lincoln, kindly: "it had to be settled, and with God's help, it has been. Now I can sleep. But I must have a breath of air first. There's nothing?"

"Only the matter of those deserters, Sir, and that can wait."

The President passed his hands over his deep-lined face. "Only!" he murmured. "*Only!* How wicked this war is! It leads us to consider lives by the dozen, by the bale, wholesale. How many in this batch, Stoddard?"

The secretary turned some papers. "Twenty-four, sir. You remember the interview with General Scanlon yesterday."

Lincoln hesitated, saying, "Twenty-four! Yes, I remember. Scanlon said that lenience to the few was injustice to the many. He is right, too." Lincoln held out his hand for the papers, then drew it back and looked up at Stoddard. "I can't decide," he said in a low voice, "not now. Stoddard, you see a weak man. But I want to thresh this out a little longer. I must walk. These cases are killing me; I must get out."

"Let me call an attendant, Mr. Lincoln."

"They're all asleep. No, I'll take my chances with God. If anybody wants to kill me, he will do it. You must go to bed, Stoddard."

The two men, each concerned for the other, shook hands in good night, and Lincoln slipped out into the dark, his long legs bearing him rapidly northward. During the heat he usually slept at the Soldiers' Home, being escorted thither by cavalry with sabers drawn. But he hated the noise of it, and during Mrs. Lincoln's absence, was playing truant to her rules. When he neared the Home, he felt slightly refreshed, and turned into a wood road. The sky to his right began to lighten.

By the time dawn showed the ruts in the road, Lincoln realized that he was tired. "Abe, Abe," he said half aloud, "they tell me you used to be great at splitting rails, and now a five-mile stroll before breakfast—well! What have we here?"

The exclamation was occasioned by his nearly stepping on a lone youngster lying in the road. The boy raised his head from a small bundle of clothes. The tall man stooped with tenderness, saying, "Hello, sonny. So you got old Mother Earth to make your bed for you! How's the mattress?"

Dan sat and rubbed his eyes. "What are you doin'?" he asked.

"I appear to be waking you, and making a bad job of it," said Lincoln.

"You didn't come to take me, then," exclaimed Dan, greatly relieved. "I wouldn't 'a' gone!" he added defiantly.

Lincoln looked at him sharply, his interest aroused by the trace of tears in the boy's eyes and the bravado in his voice. "There's a misunderstanding here," said Lincoln, "almost as bad a misunderstanding as Mamie and her mother had over Mr. Riggs, who was the undertaker back home." Here the gaunt man gave a preliminary chuckle. "Ever hear that story, sonny?"

Dan shook his head, wondering how such a homely man could sound so likable. Lincoln seated himself on a fallen tree trunk. "Well, it was this way—" And he told the story.

Dan's quick, impetuous laugh might have disturbed the early-rising birds. Lincoln joined in, and for an instant Dan completely forgot dead Jack and his deserted home. For the same fleet instant Lincoln forgot his troubles in Dan's laugh. The boy chuckled again. "I'll have to tell that to fa—" He didn't finish the word, remembering with a pang that he was not going to see his father again.

Lincoln caught the swift change on his face, and it was his turn to wonder. He knew better than to ask questions. You can't fish for a boy's heart with question marks, neat little fishhooks though they be. So he said, "Our sitting here when we ought to be getting back home reminds me of another story."

"Tell me," said Dan, well won already to this man, despite the gray, lined cheeks and the sadness that colored his voice. Dan didn't know yet who he was. He had not seen the cartoons that flooded the country during election. He was too young to go in alone to the inauguration, and the idea of the President of the United States sitting with him in the woods was too preposterous to even cross his mind.

When Dan had laughed heartily over the second story, Lincoln said, "Well, sonny, I reckon we ought to be moving, don't you?" He helped the lad with his bundle.

"Are you going to the war, too?" asked Dan. "I am."

"You!" exclaimed Lincoln, "why, you're no bigger than my own Tadpole, and he's only a wriggler yet. Does your father know?"

"I reckon he does by now," said the boy, darkly. "Father's an early riser. You see, he killed my dog without my knowin', and so I left without *his* knowin'."

The hardness of the boy's voice hurt Lincoln, who said, "What's your father's name, sonny?"

"William Ripley—that is, senior. Will, that's junior, my brother, is off at the war. I'm Dan. I'm going to find my brother. I don't care if I never come back. I loved Jack better than—than—" His voice choked.

Lincoln put his hand on the boy's shoulder. He was getting the situation. "Jack was your dog?" asked the big man, as gently as a mother.

"Yes. And father shouldn't 'a' killed him unbeknownst to me. I'll never forgive him for that, never!"

"Quite right," said the wise man, walking with him. "Don't you ever forgive him, Dan. Or don't ever forget it—under one condition."

"What's that?" asked the boy, a trifle puzzled at the unexpected compliance of his elder with his own unforgiving mood.

"Why, that you also never forget all the kind and just things that your father has done for you. Why did he kill the dog, Dan?"

"Well—he—killed—some sheep," said the boy. He would be honest with this tall, gentle, and grave person who understood so readily.

"How old are you, Dan?"

"Fourteen, going on fifteen."

"That's quite a heap," said Lincoln, musingly, "quite a heap! In fourteen years a father can pile up a lot of good deeds. But I suppose he's done a lot of mean ones to cancel 'em off, has he?"

"No," admitted Dan.

His frankness pleased the President. "I congratulate you, Dan. You're honest. I want to be honest with you, and tell you a story that isn't funny, for we're both in the same boat, as I size up this proposition—yes, both in the same boat. I am in the Army, in a way. At least, I'm called commander in chief, and occasionally they let me meddle a little with things."

"Honest?" said Dan, opening his eyes very wide. He had been so absorbed in his own disasters that he had accepted this strange, friendly acquaintance without question. But now, although the forefront of his consciousness was very active with the conversation, the misty background was trying to make him compare this man with a certain picture in the big family album, with another one pasted on the dining room cupboard door, the same loose-hung person, only this one had a living rawness—maybe it was bigness—about him that the pictures didn't give, like a tree, perhaps. But it *couldn't be* the President talking to him, Dan. If it was, what would the folks at home—And again his thought stopped. There were to be no more "folks at home" for him.

"Honestly, Dan. But sometimes they don't like it when I do meddle. There's a case on now. Last night I pretty nearly had twenty-four men shot."

"Whew!"

"But I hadn't quite decided, and that's the reason I came out here in God's own woods. And I'm glad I came, for you've helped me decide."

"I have!" said Dan, astonished, "to shoot them?"

"No! Not to. You showed me the case in a new light. Here you are, deserting home, deserting your father, bringing sorrow to him and to your mother, who have sorrowed enough with Will in danger and all; you're punishing your father because he did one deed that he couldn't very well help, just as if he'd been a mean man all his life. And it's like that with my twenty-four deserters, Dan, very much like that. They've served for years, faithfully. Then, can any one thing they do be so gross, so enormously bad, as to blot out all the rest, including probably a lifetime of decent living? I think not. Is a man to blame for having a pair of legs that play coward once? I think not, Dan. I tell you what I'll do, sonny," and the tall man stopped in the road, a new light shining in his cavernous, sad eyes, "I'll make a bargain with you. If you'll go home and forgive your father, I'll go home and forgive my twenty-four deserters. Is that a bargain?"

The boy had been shaken, but it was difficult to change all at once. "It is hard to forgive," he murmured.

"Someday you'll find it hard not to," said the great man, putting out his huge palm for the boy to shake. "Isn't that a pretty good bargain, Dan? By going home, by ceasing to be a deserter yourself, you will save the lives of twenty-four men. Won't you be merciful? God will remember, and perhaps forgive you some trespass sometime even as you forgive now."

Something of last night's horror, when he could not say that prayer, and something of the melting gentleness of the new friend before him, touched the boy. He took Lincoln's hand, saying, "All right. That's a go."

"Yes, a go home," smiled Lincoln. "I suppose I'll have to turn, now."

"Where's your home?" asked the boy, knowing, yet wishing to hear the truth, to be very sure; for now he *could* tell the folks at home.

"The White House," replied Lincoln, "but I wish I were going back to the farm with you."

The boy heard him vaguely, his jaw was sagging. "Then you—are the President?"

Lincoln nodded, enjoying the boy's wonder. "And your servant, don't forget," added Lincoln. "You have been a help to me in a hard hour, Dan. General or no generals, I'll spare those men. Any time I can do anything for you, drop in, now that you know where to find me."

The boy was still speechless with his assured elation.

"But you'd better—Wait," and Lincoln began hunting through his pockets; "you'd better let me give you a latchkey. The man at the door's a stubborn fellow, for the folks will bother him. Here—"

And finding a card and a stub of a pencil, he wrote:

"PLEASE ADMIT DAN'L RIPLEY ON DEMAND.

A. Lincoln."

"How's that?"

"Thank you," said Dan, proudly. "I reckon I should 'a' guessed it was you, but those stories you told kind o' put me off."

"That's sometimes why I tell them." And Lincoln smiled again. "It's not a bad morning's work—twenty-four lives saved before breakfast, Dan. You and I ought to be able to eat a comfortable meal. Good-by, sonny."

And so they parted. The man strode back the way he had come; the boy stood looking, looking, and then swiftly wheeled and sped. He had been talking to the President, to Abraham Lincoln, and hearing such talk as he never had heard before; but especially the words, "You have been a help to me in a hard hour, Dan"—those words trod a regular path to his brain. He ran, eager to get to the very home he had been so eager to leave. Forgiveness was in his heart, but chiefly there was a warm pride. He had been praised by Abraham Lincoln! Of this day he would talk to the end of his days. Dan did not know that the major part of the day, the greatest in his life, was still to come. Certainly the dawning of it had been very beautiful.

Breathless and with eyes bright in anticipation of telling his tale, he leaped the fences, ran up to the back door, and plunged into the house. The kitchen was quiet. A misgiving ran over him. Were they all out in search of him? Would he have to postpone his triumph?

In the dining room a half-eaten meal was cooling. He explored on, and coming out to the spacious front of the house, found them—found them in an inexplicable group around a uniformed officer. Tears were streaming down his mother's cheeks. His father, still pale from his recent accident, looked ashen and shriveled. They turned at Dan's approach. He expected that this scene of anguish would turn to smiles upon his arrival. He was amazed to find that his return gave them the merest flurry of relief, and alleviated their sorrow not at all.

"Danny, dear, where have you been?" asked his mother.

"The Lord must have sent you home in answer to our prayers," said his father.

Then they turned back to the officer, pleading, both talking at once, weeping. Dan felt hurt. Did his return, his forgiveness, mean so little to them? He might as well have gone on. Then he caught the officer's words, "Colonel Scott can do no more, madam. The President cannot see him, and more pardons are not to be hoped for."

Mrs. Ripley turned and threw her arm across Dan's shoulders. "Danny—Danny—you are our only son now. Will was—" and she broke down completely.

"Will was found asleep while on duty, Dan, and—"

"Is to be shot?" asked the boy. "I wonder if he was one of the twenty-four." They looked at him, not understanding.

"The Lord has restored you to us. If we could only pray in sufficient faith, He could restore Will," said Farmer Ripley, devoutly. "Dear, let us go in and pray. We should release this gentleman to his duty. We can talk to the Father about it."

Dan realized with a sudden clearness that his brother, his beloved, was to be taken from him as Jack had been taken. It shook his brain dizzy for a moment; but he knew that he must hold onto his wits—must think. There was Abraham Lincoln, *his friend*!

"You pray," he cried to his father, shrilly, "and I'll run."

"Run where, dear? Will is in Pennsylvania."

"To the White House, Mother. He said, 'Any time I can do anything for you, drop in.' *Anything*, mother. Surely he'll—"

"Who?" cried both his parents.

"Why, the President, Mr. Lincoln!"

"But the President is busy, dear."

"He'll see me—I know he will!" said Dan. "Look! We have a secret together, the President and I have." And the boy showed his card and poured out his story.

The mother saw a break in her gray heaven, saw the bright blue of hope.

"We must go at once," she said. "Father, you are not able to come with us, but pray here for us."

"Please take my horse and carriage," said the officer.

"Yes," said Dan, "let's hurry. Oh, I'm glad, I'm so glad!" And the joy at his lucky turning back shone in his face as he helped his mother into the vehicle.

"May God help you!" said the officer.

"He does," said the boy, thinking.

It was high noon when the doorkeeper of the White House, hardened into a very stony guard by the daily onslaught of Lincoln seekers, saw an impetuous youth leap from a light carriage and help a woman up the portico steps toward him.

"In which room is the President?" asked Dan.

"He's very busy," said the doorkeeper, probably for the five-hundredth time that morning. "Have you an appointment?"

"No, but he said I should drop in when I wanted to; and what's more, here's my 'latchkey'"; and Dan, trembling a little with haste and pride, showed him the card "A. Lincoln" had written.

The man looked quizzically at it and at him. "In that case," he said, dryly, "you'd better step into the waiting room there."

There must have been forty or fifty people crowded into the ante-room, each on some urgent errand. Some were in uniform; all looked tired, impatient, important. Dan saw the situation, and knew that Lincoln could never see them all. He whispered to his mother and showed her to a chair, then went up to the doorboy and asked if the President was in the next room. The boy admitted the fact, but would not admit anything further, including Dan. The annoyed looks on the faces of the waiting people deepened. *Does this urchin [said their looks] expect to see the President today, when so many more important persons (such as we) are kept waiting?*

Dan, not caring for etiquette when his brother might be shot at any moment, slipped under the arm of the doorboy and bolted into the room.

Lincoln was standing by the window. He looked around in surprise at the noise of Dan Ripley's entry. He recognized his walking partner, made a motion for the doorboy, who had one irate hand on Dan, to withdraw, and said: "Why, Dan, I'm glad to see you so soon again. You're just in time to back me up. Let me introduce you to General Scanlon."

Dan looked into the amazed and angry eyes of a Union general who, practically ignoring the boy, went on to say: "Mr. President, I repeat that unless these men are made an example of, the Army itself may be in danger. Mercy to these twenty-four means cruelty to near a million."

The President, worn not only from his sleepless night, but from the incessant strain of things, looked grave, for the general spoke truth. He turned to Dan, "Did you go home, sonny?"

Dan nodded.

"Then I shall keep my half of the bargain. General, this boy and I each walked the woods half the night carrying similar troubles, trying to decide whether it was best to forgive. We decided that it was best, as the Bible says, even to seventy times seven. Dan, how did your folks take it?"

Dan spoke quickly. "It would 'a' killed them if I'd run off for good, for they just got word that my brother Will—you know I told you about him—is to be shot for sleeping on watch. I just know he was tired out— he didn't go to sleep on purpose. I told my mother that you wouldn't let him be shot, if you knew."

Lincoln groaned audibly and turned away to the window for a moment. The general snorted.

"I brought my mother in to see you, too," said Dan, "seeing as she wouldn't quite believe what I said about our agreement."

Lincoln looked at the boy, and his sunken eyes glistened. "I agreed for twenty-four lives," he said; "but I don't mind throwing in an extra one for you, Dan."

And this time the general groaned.

"Stoddard," added the President, "will you see if there is a Will Ripley on file?"

The secretary left the room. Lincoln turned abruptly to the general. "You have heard me," he said. "I, with the help of God and this boy, threshed out the matter to a conclusion, and we only waste time to discuss it further. If I pardon these deserters, it surely becomes a better invest-ment for the United States than if I had them shot—twenty-four live fighters in the ranks, instead of that many corpses underground. There are too many weeping widows now. Don't ask me to add to that number, *for I won't do it*!"

It was rarely that Lincoln was so stirred. There was a strange silence. Then the secretary entered with, "Yes, sir, a Will Ripley is to be executed tomorrow, for sleeping on duty. The case was buried in the files; it should have been brought to you earlier."

"Better for the case to be buried than the boy," said the President. "Give me the paper, Stoddard."

"Then you will!" said Dan, trembling with joy.

"I don't believe that shooting the boy will do him any good," said Lincoln, as the pen traced the letters of his name beneath this message, "Will Ripley is not to be shot until further orders from me."

Dan looked at it. "Oh, thank you!" he said. "Can I bring Mother in to see it—and to see you?" he asked.

The President looked down into the shining face and could not refuse. In a moment, Dan's mother was in the room. She was all confused; the general was red with irritation.

She read the message. It didn't seem quite clear to her. "Is that a pardon? Does that mean that he won't be shot at all?"

"My dear madam," replied Lincoln, kindly, "evidently you are not ac-quainted with me. If your son never looks on death till orders come from me to shoot him, he will live to be a great deal older than anyone else."

She stretched out both her hands, crying, "I want to thank you, sir. Oh, thank you, thank you!"

"Thank Dan here," said Lincoln. "If he had not let the warmth of forgiveness soften his heart, Will Ripley would have died. And perhaps, if I had not met him in the woods at dawn, I might have gone into eternity with the blood of these twenty-four men on my hands. Dan helped me.

"True, they are erring soldiers, Mrs. Ripley. But we must consider what they have done and what they will do, as intently as we consider the wrong of the moment. Good-by, Dan; we shall both remember today with easy consciences."

The waiting crowd in the anteroom could not understand, of course, why that intruder of a boy who had fairly dragged the woman in to see the President so unceremoniously, should bring her out on his arm with such conscious pride. They could not understand why the tears were rolling down her cheeks at the same time that a smile glorified her face. They did not see that the boy was walking on air, on light. But the dullest of them could see that he was radiant with a great happiness.

And if they could have looked past him and pierced the door of the inner room with their wondering glances, they would have seen a reflection of Dan's joy still shining on the somber, deep-lined face of the man who had again indulged himself in—mercy.

Woodcut by an unknown artist.

RANSOM'S PAPERS

Mary Wells

In an old southern mansion made into an army hospital, a man lay, growing weaker each day. Only a miracle could save his life. A nurse determined to make one last try: it was only a letter, but perhaps . . . who knew what it might do! Almost impossible odds, for who could possibly cut through all that red tape in time to save this one flickering life?

The old Southern mansion made an ideal army hospital. Standing as it did on the outskirts of Fernandina, it caught the slightest breeze from Amelia Harbor on one side of the island and from the ocean on the other. The broad windows gave a view of the white sandy beaches and the blue waters of the bay beyond.

The beauty of the scene, however, had little charm for Ransom, the gaunt soldier in the east corner room. His hollow eyes were fixed wistfully on a flitting sail, the progress of which he watched until the little craft had passed beyond his field of vision. Then he turned to the sweet-faced young nurse, who was busy about the room.

"I suppose Fernandina's a pretty old town?" he said, with his slow New England drawl.

Miss Eliot straightened deftly the pillows with which Ransom was propped. "It was settled by the Spaniards in 1632," she said, "so it *has* had quite a history. There are some interesting places near here. Cumberland Island was the home of General Nathaniel Greene, and 'Light-Horse Harry' Lee is buried there."

A look of interest came into Ransom's face. "You don't say!" he exclaimed. "They was big men, both of 'em. Now I ain't so surprised about General Lee, but it seems kind of funny that Nathan'el Greene would want to come off down here to live, don't it, now?"

Miss Eliot's blue eyes twinkled. "Where is your home, Ransom?"

"Maine," said the soldier, promptly, "and I'm proud of it, too. You ain't ever been in Maine, have you, Miss Eliot?" His tone was wistful.

"No, I never have, Ransom, but I mean to go there some day," she said, pleasantly. "All of my great-great-ancestors were New Englanders, though my own family has always lived in Ohio."

"Ohio's a great state," said Ransom, gallantly, "but I don't know as it quite comes up to Maine. It's a great country, all right, but Maine's a kind of long stretch from Fernandina," Ransom added, with a sigh.

"Oh, not so far," said Miss Eliot, cheerfully. "It takes only a few weeks for the transports to make the trip. You must hurry to get strong and well, or you won't be ready."

"That's right," said Ransom. "It won't be very long now before my discharge papers come, and just as soon as I git up among the pines I'll begin to pick up. This here climate sort of takes the stiffenin' out of you, don't it?"

"It is enervating," acknowledged Miss Eliot. "By the way, how do you happen to be here, Ransom? I've never thought to ask you before."

"Guess you was too busy takin' care of me," said the soldier, shyly. "You've been pretty good to me, Miss Eliot. I must have been an awful nuisance, specially when I was out of my head so long."

"An awful nuisance, Ransom," said the girl, with mock seriousness. "But about your being in Fernandina?"

"Does seem kind of funny; but it come about natural enough. I was in the 42nd Maine, Army of the Potomac, and our regiment got orders to join Grant in Vicksburg. I was kind of ailin' before we set out from Fortress Monroe; got a cold doin' sentinel duty in the rain.

"It hung on and hung on, and it's hangin' on yet. So when we got to Fernandina they dropped me off. 'Unfit for service,' they said." Ransom's voice faltered. "And here I am, a-waitin' for my discharge papers to come.

"It was hard to feel that I wasn't no more use, so to speak, when I'd just turned thirty-seven. Seems as if all the things I thought was hard before wa'n't nothin' to it. At first I thought I couldn't stand it, but land sakes, folks can stand most anything in this world! They have to."

Miss Eliot nodded sympathetic comprehension.

"I've been doin' considerable thinkin' since I've been lyin' here," he went on. "War's a terrible thing, a cruel thing, with a lot of sufferin' for folks that ain't in any ways to blame—the women, the old folks and the little children." His voice grew tender. "Don't seem right, somehow. Of course a man's got to do his duty. Now I could no more help enlistin' than I can help breathin', so that's no credit to me. When the call come, I just left Pa to run the farm and look after Adelaide and little Mary. Then there's them on the other side, the fellers that's goin' to be beat, sure. They're such plucky fighters. I believe I'm right, and I'd fight 'em to a finish, but they don't see it that way, and it *is* kind of hard on 'em, ain't it, now?"

"That's the hard part of it," said the nurse, gently. "The victory of one always means the defeat of the other." Something in Ransom's unspoken sympathy led her to open her heart. "Father's with Thomas in Tennessee. One brother's in the Navy, and the youngest"—her voice broke—"is with Lee in Virginia. We were always great chums, Bob and I. He was Father's favorite, too. It was hard for Father."

She was silent; then, as her eyes met Ransom's direct look of gentle compassion, she went on almost as if the words were forced from her:

"And a man of whom I was very fond died at Shiloh, Ransom." Her voice lapsed into silence.

The bearded soldier reached out his thin hand and stroked the girl's sleeve. "I suspected you had a story, but I never dreamed it was like that.

You're a brave little woman," he said, tenderly, "way down here lookin' after us battered veterans."

Miss Eliot smiled through her tears.

"Oh, I couldn't help it, Ransom, any more than I can help breathing, so you see it's no credit to me."

Day followed day in the cool old mansion over which fluttered the Stars and Stripes. At intervals came letters, official and unofficial, bulky documents with imposing government seals, communications for the commandant of the fort, papers galore; but among them all, Ransom's papers were not.

When the next transport sailed without him, he bade a cheerful adieu to the men going North. "I'm right down glad for you boys," he said to a soldier who had come to say good-by. "It won't be long now before I'll be a-followin' you."

"That's right, Ransom," said the man, heartily. "Good-by, old fellow, and good luck!"

Outside the room he shook his head gravely. "That cough is pretty serious. It's too bad he isn't going up on this boat. There's so much confounded red tape in these government affairs a man could die fifty times before they get round to him."

The next day was Sunday, and as a special treat, Ransom was taken out on the veranda for a few hours. He was delighted.

"I'm a-pickin' up right along," he said to the nurse. "Perhaps it's just as well I couldn't go with the transport. Next time I'll be a good deal stronger." He looked out across the landscape with wistful eyes. "You ain't ever seen the pictures of my wife and little girl, have you?"

Miss Eliot shook her head, whereupon Ransom reached his hand into his breast pocket, and drew out a little carved wooden case, which he opened with much care, disclosing two daguerreotypes.

From one compartment looked the face of a woman with broad brow, plain-banded hair, and firm yet sweet mouth. The eyes had a strangely direct gaze, and the entire countenance bore the stamp of strength and sincerity. Through the almost austere reserve shone a divine tenderness.

The nurse instinctively recognized one of those rare natures which are not baffled by difficulties, but which persevere through suffering, even through defeat, to final triumph.

"Adelaide was teaching in our district when I married her," said Ransom. "I never quite see how she come to take me. I was older, and hadn't had her schoolin', and I ain't much to look at; but she always allowed she was satisfied, and we've been mighty happy together." There was a ring of pride in Ransom's voice.

The other picture was that of a little girl, four years old. Her parted hair hung in short curls each side of a round, serious little face. The big eyes had a questioning look, and the lips were slightly parted. The low-cut frock and short sleeves left uncovered a beautiful neck and chubby, dimpled arms.

The nurse gave a cry of delight. "The quaint little darling!" she exclaimed. "I'd just like to give her a good hug."

"I guess maybe I'd better go in now, Miss Eliot."

"Tired, Ransom?" she said, gently.

"Guess I am a little mite," he said, reluctantly. "When I git up home how—" A severe fit of coughing interrupted the last sentence.

In the hall, a few minutes later, she encountered the old doctor. He was a tall man, with bushy eyebrows and a pair of keen eyes.

Miss Eliot looked him squarely in the eye. "What are Ransom's chances?"

The old doctor regarded her gravely.

"Unless his papers come so that we can start him off on the next transport, Ransom's chances are practically nothing. I've written to Washington, and Commandant Haskell's written, and nothing's been heard. There you have it."

Miss Eliot's lips set themselves in firm limes. "I'm going to write," she said, "but I'm going to write to Adelaide."

"Who's Adelaide?" queried the old doctor, curiously.

"Adelaide is Ransom's wife. I believe if any one can get those papers, she can."

"There's a tug going up tomorrow," he said. "Your scheme may not work, but it's worth trying."

That night the nurse wrote the letter, and her whole heart went into it.

The days went slowly by. Ransom continued sweet-tempered and cheerful, although as he grew weaker, he became daily a little more quiet. Just when he stopped asking for his papers it would be hard to say, but that time did at last come. On those occasions when the mail was brought in he would watch wistfully, but the words did not pass his lips. Only his hollow eyes questioned. Miss Eliot grew to dread those moments. From her own letter to Adelaide she had not heard.

So, in the process of time, came the day for the second transport to sail. That morning Miss Eliot stood on the broad porch, watching the busy scene at the dock. Her face was sad. "This afternoon," she found herself saying, "the boat will go, and Ransom's chance will go with it."

As she paused on the threshold, she noticed idly, far out in the harbor, a gunboat steaming toward the shore.

Slowly she climbed the stairs to Ransom's room. As she entered, he greeted her with his accustomed cheerfulness. It was as if he guessed her thoughts, and was trying to make it easy for her.

"It's a fine day," he said.

"Yes, Ransom."

"It's this afternoon the boat sails, ain't it, Miss Eliot?"

She nodded, not trusting herself to speak.

Then, at last, Ransom broke the reticence of weeks.

"I've been sort of thinkin'," he said, slowly, "and I guess it ain't goin' to be my luck to get home. It looks pretty much as if my papers was a-comin' from another world.

"Don't you feel so bad about it, Miss Eliot," he said, comfortingly, as he noted the expression on her face. "I'm real contented. I ain't denyin' it was kind of hard at first, when I began to realize how things was goin', but I'm feelin' more reconciled now. If I had to do it over, I wouldn't do no different. War does cost, and if I'm to be a part of the price, so to speak, I'm willin' to pay my share. Only—I just would like to see Adelaide and little Mary again."

There was yearning unutterable in the soldier's voice.

"If I ain't here when my papers come, Miss Eliot, I'd kind of like to have Adelaide have 'em, and there's a few things—"

"I'll see to everything, Ransom," said the girl, "but don't you give up for a moment. I can't have you give up. You see, I have set my heart on your going home."

In her agitation she had gone to the window, and with tear-filled eyes was gazing down the shady street. At the wharf the gunboat had docked, and several uniformed pedestrians were coming toward the hospital. All this she noticed mechanically; then all at once her heart gave a convulsive leap. Turning in at the gate was a tall lieutenant, with a sun-browned face. Perched on his shoulder was a little girl. Her round hat had fallen back upon her neck, so that her face, with its frame of clustering curls, was distinctly visible. She was smiling down at her tall companion in a way that betokened an established comradeship. It was the dear, quaint little girl of Ransom's daguerreotype! Miss Eliot did not need a second glance in order to recognize the tall, slender woman who followed.

Without daring to look at Ransom, she slipped quietly from the room and hurried down the stairs.

The lieutenant had set the child down on the porch, and now stood with cap in hand. "Is this Miss Eliot?" he inquired, courteously.

The nurse bowed; then she turned. "This is Mrs. Ransom, isn't it?" She held out her hand.

Then Adelaide spoke: "Am I—Is John—" Her white lips refused to frame the question.

"He's weak, Mrs. Ransom, but there is a good chance, and now that you have come—" But Adelaide, overcome by the reaction, swayed suddenly, groping blindly before her. The lieutenant sprang forward, supporting her to a chair, while the nurse ran for a glass of water.

Adelaide drank the water obediently; then when she was recovered she looked up into Miss Eliot's face. "I can see him?"

"Just as soon as I've prepared him a little. You will remember he's rather weak."

The lieutenant held out his hand. "I'm glad we found good news," he said, heartily. "I'll be around again to see if I can be of any further service." He stopped to pat Mary's curly head. "Good-by, honey," and with a military salute he strode away.

Ransom had attributed Miss Eliot's abrupt departure to the emotion which had so strongly swayed her. Now he lay in the east corner room, quietly watching a wisp of white cloud, which was drifting slowly through the blue sky. He felt that he, too, was drifting, drifting out toward the wide unknown expanse of eternity.

Miss Eliot's voice roused him.

"Ransom," she said quietly, "are you strong enough to hear some good news?"

Ransom turned toward her quickly, attracted by the joy in her tone. Her cheeks were pink and her eyes like stars.

"Good news!" he stammered. "Have—have my papers come?"

"They came in a gunboat this morning, Ransom, by special messenger."

Joy so intense as to be almost dazzling overspread the worn face.

"My—papers—have—come—and I can go home this afternoon?" It was astonishing to see how the vitality flamed up in the worn frame.

"Do you feel strong enough to see the messenger, Ransom?"

"Strong enough!" Ransom's tone was sufficient answer.

The nurse left the room. A moment later the door opened softly. On the threshold stood Adelaide and little Mary. The child had clasped in her chubby hand a long envelope with a red seal. Mindful of Miss Eliot's caution, Adelaide stood quiet. Only her eyes met her husband's with deep tenderness and passionate yearning.

"Adelaide!" whispered Ransom. "Mary!" He stretched out his arms.

The child, breaking away from her mother's restraining grasp, ran forward. "Daddy, Daddy!" she cried, in her shrill, sweet voice. "We've brought your papers!" and climbing on the bed, she threw her arms about her father's neck.

"Poor sick Daddy!" she crooned.

Bowing his head above the child's curls, Ransom broke into deep, gasping sobs. A moment later Adelaide was on her knees by the bedside, her arms stretched out across her husband, as if her love would hold him by force from that which threatened.

On the stairs outside the little nurse wept tears of joy. Here, a few moments later, the old doctor found her.

"Well, young woman," he said, jovially, "what's your faith in humanity and providence up to now? Came about like a play, didn't it? Regular climax! At critical moment, enter wife and child."

"Don't joke, Doctor!" entreated the nurse.

"Joke! Bless your soul, child, nothing was farther from my thoughts." The old doctor blew his nose vigorously.

When Miss Eliot opened the door of the east corner room, she found a happy group. Adelaide sat by the bedside, her husband's hand in hers. Ransom's other hand held the long envelope with the red seal. On the bed, Mary was stroking her father's thin cheeks affectionately. There were tears in Ransom's eyes as he turned toward the nurse.

"It doesn't seem possible, Miss Eliot," he said, huskily. "I never knew anyone could be so happy. I haven't any idea yet how it all come about. I guess Adelaide will have to untangle the mystery," and his eyes rested tenderly on his wife's face.

"It's something of a story," said Adelaide, "so perhaps I'd better begin at the first."

"Yes," said Ransom, "I want to hear it all," and with her hand still in her husband's, Adelaide, in a simple, direct way, told her story:

"Letters have been pretty uncertain up in Maine. I hadn't heard from John in months, but I kept on hoping. I *had* to." A little quiver ran over

Adelaide's face, and Ransom's grasp of her hand tightened. "Then one afternoon, along about four o'clock, Jim Fellows drove into the yard with Miss Eliot's letter."

Ransom turned toward the nurse with a little start. His eyes met hers solemnly. "So it was *you*," he said. "I had enough to thank you for before, but I guess I ain't ever going to be able to pay my debt."

"Oh, I'm more than paid," said the girl, brightly. "Go on with your story, Mrs. Ransom."

"It was a long time before I tore open the envelope, and even when I did, the words just danced before my eyes. I handed the letter to Pa, and he put on his spectacles kind of slow like. His hands trembled so he could hardly hold the paper. When he had finished, he looked at me.

"'I'm going to Washington,' I said.

"Pa never said a word, but went to the old secretary, unlocked it, and took out a big roll of bills. He handed it to me.

"'I'll go right out and hitch up,' he said. 'If we hurry, you can get the night train from Old Town.'

"He went out, and all of a sudden I felt a tug at my skirts. I looked down, and there was Mary. Quick as a flash the question came to me, what should I do with her? It seemed foolish to take her, and yet, somehow, I felt that I had to. I just couldn't leave her."

Ransom raised Mary's dimpled hand to his lips. "Father's little girl," he said.

"'You'll fetch it, Adelaide,' Pa said, when the train whistled and he had to get off. 'Good-by! God bless you!'

"Everybody was kind to Mary and me. When the conductor found I was going to Washington, he began to ask me questions, and before I knew it, I found myself telling him the whole story. He had a boy in the Army, and he seemed to know just how I felt. He lived in Washington, and when we got in late at night, he made us go home with him. His wife made us welcome. I'll never forget her.

"Early the next morning we went up to the White House. Mr. Torrey—that was the conductor's name—went with us. As early as it was, there were a lot of people waiting, and most of them looked as if they had their share of troubles, too. Mr. Torrey seemed to know a good many men. I suppose they go up and down on his train often. He spoke to one big man, who was going in to the inner room. The man looked at me, sort of keen-like, then he said, 'I'll tell Mr. Lincoln.' Then he went on.

"I couldn't keep my eye off that door. Sometimes it would be awfully quiet in there; then again I'd hear somebody laughing. After a time the big man came out. He was chuckling to himself as if he had heard something mighty funny. He nearly went by us; then he seemed to remember, and he turned to me. 'The President will see you, madam,' he said; then he went up and held the door open.

"Mary held on to my hand as tight as if she never meant to let go, and I felt my own heart beating pretty fast; but I just thought of John, and how I *must* get the papers. When we went in, the President was standing, looking out of the window, with his hands in his pockets. He turned round, and when I saw his face all my fear left me. It was so sort of homely and good and kind. He just made me think of our own Maine folks. He's a good deal like Pa, only I guess maybe Pa's better-looking.

"He came over and shook hands with me, then he motioned me to a chair. Mary stood looking at him doubtfully for a moment, then all at once she smiled up at him. He leaned over and lifted her onto his lap, and in a minute they were talking away as if they'd known each other all their lives. I heard her telling him about her kittens."

"He likes kittens," interrupted Mary, "the President does, and he likes little girls, too. He hasn't any, though; his little girls are all boys. He told me so, and I told him about Daddy, and then he and Mother talked."

"I told him all about your war record, John," said Adelaide, "and then I gave him Miss Eliot's letter. He read it carefully, looked sort of thoughtful, then he rang a bell, and a young fellow with spectacles came in.

"'Look through the files,' said Mr. Lincoln, 'and see what you can find about John Ransom, 42nd Maine.' His tone was real curt.

"Pretty soon the young fellow came back with a slip of paper in his hand. 'John Ransom, 42nd Maine, Army of the Potomac; in hospital at

Fernandina; made application some months ago for his discharge papers; several letters about him.' He recited it all off as if he were saying a lesson.

"'If the record's right, why hasn't the case been attended to?' asked the President.

"'We haven't got round to it,' said the young fellow, his face getting red. 'We're just working on the J's.'

"'A man's life can't go according to the alphabet,' said Mr. Lincoln. 'Make out the papers at once, and send them this afternoon to Mrs. Ransom at—' He looked at me, and I told him where I was staying.

"All of a sudden he kind of laughed; then he looked at me over his spectacles. 'How would you like to take the papers to your husband yourself?' he said. 'There's a gunboat going down to-morrow.'

"I just looked at him. I couldn't say a word, and he smiled. 'I reckon it would be a good thing,' he said, 'and I don't know but that it would be the surest way of getting them there.'

"He wrote a few words on a piece of paper, signed his name, and gave the paper to me. Then he held out his hand. I couldn't say anything but 'God bless you!' but he seemed to understand. Mary piped up, 'Good-by, Mr. President!' He took her up in his arms and kissed her, and she put her arms round his neck, just as she does round Pa's, and said, 'I like you, Mr. President,' and he laughed again.

"'And I like you, Mary, so I reckon it's mutual.' Then we came away.

"That afternoon a messenger brought the papers, and the next morning Lieutenant Callahan came to take us to the boat. He was the one who came up with us this morning."

"That was Jerry," said Mary, gravely. "He told me to call him that."

"I can't tell you," went on Adelaide, "what a relief it was when I actually held that envelope in my hand. Then my only thought was to get to Fernandina. We made a quick trip, they said, but it seemed long to me, for I didn't know—" She stopped, her gray eyes meeting Ransom's with ineffable tenderness.

When Ransom was carried downstairs that afternoon, all the household had gathered to bid him Godspeed: but his last words and last glance were for Miss Eliot. As he bade her good-by he placed in her hand the little carved wooden case. The tears were streaming down his cheeks. "I hope it will be made up to you," he said.

Mary departed, jubilantly perched on the shoulder of the helpful young lieutenant, and Adelaide's face was wonderful in its new-found happiness.

On the porch the nurse stood long, watching the boat which was bearing Ransom toward home and health. At last, with a little smile, she went slowly into the house, and up into the east corner room.

Portrait of Edwin M. Stanton (the so-called iron secretary)
possibly adapted from an old photograph.

TAD LINCOLN

Wayne Whipple

No one wanted to play with the President's son, and his father was busy with Cabinet meetings. One Cabinet member openly expressed his dislike of the boy.

Tad waited until just the right time . . .

A lonely boy stood a long time gazing out between the thick iron rods of the great closed gate forming the northern entrance to the White House. A group of urchins stopped and stared at him.

"That's Tad Lincoln," said one of the street Arabs, nudging the next boy. "Used to be a brother Willie, but he's dead."

"Hello, Tad," shouted another boy—"hel-lo!"

Tad did not answer, he looked suspicious, yet wistful.

"Cayn't yuh talk?" sneered the dirtiest of the gang. "Cat gotcha tongue?"

"Don't," murmured the decent-looking boy—"*don't!* He *can't*—not plain, anyway. Something the matter."

"Oho!" shouted the Arab chief. "Let's get 'im mad and make 'im holler. Then we'll have fun with 'im."

All but the decent lad joined in a chorus of jeers that made the Lincoln boy's chubby face turn scarlet. Still he stood with his fat fists clenched, and his cherubic lips pressed tight.

A soldier—one of the guards stationed at the Executive Mansion—walked slowly by, outside the gate, and stopped, respectfully saluting the President's son without paying heed, apparently, to the other boys. They hesitated, but watchfully stood their ground. The guard, stooping to speak to Tad, jumped, grabbed the freckled ringleader's arm, and jerked him up to the gate. The other boys ran across the street while their captured leader kicked and struggled in vain.

"What shall we do to him?" the guard asked Tad.

The President's son twisted and turned, eying the toe of his little top boot as he rubbed it back and forth in the sand, but he did not answer.

"Shall we let him off this time?"

Tad smiled and nodded.

The soldier assumed a fierce expression and spoke sternly, loud enough for the other boys to hear.

"Skedaddle, you and all your gang! And if I ever catch you annoying Tad again I'll settle with you."

Tad, paying no further heed, turned about and dragged his heels toward the north entrance of the Mansion.

Thomas Pendel, doorkeeper of the White House, admitted the boy and noticed his sad face.

"Why, Taddie!" he exclaimed, "what's the matter?"

"Tom Pen," answered the boy, "I'm tired of playing by myself. I want to play together."

"Poor Taddie!" murmured the doorkeeper. "You do miss Willie, don't you? Wouldn't those boys play with you?"

Tad shook his head.

"What did they say?"

The head shook again.

"What did he say to them?"

A smile, but no reply.

"What did he *do* to that boy?"

The lad looked up warily and grinned, as if to say, "If you know all about it, why ask so many questions?"

Then, by force of habit, Tad turned toward his father's office.

"Wouldn't go in there, Taddie," pleaded the doorkeeper. "Cabinet's in session, you know."

Without paying the least heed, Tad went in—bumping the door with his new boot in lieu of a knock.

The Cabinet was deep in a discussion, but the boy marched straight over to the President, who sat in a swivel chair at the head of the long table, and began quavering to his father as if they two were there alone.

"Papa-day, I'm tired!"

The President responded as if there were no one else in the room.

"Tired, Taddie, tired?"

No one knew the origin of "Papa-day," the boy's name for his father, just as no one knew how he came to be called "Tad."

"Yes, I'm tired of playing by myhelf" [myself]. Tad had a cleft palate and could not pronounce "S" properly. "I want hum [some] one to—"

The Secretary of War, with a shock of iron-gray hair and a beard which looked like a lion's mane, had snorted when Tad broke into their conference, and now looked about in exasperation, apparently hoping to lead the other secretaries in a mutiny against the President. That snort was not lost on Tad, but he did not pay special attention to it at that time. The President also observed the signs of dissatisfaction, but they only made him bend over his afflicted boy with an expression of ineffable tenderness.

Many seemed to have difficulty in understanding Tad, and this exasperated the child. The Bible speaks of understanding with the heart. The heart of "Father Abraham" understood Tad's every word—even before it was uttered.

"But, Taddie," the President demurred, "I can't go now. I've got to play jest a leetle longer with Governor Seward and his little playmates."

Tad's eyes turned toward Secretary Stanton, who was still shrugging his shoulders and casting indignant glances toward the other secretaries—

but they, quickly melted by the President's mood, were smiling kindly at the boy.

"Run along now," said Mr. Lincoln, "I'll come out just as soon as I can."

But Tad flung himself down at his father's feet like a watchdog, to see what was going on. Provoked past all patience, Mr. Stanton's mane bristled and his eyes snapped as he blurted out,

"Where is that boy's *mother*? For one, I protest, Mr. President—"

"Tad," said Mr. Lincoln coolly, "go tell your mother that the Secretary of War—"

"Never mind that," snarled Stanton, looking angrily around at the other members who were all laughing. "I only meant, Mr. Pres—"

"With these remarks we will dismiss the subject," said the President with a grim smile and a peremptory tone new to him, "and proceed with the business before—and not *behind*!—this house."

Tad, who had started up at his father's request, now stood, perplexed and irresolute. What did that man mean by speaking of his mother, and why did they all laugh? As no one seemed to pay further attention to him, he darted a look of resentment toward the War Secretary and sank again beside his father's chair.

On other occasions he had fallen asleep during their long discussions, but today his wrath kept him awake. He had never relished Mr. Stanton's snappish remarks to his father, but today he watched the irate secretary like a lynx at bay. The more he observed and thought of that man's manner, the more he became convinced that something ought to be done to him!

When the session adjourned, the last secretary to leave—as always!—was Stanton. Tad sometimes thought the man kept staying and staying and talking and talking just to spite him. The south door had hardly closed behind the War Secretary before Tad was taking his father to task.

"Papa-day," he began, "why don't you take that 'Tanton over your knee and give him a good '*pankin*'?"

Mr. Lincoln burst out laughing at the novelty of the idea.

"Why, Taddie," he answered, with a wide smile, "you mustn't mind Brother Stanton. He's such a good man that I'm always willing to put up with his odd ways for the great good he can do the country. We can't win the war without Stanton."

A boy convinced against his will is of the same opinion still. Tad shook his head vehemently and set his teeth, but dropped the subject.

"You hed [said] you'd play with me," was his next rejoinder.

"All right—I'm here. What'll we play."

"Injun!"

With a blood-curdling yell, the Great White Chief snatched his boy up and set him on one shoulder, then on the other. Tad seized his father's shock of coarse black hair with both hands, and slid down pickaback, while his human steed pranced and champed about, letting out a series of whoops worthy of a Comanche on the warpath. Tad soon forgot about Stanton and all his other troubles, as he gurgled and squealed, "Papa-day! O Papa-day!"

The President seemed to throw off the cares of state and the worries of the war while leaping and capering through the spacious chambers of the Executive Mansion. A White House lifeguard wrote, years afterward, that the only happy moments Abraham Lincoln seemed to enjoy were while playing horse, Indian, and soldier with "Little Tad."

Within a week after that Cabinet meeting Tad offered to help the head gardener water the south lawn with the hose, to which was attached a newly invented nozzle variation. With the delight of an imaginative child, Tad played that the White House was on fire, and by turning the nozzle this way and that, learned how to make it sprinkle and spray, and do a sudden spurt, then turn into a steady stream. While he was thus experimenting, who should burst out of the south door and come stamping down the long, curved stairway from the south portico, but the Secretary of War? He kept turning back to brandish a paper at the President, who was following and struggling to appease Mr. Stanton's blustering wrath.

The President had just written a dispatch to be sent to the front, forbidding a certain young soldier to be shot next day, and the exasperated

Secretary of War was still menacing him with a telegram from General Butler, beseeching the President not to interfere with the regular order, in this case, as it would further demoralize the discipline of the Army.

As he descended to the lawn, ready to cut across the grass, as usual, to the War Department, Stanton made a final stand for a Parthian shot.

"I tell *you*, Mr. President, if this don't stop—"

Bzt!—a spurt through the new nozzle attachment knocked that paper out of the secretary's hand and sent it fluttering down the grass, and a firm stream struck the astounded functionary full in the face, then played steadily up and down his shuddering form. Stanton stood gurgling, gasping, and strangling, hardly uttering a medley of sublimated profanity while making frantic clutches in the direction of the grinning cause of his sudden discomfiture.

Even Abraham Lincoln had to laugh at the sorry spectacle of his would-be-terrible Secretary of War with his habitually bristling mane wet down like a disconsolate poodle's, as he stood there, shivering in the midst of a compulsory bath.

"Gannon! Captain Gannon!" shouted the President to one of the soldier guards. "Take that hose away from the boy!"

As the soldier sprang at Tad, he, being no respecter of persons, turned the hose on the guard, then dropped it and started to run

"You little skeesicks!" Gannon yelled as he chased the boy down the slippery lawn, and finally grabbed him by the tail of his jacket. Falling on one knee, he turned Tad across the other, as he muttered through clenched teeth:

"There! I'll teach *you* (spank) to turn the hose (spank, spank) and on me, too, you little villain!" (Spank, spank, spankety-spank.)

"There, Captain, I reckon that's about enough," shouted the President, coming down the steps. "Thank *you*!—Say, Gannon, as you go to change your clothes, won't you please take the boy to his mother or someone in the house? *He's* all wet, *too*!"

As the angry young soldier, still glaring in righteous wrath, led the lad through the basement door, Mr. Lincoln smiled and said to the secretary,

"You ought to make Gannon a colonel for that!"

Stanton, still shivering, replied with the raucous rant of a beleaguered walrus:

"I'd like to put that boy in the calaboose."

"No, Stanton, that would do more harm than good. I know it's mean to give you advice at such a time, but can't you see that you're to blame for this whole business? You've kept that boy's blood at the boiling point for several weeks, now. He doesn't like the way you talk to me. The other day you made a bad matter worse by what he thought was a sneer at his mother. He didn't understand what it meant, but he knew it must be all wrong, simply because *you* did it! After you went out that day he asked me why I didn't take you across my knee and give you a good spanking, and just because I laughed at the idea then, he has taken matters into his own hands, and now he's got the spanking!

"Let me give you a little fatherly counsel. You know as well as I do that men are just boys of larger growth. The Wise Man says, you know, that he that ruleth his spirit is stronger than he that taketh a city. You're getting yourself disliked on all sides by fuming and swearing at everybody, and Tad isn't the only person who resents some of the things you say about me. I don't mind it on my own account, but I can't bear to see you do yourself such an injustice. The habit seems to be growing on you. For your own sake, Stanton, as well as for the sake of the Army and the nation, won't you try to exercise jest a leetle more self-control? If you can make that boy your friend, you will be better able to win the war and save the Union."

Depiction of the cast of Lincoln's right hand made by Leonard W. Volk in 1860.

THE HEART OF LINCOLN

Louis B. Reynolds

It is hard to envision any other president in American history respond-ing as Lincoln did, during just one of the many, many visits he made to hospitals during the war.

The irony of life was never more strikingly illustrated than when the conduct of the bloodiest war in history fell into the hands of one who, perhaps more than any other man of history, shrank from the thought of human suffering. Of all the characteristics of Abra-ham Lincoln, his encompassing tenderness, coupled with his own mel-ancholy, has most endeared him to the hearts of the human race. "The great, gentle giant," wrote one of his biographers, "had a feeling of sym-pathy for every living creature. He was not ashamed to rock a cradle, or to carry a pail of water or an armful of wood to spare a tired woman's arms."

A day in May, 1863, found him visiting a camp hospital. He had spoken cheering words of sympathy to the wounded as he proceeded through the various wards.

Presently he was at the bedside of a Vermont boy of about sixteen years of age, who lay mortally wounded. Taking the dying boy's thin, bleached hands in his own, the President said in a tender tone: "Well, my boy, what can I do for you?"

The young soldier looked up into the President's kindly face and asked: "Won't you write to my mother for me?"

"That I will," responded the President, and, calling for writing materials, he seated himself by the side of the cot and wrote from the boy's dictation. It was a long letter, but he betrayed no sign of weariness, and when it was finished he arose, saying: "I will post this as soon as I get back to my office. Now, is there anything else that I can do for you?"

The boy looked up appealingly to the President. "Won't you stay with me? I do want to hold on to your hand."

Mr. Lincoln at once perceived the lad's meaning. The appeal was too strong for him to resist; so he sat down by his side and took hold of his thin hand. For two hours the President sat there patiently, as though he had been the boy's father.

When the end came, he bent over and folded the pale hands over the young soldier's breast, and left the hospital in tears.

Illustration drawn by F. Walter Taylor for
Scribner's Magazine *in 1906.*

THE PERFECT TRIBUTE

MARY RAYMOND SHIPMAN ANDREWS

He was bone-weary, and yet another speech was expected of him. It didn't have to be great, for he wasn't the main speaker of the event—but he'd try his best, in the short time he had in which to prepare.

But when nobody clapped at all—

O n the morning of November 18, 1863, a special train drew out from Washington, carrying a distinguished company. The presence with them of the Marine Band from the Navy yard indicated a public occasion to come, and among the travelers there were those who might be gathered only for an occasion of importance. There were judges of the Supreme Court of the United States; there were heads of departments; the general-in-chief of the Army and his staff; members of the Cabinet. In their midst, as they stood about the car before settling for the journey, towered a man sad, preoccupied, unassuming; a man awkward and ill-dressed; a man, as he leaned slouchingly against the wall, of no grace of look or manner, in whose haggard face seemed to be the suffering of the sins of the world. Abraham Lincoln, President of the United States, journeyed with his party to assist at the consecration, the next day, of the national cemetery at Gettysburg.

The quiet November landscape slipped past the rattling train, and the President's deep-set eyes stared out at it gravely, a bit listlessly. From time to time he talked with those who were about him; from time to time there were flashes of that quaint wit which is linked, as his greatness, with his name, but his mind was today dispirited, unhopeful. The weight on his shoulders seemed pressing more heavily than he had courage to press back against it, the responsibility of one almost a dictator in a wide, war-torn country came near to crushing, at times, the mere human soul and body. There was, moreover, a speech to be made tomorrow to thousands who would expect their President to say something to them worth the listening of a people who were making history; something brilliant, eloquent, strong. The melancholy gaze glittered with a grim smile. He—Abraham Lincoln—the boy bred in a cabin, tutored in rough schools here and there, fighting for, snatching at crumbs of learning that fell from rich tables, struggling to a hard knowledge which well knew its own limitations—it was he of whom this was expected. He glanced across the car. Edward Everett sat there, the orator of the following day, the finished gentleman, the careful student, the heir of traditions of learning and breeding, of scholarly instincts and resources. The self-made President gazed at him wistfully. From him the people might expect and would get a balanced and polished oration. For that end he had been born, and inheritance and opportunity and inclination had worked together for that end's perfection. While Lincoln had wrested from a scanty schooling a command of English clear and forcible always, but, he feared, rough-hewn; lacking, he feared, in finish and in breadth. Of what use was it for such a one as he to try to fashion a speech fit to take a place by the side of Everett's silver sentences? He sighed. Yet the people had a right to the best he could give, and he would give them his best; at least he could see to it that the words were real and were short; at least he would not, so, exhaust their patience. And the work might as well be done now in the leisure of the journey. [It is now known that Lincoln had written the original drafts in Washington before boarding the train.] He put a hand, big, powerful, labor-knotted, into first one sagging pocket and then another, in search of a pencil, and drew out one broken across the end. He glanced about inquiringly—there was nothing to write upon. Across the car the Secretary of State had just opened a package of books and their wrapping of brown paper lay on the floor, torn carelessly in a zigzag. The President stretched out a long arm.

"Mr. Seward, may I have this to do a little writing?" he asked, and the Secretary protested, insisted on finding better material.

But Lincoln, with few words, had his way, and soon the untidy stump of a pencil was at work and the great head, the deep-lined face, bent over Seward's bit of brown paper, the whole man absorbed in his task.

Earnestly, with that "capacity for taking infinite pains" which has been defined as genius, he labored as the hours flew, building together close-fitted word on word, sentence on sentence. As the sculptor must dream the statue prisoned in the marble, as the artist must dream the picture to come from the brilliant unmeaning of his palette, as the musician dreams a song, so he who writes must have a vision of his finished work before he touches, to begin it, a medium more elastic, more vivid, more powerful than any other—words—prismatic bits of humanity, old as the Pharaohs, new as the Arabs of the street, broken, sparkling, alive, from the age-long life of the race. Abraham Lincoln, with the clear thought in his mind of what he would say, found the sentences that came to him colorless, wooden. A wonder flashed over him once or twice of Everett's skill with these symbols which, it seemed to him, were to the Bostonian a key-board facile to make music, to Lincoln tools to do his labor. He put the idea aside for it hindered him. As he found the sword fitted to his hand he must fight with it; it might be that he, as well as Everett, could say that which should go straight from him to his people, to the nation who struggled at his back towards a goal. At least each syllable he said should be chiseled from the rock of his sincerity.

So he cut here and there an adjective, here and there a phrase, baring the heart of his thought, leaving no ribbon or flower of rhetoric to flutter in the eyes of those with whom he would be utterly honest.

And when he had done he read the speech and dropped it from his hand to the floor and stared again from the window. It was the best he could do, and it was a failure. So, with the pang of the workman who believes his work done wrong, he lifted and folded the torn bit of paper and put it in his pocket, and put aside the thought of it, as of a bad thing which he might not better, and turned and talked cheerfully with his friends.

At eleven o'clock on the morning of the day following, on November 19, 1863, a vast, silent multitude billowed, like waves of the sea, over what had been not long before the battle-field of Gettysburg. There were wounded soldiers there who had beaten their way four months ago through a singeing fire across these quiet fields, who had seen the men die who were buried here; there were troops grave and responsible, who must soon go again into battle; there were the rank and file of an every-day American gathering in surging thousands; and above them all, on the open-air platform, there were the leaders of the land, the pilots who today lifted a hand from the wheel of the ship of state to salute the memory of those gone down in the storm. Most of the men in that group of honor are now passed over to the majority, but their names are not dead in American history—great ghosts who walk still in the annals of their country, their flesh-and-blood faces were turned attentively that bright, still November afternoon toward the orator of the day, whose voice held the audience.

For two hours Everett spoke and the throng listened untired, fascinated by the dignity of his high-bred look and manner almost as much, perhaps, as by the speech which has taken a place in literature. As he had been expected to speak he spoke, of the great battle, of the causes of the war, of the results to come after. It was an oration which missed no shade of expression, no reach of grasp. Yet there were those in the multitude, sympathetic as they were with the Northern cause, who grew restless when this man who had been crowned with so thick a laurel wreath by Americans spoke of Americans as rebels, of a cause for which honest Americans were giving their lives as a crime. The days were war days, and men's passions were inflamed, yet there were men who listened to Edward Everett who believed that his great speech would have been greater unlaced with bitterness.

As the clear, cultivated voice fell into silence, the mass of people burst into a long storm of applause, for they knew that they had heard an oration which was an event. They clapped and cheered him again and again and again, as good citizens acclaim a man worthy of honor whom they have delighted to honor.

At last, as the ex-Governor of Massachusetts, the ex-ambassador to England, the ex-Secretary of State, the ex-Senator of the United States—handsome, distinguished, graceful, sure of voice and of movement—took his seat, a tall, gaunt figure detached itself from the group on the platform and moved slowly across the open space and stood facing the audience. A stir and a whisper brushed over the field of humanity, as if a breeze had rippled a monstrous bed of poppies. This was the President. A quivering silence settled down and every eye was wide to watch this strange, disappointing appearance, every ear alert to catch the first sound of his voice.

Suddenly the voice came, in a queer, squeaking falsetto. The effect on the audience was irrepressible, ghastly. After Everett's deep tones, after the strain of expectancy, this extraordinary, gaunt apparition, this high, thin sound from the huge body, were too much for the American crowd's sense of humor, always stronger than its sense of reverence. A suppressed yet unmistakable titter caught the throng, ran through it, and was gone. Yet no one who knew the President's face could doubt that he had heard it and had understood. Calmly enough, after a pause almost too slight to be recognized, he went on, and in a dozen words his tones had gathered volume, he had come to his power and dignity. There was no smile now on any face of those who listened. People stopped breathing rather, as if they feared to miss an inflection. A loose-hung figure, six feet four inches high, he towered above them, conscious of and quietly ignoring the bad first impression, unconscious of a charm of personality which reversed that impression within a sentence. That these were his people was his only thought. He had something to say to them; what did it matter about him or his voice?

"Fourscore and seven years ago," spoke the President, "our fathers brought forth on this continent a new nation, conceived in liberty and dedicated to the proposition that all men are created equal. Now we are engaged in a great civil war, testing whether that nation, or any nation, so conceived and so dedicated, can long endure. We are met on a great battle-field of that war. We have come to dedicate a portion of it as a final resting-place for those who here gave their lives that that nation might live. It is altogether fitting and proper that we should do this.

"But in a larger sense we cannot dedicate, we cannot consecrate, we cannot hallow, this ground. The brave men, living and dead, who struggled here, have consecrated it far above our poor power to add or to detract. The world will little note nor long remember what we say here, but it can never forget what they did here. It is for us, the living, rather, to be dedicated here to the unfinished work which they who fought here have thus far so nobly advanced. It is rather for us to be here dedicated to the great task remaining before us—that from these honored dead we take increased devotion to that cause for which they here gave the last full measure of devotion—that we here highly resolve that these dead shall not have died in vain, that this nation, under God, shall have a new birth of freedom, and that government of the people, by the people, for the people shall not perish from the earth."

There was no sound from the silent, vast assembly. The President's large figure stood before them, at first inspired, glorified with the thrill and swing of his words, lapsing slowly in the stillness into lax, ungraceful lines. He stared at them a moment with sad eyes full of gentleness, of resignation, and in the deep quiet they stared at him. Not a hand was lifted in applause. Slowly the big, awkward man slouched back across the platform and sank into his seat, and yet there was no sound of approval, of recognition from the audience; only a long sigh ran like a ripple on an ocean through rank after rank. In Lincoln's heart a throb of pain answered it. His speech had been, as he feared it would be, a failure. As he gazed steadily at these his countrymen who would not give him even a little perfunctory applause for his best effort he knew that the disappointment of it cut into his soul. And then he was aware that there was music, the choir was singing a dirge; his part was done, and his part had failed.

When the ceremonies were over Everett at once found the President. "Mr. President," he began, "your speech—" but Lincoln had interrupted, flashing a kindly smile down at him, laying a hand on his shoulder.

"We'll manage not to talk about my speech, Mr. Everett," he said. "This isn't the first time I've felt that my dignity ought not to permit me to be a public speaker."

He went on in a few cordial sentences to pay tribute to the orator of the occasion. Everett listened thoughtfully and when the chief had done, "Mr. President," he said simply, "I should be glad if I could flatter myself that I came as near the central idea of the occasion in two hours as you did in two minutes."

But Lincoln shook his head and laughed and turned to speak to a newcomer with no change of opinion—he was apt to trust his own judgments.

The special train which left Gettysburg immediately after the solemnities on the battle-field cemetery brought the President's party into Washington during the night. There was no rest for the man at the wheel of the nation next day, but rather added work until, at about four in the afternoon, he felt sorely the need of air and went out from the White House alone, for a walk. His mind still ran on the events of the day before—the impressive, quiet multitude, the serene sky of November arched, in the hushed interregnum of the year, between the joy of summer and the war of winter, over those who had gone from earthly war to heavenly joy. The picture was deeply engraved in his memory; it haunted him. And with it came a soreness, a discomfort of mind which had haunted him as well in the hours between—the chagrin of the failure of his speech. During the day he had gently but decisively put aside all reference to it from those about him; he had glanced at the headlines in the newspapers with a sarcastic smile; the Chief Executive must be flattered, of course; newspaper notices meant nothing. He knew well that he had made many successful speeches; no man of his shrewdness could be ignorant that again and again he had carried an audience by storm; yet he had no high idea of his own speech-making, and yesterday's affair had shaken his confidence more. He remembered sadly that, even for the President, no hand, no voice had been lifted in applause.

"It must have been pretty poor stuff," he said half aloud; "yet I thought it was a fair little composition. I meant to do well by them."

His long strides had carried him into the outskirts of the city, and suddenly, at a corner, from behind a hedge, a young boy of fifteen years or so came rushing toward him and tripped and stumbled against him, but Lincoln kept him from falling with a quick, vigorous arm. The lad righted himself and tossed back his thick, light hair and stared haughtily, and the President, regarding him, saw that his blue eyes were blind with tears.

"Do you want all of the public highway? Can't a gentleman from the South even walk in the streets without—without—" and the broken sentence ended in a sob.

The anger and the insolence of the lad were nothing to the man who towered above him—to that broad mind this was but a child in trouble. "My boy, the fellow that's interfering with your walking is down inside of you," he said gently, and with that the astonished youngster opened his wet eyes wide and laughed—a choking, childish laugh that pulled at the older man's heart-strings. "That's better, sonny," he said, and patted the slim shoulder. "Now tell me what's wrong with the world. Maybe I might help straighten it."

"Wrong, wrong!" the child raved; "everything's wrong," and launched into a mad tirade against the government from the President on down.

Lincoln listened patiently, and when the lad paused for breath, "Go ahead," he said good-naturedly. "Every little helps."

With that the youngster was silent and drew himself up with stiff dignity, offended yet fascinated; unable to tear himself away from this strange giant who was so insultingly kind under his abuse, who yet inspired him with such a sense of trust and of hope.

"I want a lawyer," he said impulsively, looking up anxiously into the deep-lined face inches above him. "I don't know where to find a lawyer in this horrible city, and I must have one—I can't wait—it may be too late—I want a lawyer *now*," and once more he was in a fever of excitement.

"What do you want with a lawyer?" Again the calm, friendly tone quieted him.

"I want him to draw a will. My brother is—" he caught his breath with a gasp in a desperate effort for self-control. "They say he's—dying." He finished the sentence with a quiver in his voice, and the brave front and the trembling, childish tone went to the man's heart. "I don't believe it—he can't be dying," the boy talked on, gathering courage. "But anyway, he wants to make a will, and—and I reckon—it may be that he—he must."

"I see," the other answered gravely, and the young, torn soul felt an unreasoning confidence that he had found a friend. "Where is your brother?"

"He's in the prison hospital there—in that big building," he pointed down the street. "He's captain in our army—in the Confederate army. He was wounded at Gettysburg."

"Oh!" The deep-set eyes gazed down at the fresh face, its muscles straining under grief and responsibility, with the gentlest, most fatherly pity. "I think I can manage your job, my boy," he said. "I used to practice law in a small way myself, and I'll be glad to draw the will for you."

The young fellow had whirled him around before he had finished the sentence. "Come," he said. "Don't waste time talking—why didn't you tell me before?" and then he glanced up. He saw the ill-fitting clothes, the crag-like, rough-modeled head, the awkward carriage of the man; he was too young to know that what he felt beyond these was greatness. There was a tone of patronage in his voice and in the cock of his aristocratic young head as he spoke. "We can pay you, you know—we're not paupers." He fixed his eyes on Lincoln's face to watch the impression as he added, "My brother is Carter Hampton Blair, of Georgia. I'm Warrington Blair. The Hampton Court Blairs, you know."

"Oh!" said the President. The lad went on.

"It would have been all right if Nellie hadn't left Washington today—my sister, Miss Eleanor Hampton Blair. Carter was better this morning, and so she went with the Senator. She's secretary to Senator Warrington, you know. He's on the Yankee side"—the tone was full of contempt—"but yet he's our cousin, and when he offered Nellie the position she would take it in spite of Carter and me. We were so poor"—the lad's pride was off its guard for the moment, melted in the soothing trust with which this stranger thrilled his soul. It was a relief to him to talk, and the large hand which rested on his shoulder as they walked seemed an assurance that his words were accorded respect and understanding. "Of course, if Nellie had been here she would have known how to get a lawyer, but Carter had a bad turn half an hour ago, and the doctor said he might get better or he might die any minute, and Carter remembered about the money, and got so excited that they said it was hurting him, so I said I'd get a lawyer, and I rushed out, and the first thing I ran against was you. I'm afraid I wasn't very polite." The smile on the gaunt face above him was all the answer he needed. "I'm sorry. I apologize. It certainly was good of you to come right back with me." The boy's manner was full of the assured graciousness of a high-born gentleman; there was a lovable quality in his very patronage, and the suffering and the sweetness and the pride combined held Lincoln by his sense of humor as well as by his soft heart. "You sha'n't lose anything by it," the youngster went on. "We may be poor, but we have more than plenty to pay you with, I'm sure. Nellie has some jewels, you see—oh, I think several things yet. Is it very expensive to draw a will?" he asked wistfully.

"No, sonny; it's one of the cheapest things a man can do," was the hurried answer, and the boy's tone showed a lighter heart.

"I'm glad of that, for, of course, Carter wants to leave—to leave as much as he can. You see, that's what the will is about—Carter is engaged to marry Miss Sally Maxfield, and they would have been married now if he hadn't been wounded and taken prisoner. So, of course, like any gentleman that's engaged, he wants to give her everything that he has. Hampton Court has to come to me after Carter, but there's some money—quite a lot—only we can't get it now. And that ought to go to Carter's wife, which is what she is—just about—and if he doesn't make a will it won't. It will come to Nellie and me if—if anything should happen to Carter."

"So you're worrying for fear you'll inherit some money?" Lincoln asked meditatively.

"Of course," the boy threw back impatiently. "Of course, it would be a shame if it came to Nellie and me, for we couldn't ever make her take it. We don't need it—I can look after Nellie and myself," he said proudly, with a quick, tossing motion of his fair head that was like the motion of a spirited, thoroughbred horse. They had arrived at the prison. "I can get you through all right. They all know me here," he spoke over his shoulder reassuringly to the President with a friendly glance. Dashing down the corridors in front, he did not see the guards salute the tall figure which followed him; too preoccupied to wonder at the ease of their entrance, he flew along through the big building, and behind him in large strides came his friend.

A young man—almost a boy, too—of twenty-three or twenty-four, his handsome face a white shadow, lay propped against the pillows, watching the door eagerly as they entered.

"Good boy, Warry," he greeted the little fellow; "you've got me a lawyer," and the pale features lighted with a smile of such radiance as seemed incongruous in this gruesome place. He held out his hand to the man who swung toward him, looming mountainous behind his brother's slight figure. "Thank you for coming," he said cordially, and in his tone was the same air of a *grand seigneur* as in the boy's. Suddenly a spasm of pain caught him, his head fell into the pillows, his muscles twisted, his arm about the neck of the kneeling boy tightened convulsively. Yet while the agony still held him he was smiling again with gay courage. "It nearly blew me away," he whispered, his voice shaking, but his eyes bright with amusement. "We'd better get to work before one of those little breezes carries me too far. There's pen and ink on the table, Mr.—my brother did not tell me your name."

"Your brother and I met informally," the other answered, setting the materials in order for writing. "He charged into me like a younger steer," and the boy, out of his deep trouble, laughed delightedly. "My name is Lincoln."

The young officer regarded him. "That's a good name from your standpoint—you are, I take it, a Northerner?"

The deep eyes smiled whimsically. "I'm on that side of the fence. You may call me a Yankee if you'd like."

"There's something about you, Mr. Lincoln," the young Georgian answered gravely, with a kindly and unconscious condescension, "which makes me wish to call you, if I may, a friend."

He had that happy instinct which shapes a sentence to fall on its smoothest surface, and the President, in whom the same instinct was strong, felt a quick comradeship with this enemy who, about to die, saluted him. He put out his great hand swiftly.

"Shake hands," he said. "Friends it is."

" 'Till death us do part,' " said the officer slowly, and smiled, and then threw back his head with a gesture like the boy's. "We must do the will," he said peremptorily.

"Yes, now we'll fix this will business, Captain Blair," the big man answered cheerfully. "When your mind's relieved about your plunder you can rest easier and get well faster."

The sweet, brilliant smile of the Southerner shone out, his arm drew the boy's shoulder closer, and the President, with a pang, knew that his friend knew that he must die.

With direct, condensed question and clear answer the simple will was shortly drawn and the impromptu lawyer rose to take his leave. But the wounded man put out his hand.

"Don't go yet," he pleaded, with the imperious, winning accent which was characteristic of both brothers. The sudden, radiant smile broke again over the face, young, drawn with suffering, prophetic of close death. "I like you," he brought out frankly. "I've never liked a stranger as much in such short order before."

His head, fair as the boy's, lay back on the pillows, locks of hair damp against the whiteness, the blue eyes shone like jewels from the colorless face, a weak arm stretched protectingly about the young brother who pressed against him. There was so much courage, so much helplessness, so much pathos in the picture that the President's great heart throbbed with a desire to comfort them.

"I want to talk to you about that man, Lincoln, your namesake," the prisoner's deep, uncertain voice went on, trying pathetically to make conversation which might interest, might hold his guest. The man who stood hesitating controlled a startled movement. "I'm Southern to the core of me, and I believe with my soul in the cause I've fought, for the cause I'm—" he stopped, and his hand caressed the boy's shoulder. "But that President of yours is a remarkable man. He's regarded as a red devil by most of us down home, you know," and he laughed, "but I've admired him all along. He's inspired by principle, not by animosity, in this fight; he's real and he's powerful and"—he lifted his head impetuously and his eyes flashed—"and, by Jove have you read his speech of yesterday in the papers?"

Lincoln gave him an odd look. "No," he said, "I haven't."

"Sit down," Blair commanded. "Don't grudge a few minutes to a man in hard luck. I want to tell you about that speech. You're not so busy but that you ought to know."

"Well, yes," said Lincoln, "perhaps I ought." He took out his watch and made a quick mental calculation. *It's only a question of going without my dinner, and the boy is dying*, he thought. *If I can give him a little pleasure the dinner is a small matter.* He spoke again. "It's the soldiers who are the busy men, not the lawyers, nowadays," he said. "I'll be delighted to spend a half hour with you, Captain Blair, if I won't tire you."

"That's good of you," the young officer said, and a king on his throne could not have been gracious in a more lordly yet unconscious way. "By the way, this great man isn't any relation of yours, is he, Mr. Lincoln?"

"He's a kind of connection—through my grandfather," Lincoln acknowledged. "But I know just the sort of fellow he is—you can say what you want."

"What I want to say first is this: that he yesterday made one of the great speeches of history."

"*What?*" demanded Lincoln, staring.

"I know what I'm talking about." The young fellow brought his thin fist down on the bedclothes. "My father was a speaker—all my uncles and my grandfather were speakers. I've been brought up on oratory. I've studied and read the best models since I was a lad in knee-breeches. And I know a great speech when I see it. And when Nellie—my sister—brought in the paper this morning and read that to me I told her at once that not six times since history began has a speech been made which was its equal. That was before she told me what the Senator said."

"What did the Senator say?" asked the quiet man who listened.

"It was Senator Warrington, to whom my sister is—is acting as secretary." The explanation was distasteful, but he went on, carried past the jog by the interest of his story. "He was at Gettysburg yesterday, with the President's party. He told my sister that the speech so went home to the hearts of all those thousands of people that when it was ended it was as if the whole audience held its breath—there was not a hand lifted to applaud. One might as well applaud the Lord's Prayer—it would have been sacrilege. And they all felt it—down to the lowest. There was a long minute of reverent silence, no sound from all that great throng—it seems to me, an enemy, that it was the most perfect tribute that has ever been paid by any people to any orator."

The boy, lifting his hand from his brother's shoulder to mark the effect of his brother's words, saw with surprise that in the strange lawyer's eyes were tears. But the wounded man did not notice.

"It will live, that speech. Fifty years from now American school-boys will be learning it as part of their education. It is not merely my opinion," he went on. "Warrington says the whole country is ringing with it. And you haven't read it? And your name's Lincoln? Warry, boy, where's the paper Nellie left? I'll read the speech to Mr. Lincoln myself."

The boy had sprung to his feet and across the room, and had lifted a folded newspaper from the table. "Let me read it, Carter—it might tire you."

The giant figure which had crouched, elbows on knees, in the shadows by the narrow hospital cot, heaved itself slowly upward till it loomed at its full height in air. Lincoln turned his face toward the boy standing under the flickering gas-jet and reading with soft, sliding inflections, the words which had for twenty-four hours been gall and wormwood to his memory. And as the sentences slipped from the lad's mouth, behold, a miracle happened, for the man who had written them knew that they were great. He knew then, as many a lesser one has known, that out of a little loving-kindness had come great joy; that he had wrested with gentleness a blessing from his enemy.

"'Fourscore and seven years ago,'" the fresh voice began, and the face of the dying man stood out white in the white pillows, sharp with eagerness, and the face of the President shone as he listened as if to new words. The field of yesterday, the speech, the deep silence which followed it, all were illuminated, as his mind went back, with new meaning. With the realization that the stillness had meant, not indifference, but perhaps, as this generous enemy had said, "The most perfect tribute ever paid by any people to any orator," there came to him a rush of glad strength to bear the burdens of the nation. The boy's tones ended clearly, deliberately.

"'We here highly resolve that these dead shall not have died in vain, that this nation, under God, shall have a new birth of freedom, and that government of the people, by the people, for the people shall not perish from the earth.'"

There was deep stillness in the hospital ward as there had been stillness on the field of Gettysburg. The soldier's voice broke it. "It's a wonderful speech," he said. "There's nothing finer. Other men have spoken stirring words, for the North and for the South, but never before, I think, with the love of both breathing through them. It is only the greatest who can be a partisan without bitterness, and only such, today may call himself not Northern or Southern, but American. To feel that your enemy can fight you to death without malice, with charity—it lifts country, it lifts humanity to something worth dying for. They are beautiful broad words and the sting of war would be drawn if the soul of Lincoln could be breathed into the armies. Do you agree with me?" he demanded abruptly, and Lincoln answered slowly, from a happy heart.

"I believe it is a good speech," he said.

The impetuous Southerner went on: "Of course, it's all wrong from my point of view," and the gentleness of his look made the words charming. "The thought which underlies it is warped, inverted, as I look at it, yet that doesn't alter my admiration of the man and of his words. I'd like to put my hand in his before I die," he said, and the sudden, brilliant, sweet smile lit the transparency of his face like a lamp; "and I'd like to tell him that I know that what we're all fighting for, the best of us, is the right of our country as it is given us to see it." He was laboring a bit with the words now as if he were tired, but he hushed the boy imperiously. "When a man gets so close to death's door that he feels the wind through it from a larger atmosphere, then the small things are blown away. The bitterness of the fight has faded for me. I only feel the love of country, the satisfaction of giving my life for it. The speech—that speech—has made it look higher and simpler—your side as well as ours. I would like to put my hand in Abraham Lincoln's—"

The clear, deep voice, with its hesitations, its catch of weakness, stopped short. Convulsively the hand shot out and caught at the great fingers that hung near him, pulling the President, with the strength of agony, to his knees by the cot. The prisoner was writhing in an attack of mortal pain, while he held, unknowing that he held it, the hand of his new friend in a torturing grip. The door of death had opened wide and a stormy wind was carrying the bright, conquered spirit into that larger atmosphere of which he had spoken. Suddenly the struggle ceased, the unconscious head rested in the boy's arms, and the hand of the Southern soldier lay quiet, where he had wished to place it, in the hand of Abraham Lincoln.

Painted by Sidney H. Riesenberg for
Harper's Magazine *in 1912.*

MARY BOWMAN, OF GETTYSBURG

ELSIE SINGMASTER

Of all the stories about Gettysburg, none come even close to this one. None as bleak, as draining to read, as raw, as revealing. To read it is to go backward in time almost fifty years from when Singmaster wrote it, and a hundred more for us readers of today. No other Civil War story I have ever read so fully captures the feelings of the women and children who somehow lived through the war's hell, and its bleak aftermath.

Quite simply it is a one-of-a-kind masterpiece.

F rom the kitchen to the front door, on the 1st of July, 1863, back to the kitchen, out to the little stone-fenced yard behind the house, where her children played in their quiet fashion, Mary Bowman went uneasily. She was a bright-eyed, slender person, with an intense joy in life. In her red plaid gingham dress, with its full, starched skirt, she looked not much older than her ten-year-old boy.

Presently she went back to her work. She sat down in a low chair by the kitchen table, and laid upon her knee a strip of thick muslin. Upon that she placed a strip of linen which she began to scrape with a sharp knife. Gradually a pile of little downy masses of lint gathered in her lap.

After a while she slipped her hands under the soft mass and lifted it to the table. Forgetting the knife, which fell with a clatter to the floor, she rose and went to the kitchen door.

"Children," she said, "remember you are not to go away."

The oldest boy answered obediently. Mounted upon a broomstick, he impersonated General Early, who a few days before had visited the town, and little Katy and the four-year-old boy represented General Early's ragged soldiers.

Their mother's eyes darkened as she watched them. Those raiding Confederates had been so terrible to look up, so ragged, so worn, so starving. The Union soldiers who had come yesterday, marching in the Emmittsburg road, through the town, and out to the Theological Seminary, were different; travel-worn as they were, they had seemed in comparison like new recruits.

Suddenly Mary Bowman clasped her hands. Thank God they would not fight here! Once more frightened Gettysburg had anticipated a battle, once more its alarm had proved ridiculous. Early had gone days ago to York; the Union soldiers were marching toward Chambersburg. Thank God, John Bowman, her husband, was not a regular soldier, but a fifer in the brigade band. Members of the band, poor Mary thought, were safe.

It was only on dismal, rainy days, or when she woke at night and looked at her children lying in their beds, that the vague, strange possibility of her husband's death occurred to her. Then she assured herself with conviction that God would not let him die. By fall the war would be over, and he would come back and resume his school-teaching, and everything would be as it had been.

She went through the kitchen again and out to the front door, and looked down the street with its scattering houses. Opposite lived good-natured, strong-armed Hannah Casey; in the next house, a dozen rods away, the Deemer family. The Deemers had had great trouble; the father was at war, and two children were ill with typhoid fever. Beyond, the houses were set closer together; the Wilson house first, where a baby was watched for now each day; and next to it, the McAtee house, where

Grandma McAtee was dying. Farther on, past the new courthouse, men were moving about, some mounted, some on foot. Their presence did not disturb Mary, since Early had gone in one direction and the Union soldiers were going in the other.

Over the tops of the houses Mary could see the cupola of the seminary lifting its graceful dome and slender pillars against the sky. She and her husband had always planned that one of their boys should go to the seminary and learn to be a preacher; she remembered their hope now. Far beyond the seminary the foothills of the Blue Ridge lay clear and purple in the morning sunshine. The sun, already high in the sky, was behind her; it stood over the tall, thick pines of the little cemetery where her kin lay, where she herself would lie, with her husband beside her. Except for that dim spot, the lovely landscape lay unshadowed.

Suddenly she put out her hand to the pillar of the porch and called her neighbor.

"Hannah!"

The door of the opposite house opened, and Hannah Casey's burly figure crossed the street. She had been working in her carefully tended garden, and her face was crimson. Hannah Casey anticipated no battle.

"Good morning to you!" she called. "What is it you want?"

"Come here!" bade Mary Bowman.

The Irishwoman climbed the three steps to the little porch.

"What is it?" she asked again. "What is it you see?"

"Look! Out there at the seminary! You can see the soldiers moving about like black specks under the trees!"

Hannah squinted a pair of near-sighted eyes in the direction of the seminary.

"I'll take your word for it," said she.

With a sudden motion Mary Bowman lifted her hand to her lips.

"Early wouldn't come back!" she said. "He would never come back!"

Hannah Casey laughed a bubbling laugh. "Those rag-a-bones? It 'ud go hard with 'em! The Unionists wouldn't jump before 'em like the rabbits here. The Bateses fled once more for their lives; it's the seventeenth time they've saved their valuable commodities. Down the street they flew, their precious tin rattling in their wagon. 'Oh, my kind sir,' says Lillian to the raggedy man you fed—'oh, my kind sir, I surrender!' 'You're right you do,' says he. 'We're goin' to eat you up!' 'Lady,' says that same snip to me, 'you'd better leave your home.' 'Worm,' says I back to him, 'you leave my home!'"

"He ate like an animal," said Mary.

"And all the cavae-dwellers was talkin' about divin' for their cellars. I wasn't goin' into no cellar. Here I stay, above ground, till they lay me out for good."

Mary Bowman laughed suddenly, hysterically.

"Did you see him dive into the apple butter, Hannah Casey? He—" She stopped and listened, frowning. She looked out once more toward the ridge with its moving spots, then down at the town with its larger spots, then back at the pines, straight and tall in the July sunshine. She could see the white tombstones beneath the trees.

"Listen!" she cried.

"To what?" said Hannah Casey.

There were still the same faint, distant sounds, but they were not much louder, not much more numerous than could be heard in the village on any summer morning.

Hannah Casey spoke irritably. "What do you hear?"

"Nothing," answered Mary Bowman. "But I thought I heard men marching. I believe it's my heart beating! I thought I heard them in the night. Could you sleep?"

"Like a log!" said Hannah Casey. "Ain't our boys yonder? Ain't the Rebs shakin' in their shoes? No, they ain't. They ain't got no shoes. Ain't the Bateses, them barometers of war, still in their castle; ain't—"

"I slept the first part of the night," said Mary Bowman. "Then it seemed to me I heard men marching. I looked out, but there was nothing stirring. It was the brightest night I ever saw. I—"

Again Hannah Casey laughed her mighty laugh. There were nearer sounds now, the rattle of a cart behind them, the gallop of hoofs in front.

The Bateses were fleeing once more, a family of eight, crowded into a little springless wagon with what household effects they could collect. Hannah Casey waved her apron at them.

"Run!" she yelled. "Skedaddle! Help! Murder!"

Her jeers could not make them turn their heads. Mrs. Bates held in her short arms a feather bed; her children tried to get under it as chicks under a mother hen. In front of the Deemer house they stopped suddenly. A Union soldier had halted them, then let them pass. He rode his horse up on the pavement and pounded with his sword at the Deemer door.

"He might terrify the children to death!" cried Mary Bowman. Already the soldier was riding toward her.

"There is sickness there!" she protested to his unheeding ears. "You oughtn't to pound like that!"

"You women will have to stay in your cellars," he shouted. "A battle is to be fought here."

"Here?" said Mary Bowman, stupidly.

"Get out!" said Hannah Casey. "There ain't nobody here to fight with!"

The soldier rode his horse to Hannah Casey's door and began to pound with his sword.

"I live there!" screamed Hannah. "You dare to bang that door!"

Mary Bowman crossed the street and looked up at him as he sat on his great horse.

"Oh, sir, do you mean that they will fight *here?*"

"Where there are women and children?" screamed Hannah. "And gardens planted? I'd like to see one of them in my garden! I—"

"Get into your cellars," commanded the soldier. "You'll be safe there."

"Sir!" Mary Bowman went closer. The crisis in the Deemer house was not yet passed; even at the best it was doubtful whether Agnes Wilson could survive the hour of her trial; and Grandma McAtee was dying. "Sir!" said Mary Bowman, earnestly, "there are women and children here whom it might kill!"

The man laughed a short laugh.

"Oh, my God!" said he. He leaned a little from his saddle. "Listen to me, sister! I have lost my father and two brothers in this war. Get into your cellars."

Mary Bowman looked down the street. The movement was more rapid, the crowd was thicker. It seemed to her that she heard Mrs. Deemer scream. Suddenly there was a clatter of hoofs; a dozen soldiers, riding from the town, halted and began to question her.

"This is the road to Baltimore?"

"Yes."

Gauntleted hands lifted the dusty reins. One of the soldiers spoke:

"You'd better protect yourself. There is going to be a battle."

"Here?" said Mary Bowman, again stupidly.

"Right here."

Hannah Casey thrust herself between them.

"Who are you going to fight with—say?"

The soldiers grinned at her. "With the Turks," answered one, over his shoulder.

Another was kinder, or more cruel. "Sister," said he, "it is likely that two hundred thousand men will be engaged on this spot. The whole Army of Virginia is advancing from the north, the whole Army of the Potomac from the south, you—"

The soldier did not finish. His galloping comrades left him; he hastened to join them. After him floated another accusation of lying from the lips of Hannah Casey.

"Hannah," said Mary Bowman, thickly, "I told you how I heard them marching. It was as though they came in every direction, Hannah—from Baltimore and Taneytown and Harrisburg and York. They were shoulder against shoulder, and their faces were like death."

Hannah Casey grew ghastly white. Superstition did what common sense and word of man could not do.

"So you did!" she whispered. "So you did!"

Mary Bowman clasped her hands. The little sounds had died away; there was now a mighty stillness.

"He said the whole Army of the Potomac. John is in the Army of the Potomac."

"That is what he said," answered the Irishwoman.

"What will the Deemers do?" asked Mary Bowman. "And the Wilsons?"

"God knows!" said Hannah Casey.

Suddenly Mary lifted her arms above her head.

"Look!" she screamed.

"What?" cried Hannah Casey. "What is it?"

Mary Bowman went backward toward the door, her eyes fixed on the distant ridge. It was nine o'clock; a shrill little clock in the house struck the hour.

"Children!" called Mary Bowman. "Come! See!"

The children dropped the little sticks with which they played and ran toward her.

"What is it?" whined Hannah Casey.

Mary Bowman lifted the little boy to her shoulder. A strange, unaccountable excitement possessed her. She wondered what a battle would be like. She did not think of wounds, of blood, of groans, but of great sounds, of martial music, of streaming flags carried aloft. She sometimes dreamed that her husband, though he had so unimportant a place, might perform some great deed of valor, might snatch the colors from a wounded bearer and lead a regiment to victory. She never thought that he might die, that he might be lost, swallowed up in the yawning mouth of some great battle trench; she never dreamed that she would never see him again; would hunt for him among thousands of dead bodies, would have her eyes filled with sights intolerable, with wretchedness unspeakable, would be tortured by a thousand agonies which she could not assuage, torn by a thousand griefs beside her own. She could not foresee that all the dear woods and fields which she loved, where she had played as a child, had walked with her beloved as a girl, would become, from Round Top to the seminary, from the seminary to Culp's Hill, a great shambles, then a great charnel-house—a vast house of death.

"See, darling!" she cried to the little boy on her shoulder. "See the bright things sparkling on the hill!

"What are they?" begged Hannah Casey.

"They are bayonets and swords!"

She put the little boy down on the floor and looked at him.

"Hark!" said Hannah Casey.

Far out toward the shining cupola of the seminary there was a sharp little sound, then another and another.

"What is it?" shrieked Hannah Casey. "Oh, what is it?"

"What is it?" mocked Mary Bowman. "It is"—

A single, thundering, echoing blast took the words from Mary Bowman's lips.

Stupidly she and Hannah Casey looked at each other.

• • • •

Four months later Mary Bowman was warned, together with the other citizens of Gettysburg, that on Thursday, the 19th of November, 1863, she would be awakened by a bugler's reveille, and that during that great day she would hear again the dread sound of cannon.

Nevertheless, hearing the reveille, she sat up in bed with a scream. Then, gasping, groping about in her confusion and terror, she began to dress. She put on a dress which had once been a bright plaid, but which now, having lost both its color and the stiff, outstanding quality of the skirts of '63, hung about her in straight and dingy folds. It was clean, but it had about it certain ineradicable brown stains on which soap and water seemed to have had no effect.

In the bed from which she had risen lay her little daughter; in a trundle-bed her two sons, one about ten years old, the other about four. They slept heavily, lying deep in their beds. Their mother looked at them with her strange, absent gaze, then she barred more closely the broken shutters and went down the stairs. The shutters were broken in a curious fashion. Here and there they were pierced by round holes, and one hung by a single hinge. The window-frames were without glass, the floor was without carpet, the beds were without pillows.

In her kitchen Mary Bowman looked about her dully. Here, too, the floor was carpetless. Above the stove a patch of fresh plaster showed where a great hole had been filled in; in the doors were the same little round holes as in the shutters of the room above. She opened the shuttered door of the cupboard, and, having made the fire, began to prepare breakfast.

Outside the house there was already, at six o'clock, noise and confusion. Last evening a train from Washington had brought to the village Abraham Lincoln; awaiting him, thousands thronged the little town. This morning the tract of land between Mary Bowman's house and the village cemetery was to be dedicated for the burial of the Union dead.

Of the dedication, of the President of the United States, of the great crowds, of the crape-banded banners, Mary Bowman and her children would see nothing. Mary Bowman would sit in her little wrecked kitchen with her children. For to her the President of the United States and others in high places who prosecuted war or who tolerated war were hateful. To her the crowds of curious people who coveted a sight of the great battle-field were ghouls, whose eyes longed to gloat upon ruin, whose feet longed to sink into the loose ground of hastily made graves.

Mary Bowman knew that field! From Culp's Hill to the McPherson farm, from Big Round Top to the poorhouse, she had traveled it, searching, searching, with frantic, insane disregard of positions or possibility. Her husband could not have fallen here among the Eleventh Corps; he could not lie here among the unburied dead of the Louisiana Tigers! If he was in the battle at all, it was at the Angle that he fell.

She had not been able to begin her search immediately after the battle because there were forty wounded men in her little house; she could not prosecute it with any diligence even after the soldiers had been carried to the hospital. Nurses were here, Sisters of Mercy were here, compassionate women were here by the score, but still she was needed to nurse, to bandage, to comfort, to pray with those who must die. Little Mary Bowman had assisted at the amputation of limbs, she had helped to control strong men torn by the frenzy of delirium, she had tended poor bodies which had almost lost semblance to humanity. Neither she nor any of the other women of the village counted themselves especially heroic; they forgot that fainting at the sight of blood was one of the distinguishing qualities of their sex; they turned back their sleeves and repressed their tears, and fed the hungry and healed the sick and clothed the naked. If Mary Bowman had been herself, she might have laughed at the sight of her dresses cobbled into trousers, her skirts wrapped round the shoulders of sick men. But neither then, nor even after, did Mary Bowman laugh at any incident of that summer. Hannah Casey laughed, and by and by she began to boast. Meade, Hancock, Slocum were non-combatants beside her. She had fought whole companies of Confederates, she had wielded bayonets, she had assisted at the spiking of guns. But all Hannah's lunacy could not make Mary Bowman smile.

Of John Bowman no trace could be found; to Mary's frantic letters no one responded. Her old friend, the village judge, wrote also, but could get no reply. Her husband was missing; it was probable that he lay somewhere upon this field, upon which he and she had wandered as sweethearts.

In midsummer a few trenches were opened, and Mary saw them opened. At the uncovering of the first great pit she actually helped with her own hands. For those of this generation who know nothing of war that fact may be written down, to be passed over lightly. She did not cry or shudder; she only helped doggedly, and looked at what they uncovered.

Immediately an order went forth that no graves were to be opened before cold weather. Already there were cases of dysentery and typhoid. Now that the necessity for daily work for the wounded was past, the village became nervous, excited. Several men and boys were killed while trying to open unexploded shells; their deaths added to the general horror. There were constant visitors who sought husbands, brothers, sweethearts; with these the Gettysburg women were still able to weep, for them they were still able to care, but the demand for entertainment by the curious irritated those who wished to be left alone to recover from the shock of battle. Gettysburg was prostrate, bereft of many of its worldly possessions, drained to the bottom of its well of sympathy. There were many, like Mary Bowman, who no longer owned any quilts or blankets, who had given away their clothes, their linen, even the precious sheets which their grandmothers had spun. Gettysburg wished nothing back; it asked only to be left in peace.

When the order was given to postpone the opening of the graves till fall, Mary began to go about the battle-field searching alone. Her children were beginning to grow thin and wan, they were shivering in the hot August weather, but their mother did not see. She gave them a great deal more to eat than she had herself, and they had far better clothes than her blood-stained rags.

She went about the battle-field with her eyes on the ground, her feet treading gently, anticipating loose soil or some sudden obstacle. Sometimes she stopped suddenly. But she found nothing.

One morning, late in August, she sat beside her kitchen table with her head on her arm. The first of the scarlet gum leaves had begun to drift down from the shattered trees; it would not be long before the ground would be covered, and those depressed spots, those tiny wooden headstones, those fragments of blue and gray, be hidden. The thought smothered her. But she did not cry.

Suddenly, hearing a sound, Mary had looked up. The judge stood in the doorway; he had known all about her since she was a little girl. She did not ask him to sit down; she said nothing at all. She had been a loquacious person; she was now an abnormally silent one. Speech hurt her.

The judge looked round the little kitchen. The rent in the wall was still unmended, the chairs were broken, there was nothing else to be seen but the table and the rusty stove and the thin, friendless-looking children. It was the house not only of poverty and woe, but of neglect.

"Mary," said the judge, "how do you mean to live?"

Mary's thin, sunburned hand stirred as it lay on the table.

"I don't know."

"You have these children to feed and clothe. Mary—" The judge hesitated for a moment. John Bowman had been a school-teacher, a thrifty, ambitious soul, who would have thought it a disgrace for his wife to earn her living. The judge laid his hand on the thin hand beside him. "Come down to my house and my wife will give you work. Come now."

Slowly Mary had obeyed him. Down the street they went, seeing fences still prone, seeing walls torn by shells, past the houses where the shock of battle had hastened the deaths of old persons and of little children, and had disappointed the hearts of those who longed for a child, to the judge's house on the square. There wagons stood about, loaded with wheels of cannon, fragments of burst caissons, or with long, narrow pine boxes, brought from the railroad, to be stored against the day of exhumation. Men were laughing and shouting to one another; the driver of the wagon on which the long boxes were piled cracked his whip as he urged his horse. Mary shivered as she listened.

Hannah Casey congratulated her neighbor heartily upon her finding work. "That'll fix you up," she assured her. She visited Mary constantly, she reported to her the news of the war, she talked of the coming of the President.

"I'm going to see him," she announced. "I'm going to shake him by the hand. I'm going to say, 'Hello, Abe, you old rail-splitter, God bless you!' Then the bands'll play, and the Johnny Rebs'll hear 'em in their graves."

Mary Bowman put her hands over her ears.

"I believe you'd let 'em rise from the dead."

"I would," said Mary Bowman, hoarsely—"I would."

"Well, not so Hannah Casey! Look at me garden, tore to bits!" And Hannah Casey departed to her house.

Details of the coming celebration penetrated to the ears of Mary Bowman, whether she wished it or not, and the gathering crowds made themselves known. They stood on her porch, they examined the broken shutters, they wished to question her. But Mary Bowman would answer no questions. To her the celebration was horrible. She saw the battling hosts, she heard the roar of artillery, she smelled the smoke of battle.

She seemed to feel in the ground beneath her a feebly stirring, suffering, ghastly host. They had begun again to open trenches, and she had looked into them.

Presently on the morning of Thursday, the 19th of November, her children dressed themselves and came down the steps. They had begun to have a little plumpness and color, but the dreadful light in their mother's eyes was still reflected in theirs. On the lower step they hesitated, looking at the door. Outside stood the judge, who had found time in the multiplicity of his cares to come to the little house.

"Mary," he said, "you must take these children to hear President Lincoln."

"What!" cried Mary.

"You must take these children to the exercises."

"I cannot!" cried Mary. "I cannot!"

"You must!" The judge came into the room. "You are a Christian; your husband was a Christian. Do you want your children to think it is a wicked thing to die for their country? Do as I tell you, Mary."

Mary got up from her chair and put on her children all the clothes they had. Then, as one who steps into an unfriendly sea, she started out with them into the great crowd. Once more poor Mary said to herself she would obey. She had seen the platform; by going round through the cemetery she could get close to it.

The November day was bright and warm, but Mary and her children shivered. Slowly she made her way close to the platform and patiently waited. Sometimes she stood with shut eyes, swaying a little. On the moonlit night of the third day of the battle she had ventured from her house to find some brandy for the dying men about her, and, as in a dream, she had seen a tall general, mounted upon a white horse with muffled hoofs, ride down the street. Bending from his saddle, he had spoken, apparently to the empty air:

"Up, boys, up!"

There had risen at his command thousands of men, lying asleep on pavement and street, and quietly, in an interminable line, they had stolen out like dead men toward the seminary to join their comrades and begin the long, long march to Hagerstown. It seemed to her now that all about her dead men might rise to look with reproach upon these strangers who disturbed their rest.

The procession was late, the orator of the day was delayed, but still Mary waited, swaying in her place. Presently the great guns roared forth a welcome, the bands played, the procession approached. On horseback, erect, gauntleted, the President of the United States drew rein beside the platform and, with the orator and the other famous men, dismounted. There were great cheers; there were deep silences; there were fresh volleys of artillery; there was new music.

Men spoke and prayed and sang, and Mary stood still in her place. The orator of the day described the battle, he eulogized the dead, he proved the righteousness of this great war; his words fell on Mary's ears unheard. If she had been asked who he was, she might have said vaguely that it was Mr. Lincoln. When he ended, she was ready to go home. There was singing; now she could slip away through the gaps in the cemetery fence. She had done as the Judge commanded; now she would go back to her little house.

With her arms round her children, she started away. Then someone who stood nearby took her by the hand.

"Madam," said he, "the President is going to speak!"

Half turning, Mary looked back. The thunder of applause made her shiver, made her even scream, it was so like those other thunderous sounds which she would hear forever. She leaned upon her little children heavily, trying to get her breath, trying to keep her consciousness. She fixed her eyes upon the rising figure before her; she clung frantically to the sight of him, as a drowning swimmer in deep waters; she struggled to fix her thoughts upon him. Exhaustion, grief, misery threatened to engulf her; she hung upon him in desperation.

Slowly, as one who is old or tired or sick at heart, he rose to his feet, the President of the United States, the commander-in-chief of the Army and Navy, the hope of his country. Then he stood waiting. In great waves of sound the applause rose and died and rose again. He waited quietly. The winner of debate, the great champion of a great cause, the veteran in argument, the master of men, he looked down upon the throng. The clear, simple things he had to say were ready in his mind; he had thought them out, written out a first draft of them in Washington, copied it in Gettysburg. It is probable that now, as he waited to speak, his mind traveled to other things—to the misery, the wretchedness, the slaughter of this field, to the tears of mothers, the grief of widows, the orphaning of little children.

Slowly, in his clear voice, he said what little he had to say. To the weary crowd, settling itself into position, the speech seemed short; to the cultivated, who had been applauding the periods of elaborate oratory, it seemed commonplace. But it was not so with Mary Bowman, nor with many other unlearned persons. Mary Bowman's soul seemed to smooth itself out like a scroll, her hands lightened their clutch on her children, the beating of her heart slackened, she gasped no more.

She could not have told exactly what he said, though afterward she learned it and taught it to her children and her children's children. She only saw him, felt him, breathed him in, this great, common, kindly man. His gaze seemed to rest upon her; it was not impossible, it was even probable, that during the hours that had passed he had singled out that little group so near him, that desolate woman in her motley dress, with her little children clinging about her. He said that the world would not forget this field, these martyrs; he said it in words which Mary Bowman could understand; he pointed to a future for which there was a new task.

"Daughter!" he seemed to say to her from the depths of trouble, of responsibility, of care greater than her own—"daughter, be of good comfort!"

Unhindered now, amid the cheers, across ground which seemed no longer to stir beneath her feet, Mary Bowman went back to her little house. There, opening the shutters, she bent solemnly and kissed her children, saying to herself that henceforth they must have more than food and raiment, they must be given joy in life.

• • • •

Outside the broad gateway which leads into the National Cemetery at Gettysburg stands a little house on whose porch may be seen on summer days an old woman. The cemetery with its tall monuments lies a little back of her and to her left; before her is the village; beyond, on a little ridge, the buildings of the Lutheran Theological Seminary; and still further beyond, the foothills of the Blue Ridge. The village is tree-shaded, the hills are set with fine oaks and hickories, the fields are green. It would be difficult to find an expanse more lovely. Those who have known it in their youth grow homesick for it, their throats tighten as they remember it. At sunset it is bathed with purple light, its trees grow darker, its hills more shadowy, its hollows deeper and more mysterious. Then, lifted above the dark masses of the trees, one may see marble shafts and domes turn to liquid gold.

The little old woman sitting with folded hands is Mary Bowman, whose husband was lost on this field. The battle will soon be fifty years in the past; she has been for that long a widow. One of her sons is a merchant, the other is a clergyman, and her daughter is happily married. Her own life of activity is past; she is waited upon tenderly by her children and her grandchildren. She was born in this village; she has almost never been away. From here her husband went to war, here he is buried among thousands of unknown dead, here she nursed the wounded and dying, here she will be buried in the Evergreen Cemetery, beyond the National Cemetery.

She has seen beauty turn to desolation, trees shattered, fields trampled, walls broken, all her dear, familiar world turned to chaos; she has seen also desolation grow again to beauty. These hills and streams were always lovely; now a nation has determined to keep them forever in that same loveliness. Here was a rocky, wooded field, destined by its owner for cultivation; it has been decreed that its rough picturesqueness shall endure forever. Here is a lowly farmhouse; upon it no hand of change shall be laid while the nation endures. Preserved, consecrated, hallowed are the woods and lanes in which Mary Bowman walked with the great love of her youth.

Broad avenues lead across the fields, marking the lines where thousands of men died. Big Round Top, to which one used to journey by a difficult path, is now easily accessible; Union and Confederate soldiers, returning, find their way quickly to old positions; young men from West Point are brought to see, spread out before them as on a map, that Union fish-hook five miles long, that slightly curved Confederate line.

Monuments are here by hundreds, names by thousands, cast in bronze, as endurable as they can be made by man. All that can be done in remembrance of those who fought here has been done, all possible effort to identify the unknown has been made. For fifty years their little trinkets have been preserved—their pocket Testaments, their photographs, their letters—letters addressed to "My precious son," "My dear brother," "My beloved husband." Seeing them today, you will find them marked by a number. This stained scapular, these little rusty scissors, this unsigned letter, dated in '63, belonged to him who lies in Grave No. 20 or Grave No. 3,500.

There is almost an excess of tenderness for these dead, yet mixed with it is a strange feeling of remoteness. We mourn them, praise them, laud them, but we cannot understand them. To this generation war is strange; its sacrifices are uncomprehended, incomprehensible. It is especially so in these latter years, since those who came once to this field come now no more. Once the heroes of the war were familiar figures upon these streets: Meade, with his serious, bearded face; Slocum, with his quick, glancing eye; Hancock, with his distinguished air; Howard, with his empty sleeve. They have gone away, and with them have marched two-thirds of Gettysburg's two hundred thousand.

Mary Bowman has seen them all, has heard them speak. Sitting on her little porch, she has watched most of the great men of the United States go by—Presidents, cabinet officers, ambassadors, soldiers, and also famous visitors from other lands, who know little of the United States, but to whom Gettysburg is as a familiar country. She has watched also that great, rapidly shrinking army of private soldiers in faded blue coats, who make pilgrimages to see the fields and hills upon which they fought. She has tried to make herself realize that her husband, had he lived, would be like these old men—maimed, feeble, decrepit—but the thought possesses no reality for her. He is still young, still erect; he still goes forth to battle in the pride of life and strength.

Mary Bowman will not talk about the battle. To each of her children and each of her grandchildren she has told once, as one performs a sacred duty, its many-sided story. She has told each one of wounds and suffering, but she has not omitted tales of heroic death, of promotion on the field, of stubborn fight for glory. By others than her own she will not be questioned. Her neighbors who suffered with her, some just as cruelly, have recovered, their wounds have healed, as wounds do in the natural course of things. But Mary Bowman has remained faithful; she has been for all these years widowed indeed.

Her faithful friend Hannah Casey is the great joy of the visitor to the battle-field. She will talk incessantly, enthusiastically, with insane invention. The most morbid listener will be satisfied with Hannah's wild account of a Valley of Death filled to the rim with dead bodies, of the trickling rivulet of Plum Creek swollen with blood to a roaring torrent. But Mary Bowman is different.

Her granddaughter, who lives with her, is curious about her emotions.

"Do you feel reconciled?" she will ask. "Do you feel reconciled to the sacrifice, Grandmother? Do you think of the North and South as reunited, and are you glad you helped?"

Her grandmother answers with no words, but with a slow, tearful smile. She does not analyze her emotions. Perhaps it is too much to expect of one who has been a widow for fifty years that she philosophize about it!

Sitting on her porch in the early morning, she remembers the 1st of July, fifty years ago.

"Here?" she had answered, stupidly. "Here?"

Sitting there at noon, she hears the roaring blasts of artillery, she seems to see shells, as of old, curving like great ropes through the air; she remembers that somewhere on this field, struck by a missile such as that, her husband fell.

Sitting there in the moonlight, she pictures Early on his white horse with muffled hoofs, riding spectralwise down the street among the sleeping soldiers.

"Up, boys!" he whispers, and is heard even in that heavy stupor. "Up, boys; we must get away!"

She hears the pouring rain of July 4th falling upon her little house, upon that wide battle-field, upon her very heart. She sees the deep, sad eyes of Abraham Lincoln, she hears his voice in the great sentences of his simple speech, she feels his message in her soul.

"Daughter," he seems to say, "daughter, be of good comfort."

So still Mary Bowman sits waiting. She is a Christian, she has great hope; as her waiting has been long, so may the joy of her reunion be full.

Photograph by Mathew Brady, engraved by R. G. Tietze.

TAD LINCOLN'S GOAT

Seth Harmon

This remarkable story was lost for eighty-four years, buried as it was in one of Lincoln's personal letters. It saw the light of day for the first time in July of 1947.

August in our nation's capital can be hot and humid. Peter, the gardener, who was trimming the White House lawn felt it. So did Mrs. Cuthbert, the housekeeper, who fanned herself wearily as she approached the panting gardener.

"Where are the flowers for the table?" she wanted to know. "Mrs. Lincoln's guests will arrive any minute."

It was the year 1863, an anxious time for our country. Mrs. Mary Lincoln had invited some friends to luncheon to discuss what they, as women, could do to help.

"The flowers are behind the lilacs in a bucket of water," replied the gardener.

Mrs. Cuthbert hurried toward the lilac bushes. An instant later she shrieked, "Gracious to Betsy! Peter, come quick."

Peter trotted across the lawn. Mrs. Cuthbert nodded toward the wilted greens scattered on the ground. Not a bloom remained on the broken stems.

"It's that pesky Nanny goat again!" Peter groaned. "Yesterday she tackled the boxwood, day before the roses. Young Tad is simply going to *have* to keep her out of this garden!"

Mrs. Cuthbert wrung her hands. "Dear me, you'll have to pick other flowers. Hurry, Peter. Anything!"

The gardener scowled. "They were my finest blooms, too," he lamented. He took his shears and set about clipping a last-minute bouquet.

"Baa-a!" The gardener swung around.

An impish face was peering at him quizzically through the hedge. Nanny seemed to be reproving him for taking blooms which she had planned to nibble off herself.

"Get out of here!" Peter shouted. Nanny didn't budge. She nipped off a pink petunia bloom and started chewing. That was too much for the gardener. He broke off a switch and started after the goat. She began bleating so plaintively she brought her young master himself running down the path.

"Don't do that to Nanny!" the boy said, sweeping his pet up awkwardly into his arms just as Peter caught up with her. "You might hurt her."

"Hurt her indeed!" the panting man grunted. "I'll be tempted to do worse than that if you don't keep her out of this garden!"

"I'll keep Nanny out of your way," Tad promised. He carried her back toward the White House. The astonished housekeeper met him in the doorway.

"Hold on, Master Tad. You don't mean to bring that animal in here!"

That certainly seemed to be Tad's exact intention. Straight up the broad stairs to his room he carried Nanny. He settled down on the rug with his book again. Nanny settled down also—right in the middle of Tad's bed. There she lay, innocently chewing her cud, when Mrs. Cuthbert marched into the room.

"Well, I never! Are my poor over-worked eyes deceiving me? A goat on your bed? Young man, I mean to tell your mother about this. Yes, and your father, too!"

"Please, Mrs. Cuthbert," Tad pleaded in Nanny's behalf. "She's such a nice goat. And splendid company."

"Company? I suppose you'll be installing her in one of the company's guest rooms next. No, indeed, that goat has got to go!"

• • • •

Tad decided he'd better speak to his father about Nanny before the irate Mrs. Cuthbert did so.

"I know you're very busy with affairs of state, Father," the boy apologized, "but war has also been declared by Peter and Mrs. Cuthbert on my poor, innocent Nanny. Won't you help me restore peace?"

Tad was telling his father the events of the day when Mrs. Cuthbert knocked on the library door. Ignoring Tad's pleading glance, she suggested immediate banishment from the White House and its vicinity of Nanny, the goat. The President's deep-set eyes twinkled.

"Mrs. Cuthbert, you have probably heard the saying that a man's home is his castle? Well, I'm afraid Tad's room is his home and his castle. If he wants to share it with a goat, I reckon there's nothing we can do about it."

Tad hugged his father to express his thanks, and Nanny stayed.

Next morning Tad dutifully took Nanny for her daily walk, and afterwards once more installed her in his room while he went on an errand. When he returned, Mrs. Cuthbert was quite upset.

"It's my nerves, I'm afraid," she told the boy. "I'm so jumpy! Half an hour ago the dumb-waiter crashed into the basement and I do declare I jumped a foot. The rope must have broken. Tad, will you look at it? Everybody else is so busy."

Tad Lincoln, like his father, was a tinkerer by nature. He liked to fix things. But he found nothing wrong with the little wooden elevator which was used to lift small articles from the basement to the upper floors of the White House. Puzzled, he went up to his room.

He pushed open his door and started looking for Nanny. She wasn't on the bed or under it. She wasn't in the closet or beneath the easy chair. Then Tad remembered that the door had not been tightly closed. Down the corridor he went, looking right and left.

At last his glance fell on the opening into the dumb-waiter shaft. Then he knew. The curious goat had wandered into the dark opening and her weight had sent the elevator crashing to the basement. Tad ran downstairs to catch her if he could.

As he expected, the basement door stood open, too. He ran down the rear driveway and out onto the side street. A bit of chewed hedge here, a nipped-off blossom there, told him Nanny had passed that way. Down a narrow street and through an alley he trailed her.

"Yes, I saw a white goat. She went that way," an obliging newsboy said. Tad hurried on. At last he reached an unpaved street lined with shabby houses. Some children, even shabbier than their house, were gathered around something in their very shabby front yard.

No one noticed Tad approach—not even Nanny.

"Isn't she beautiful?" a girl of about ten was saying.

"It seems like a fairy tale to have a real, live goat in our yard," a smaller boy declared.

"And nobody seems to own her," a boy of about Tad's age put in. "I asked at every house in the block."

"Then she's our goat until someone claims her," the girl decided. "She'll give us milk we can't afford to buy. We'll feed her wild hay, and Mother's parsley bed is always overgrown."

• • • •

Suddenly the girl stopped talking. The other children's eyes followed her stare. She had noticed Tad standing outside the gate. She knew of course that he was a stranger. She said, "I suppose you've come to take the goat away from us. I thought this was too good to be true." That, to be sure, had been Tad's original intention. Now he found it very difficult to do so.

"I do happen to know who owns that goat," he confessed, "but I don't think I'll take her right away."

"But you'll tell her owner and he'll come and take her away," wailed the little boy.

"Quiet," the older brother scolded. "If the goat belongs to someone else, we wouldn't want to keep her. I think you should take her to her owner right away."

"No, I'll be back tomorrow," Tad replied. "I'll let you know what the owner decides to do."

"Take her now," the other boy urged. "Why should anyone want to lose such a handsome goat?"

"Well, you see, the owner might not need a goat as much as you do. And I happen to know he's been having a lot of trouble finding a place for his goat."

Tad saw the others' thin faces brighten. Then his hand touched his beloved Nanny's soft fur. She looked up at him and baa-ed. He felt sure then that he would never be able to part with her.

"Well, anyway, you may keep her until tomorrow," he said.

• • • •

Back at the White House, Tad noticed the door of his father's study was open. He ventured in. "It's about Nanny again," he began. His father put a big long arm around his son's shoulders.

"And what's that rascal up to this time, Son?" Tad didn't know exactly how to say what he was feeling inside.

"Father, if you liked something very much yourself, but you knew someone else who needed that something much more than you, would you give it away?"

Mr. Lincoln raised his heavy brow thoughtfully. "That would require a real sacrifice, my boy."

Tad nodded. "I know. It wouldn't be easy."

"On the other hand," the great man continued, "I'm not so sure keeping this prized possession to yourself would bring you so much pleasure if you knew it was needed by someone else. Had you thought of that?"

Again Tad nodded. "If that weren't troubling me, I don't think it would be so hard for me to decide."

"Well then, Son," said Mr. Lincoln with an understanding smile, "I reckon it's just a matter of simple arithmetic, only this time your heart as well as your head must find the answer. You've got to figure out whether keeping something will bring you more or less pleasure than the joy of giving. No one but you can find the answer."

Tad nodded a third time and went back to do his figuring. Next morning, with winged feet, he retraced yesterday's route. Three eager children were expecting him.

"Where's the man who owns the goat?" the youngest one wanted to know.

"Of course if he doesn't really need a goat," the little girl hinted, almost too eagerly, "and if he hasn't any suitable place to keep her—"

"The owner wants you to keep the goat for him," Tad managed at last. "He hopes Nanny comes to mean as much to you as she always has to him."

• • • •

This good news made the three children so happy they almost over whelmed Tad with thank-you's. Nanny looked up from her parsley only long enough to say "Baa-a!" How were the children to guess she was saying farewell to her former master?

That evening Tad once more poked his head into his father's study. "I won't disturb you again, Father. I just wanted to tell you I found the answer to my arithmetic problem."

For a moment the worries of his office seemed to lift from the President's stooping shoulders. "I'm glad of that, Son. And I can see by the smile on your face that you found the right answer."

Drawn by D. W. Clinedinst for Century Magazine *in 1897.*

PRESIDENT LINCOLN'S VISITING CARD

John M. Bullock

It was a fruitless request—everyone told the fifteen-year-old boy that. Even if the request wasn't for a dying Confederate officer. Nevertheless, in desperation, the boy found his way over to the White House.

In the early summer of 1864, my eldest brother, Waller R. Bullock of Kentucky, was wounded and captured while acting as captain of a detachment of General John H. Morgan's dismounted Confederates at Mount Sterling, Kentucky, Morgan's men being defeated by the troops of General Stephen G. Burbridge of the Union army. After having been left for dead upon the battlefield, and finally brought back to life in an almost miraculous manner, he was allowed, through the kind efforts of some of my father's Union friends, to be carried to the home of a relative and cared for until he was in a condition to be sent to prison at Johnson's Island, near Sandusky, Ohio. After his removal to prison, we often received letters from him, telling us of his daily life of enforced idleness, but nothing regarding his health that caused us any uneasiness until the cold and icy winds of winter had set in. Then it was he wrote of a cough and

some slight indisposition, but nothing that could awaken the watchful-
ness of even a mother's love.

Early in February, 1865, Colonel Holliday of Kentucky, a Confederate
officer, came through Baltimore on special exchange. My father, the Rev.
Dr. Bullock, had left Kentucky at the beginning of the war, and accepted
a call to the Franklin Street Presbyterian Church of Baltimore, where
he resided for ten or eleven years. He afterward removed to Alexandria,
Virginia, where he resided when he was elected Chaplain of the United
States Senate. Later he made his home in Washington City. Colonel Holliday took tea with us the evening of his arrival; but although we asked
him many questions regarding my brother's condition of health, he gave
us no cause for alarm, only telling us that he suffered occasionally from
his wounds, which had not entirely healed, and was troubled more or less
by a cough. After bidding the family good-by, he requested me to walk
with him to Barnum's Hotel, as he was not familiar with the streets of
our city.

After leaving the house, he delivered to me a message from my
brother, to the effect that he was a very sick man, and had not long to
live, owing to trouble with his wounds and a severe attack of pleurisy and
pneumonia. As I was the only son living at home, he had sent this word
to me in order that I might break the sad news to my parents. My mother
being an invalid, it was my brother's wish that the information should
be given to her in such a way as to alarm her as little as possible. That
night I lay awake, in deepest anxiety and perplexity as to what was the
best course to pursue to keep my mother in ignorance of my brother's real
condition while I could put into execution some plan that would enable
me to win the race from death. Though a school-boy at the time, my
mind was made up before the morning dawned; and so, after a few hours
of troubled slumber, I arose, dressed myself with unusual care, ate my
breakfast, and then took my way, not to school, but to the station of the
Baltimore and Ohio Railroad; and in about an hour I was in Washington
City.

As soon as I arrived in the capital I inquired the way to the home of

Postmaster-General Montgomery Blair. Mr. Blair was a relative of my mother's, and had been a classmate of my father's at Transylvania University, Lexington, Kentucky, when they were both young lads. I found Mr. Blair at home, and apparently not very busy. In as few words as possible I stated the object of my visit—namely, that I desired to secure from President Lincoln the release from prison, upon parole, of my brother, Waller R. Bullock, who was sick and wounded; and that the first step toward the accomplishment of my mission was an introduction to Mr. Lincoln through some influential person or common friend. I further informed him that I had come to request his good offices in the matter of the introduction to the President.

Mr. Blair's reception of me had been most cordial, but as soon as he learned the true object of my visit, the warmth of his manner visibly cooled, and in very decided language he said: "Such a request to the President will be altogether useless. I can assure you that there are many members of Congress, and others high in authority, who would be glad to have their friends and relatives released from prison on such terms as you ask, and are unable to accomplish it. Don't bother your head about such matters, my son. Come, take your lunch with us, and then go out and see some of the sights of Washington; and I assure you it will be time far more profitably spent than in seeking an interview with the President that will do you no good."

In a most emphatic manner I declined both Mr. Blair's advice and hospitality; and learning that Mr. Lincoln was that morning holding a levee at the White House, I took my leave of the Postmaster General, after thanking him for all he had done for me, and strolled over in that direction. I had never before been present at a presidential reception, and the sight was indeed a novel one.

Mr. Lincoln was standing in the center of one of the small rooms— the "Blue Room," I believe; and near him were Mrs. Lincoln and some half-dozen ladies, wives of members of the Cabinet. In animated conversation with Mrs. Lincoln and her guests were a number of officers of the Army and Navy, several generals and admirals among them. The

President stood alone. There were no introductions. Each person came up and shook his hand, and passed on to give place to those who followed.

During this ceremony the Marine Band, stationed in the "East Room," played for the marching throng. I had noticed one thing of which I had determined to take advantage. In the interval between the time the band ceased to play one selection and the beginning of another piece, the people stopped passing through the Blue Room, and for the time being left the President entirely alone. He stood with his hands clasped in front of him, his head slightly bowed, in his eyes that far-away look so often spoken of by those who knew him well. I thought this a splendid opportunity to get speech of him. Had I been older, I should not have thrust myself upon him at such a time; but youth does not stop to inquire too closely into the courtesies of life.

Just as the band ceased playing, I stepped up to Mr. Lincoln, shook him by the hand, and said, "Mr. President, I am a son of the Rev. Dr. Bullock of Baltimore, whom you know; and I have come to ask that you will parole my brother, Waller R. Bullock, who is a Confederate lieutenant, now in prison at Johnson's Island, wounded and sick." I of course supposed Mr. Lincoln would reply to my petition by granting it or dismissing me with a refusal. But ignoring what I had said altogether, he asked in quite a loud voice—enough so to attract the notice of all those about him: "You are a nephew of John C. Breckinridge, ain't you?"

"Yes, sir," I replied.

"Then I suppose, when you are old enough, you will be going down to fight us," said Mr. Lincoln, in rather a laughing tone.

"Yes, sir," I replied; "I suppose, when I am old enough, I will join the Army."

Mr. Lincoln seemed to be somewhat amused at my answer, and placing his hand upon my shoulder, said in a kind, fatherly way: "My son, you come back here at four o'clock this afternoon, and I will see you then."

I could see, from the cessation of all conversation by the persons about the President, including both Mrs. Lincoln and her guests, that they were interested listeners to our interview.

As the first person came up to shake Mr. Lincoln's hand after the band began to play once more, I retired, bowing myself out, only too well pleased to have an engagement with so important a person as the President of the United States, the man who held the life of my brother in his keeping. Thinking I would speak to the doorkeeper at the main entrance of the mansion as to my prospects of gaining admittance to Mr. Lincoln's presence, at four o'clock, I asked that official how it would be, telling him what the President had said.

"He just said that to keep from hurting your feelings, young fellow; for I have positive orders from Mr. Lincoln in person to close these doors at two o'clock sharp, and not allow anybody to come in—not even members of the Cabinet."

I had more confidence in Mr. Lincoln's word than the doorkeeper of the White House, and went my way without fear and full of hope. After satisfying a growing boy's appetite at Willard's Hotel—a matter of time—I counted the minutes until the hour named.

As I approached the White House, to my surprise and gratification I saw Mr. Lincoln standing upon the west end of the front portico, with his son Robert by his side. Robert had lately been appointed assistant adjutant-general and assigned to duty with General Grant; and he and his father, I discovered, were negotiating for the purchase of a horse suitable for service in the field. As I stepped up and took a position near the President, an orderly was in the act of riding a stylish-looking animal up and down one of the driveways in front of the mansion. I stood silently by, listening to the comments of the quiet, businesslike father and the more enthusiastic son, until suddenly Mr. Lincoln turned to where I stood, and said: "My son, you are a Kentuckian, and ought to know something about the value of horses. Tell me, what do you think, that one is worth?" pointing to the animal in question.

I replied, "I should like to see how he is gaited, sir, before I decide."

"Ride that horse around a little more," called the President to the orderly, "and let us see how he goes."

After looking him over for a few minutes, and noticing the fact that he was a fairly good saddle-horse, I gave my opinion that he was worth about one hundred and fifty dollars. My decision seemed to have coincided with that of Mr. Lincoln; for he said in a rather loud voice, easily heard by the rider, who had stopped his horse near the end of the portico: "Just what I said he was worth—just what I offered him; but he wanted two hundred dollars for him—more than I thought he was worth."

In a few moments, however, the sale was made at the President's figure; and, seemingly much to Robert's delight, the horse was ordered to be delivered to the White House stables. Upon the conclusion of the purchase, Mr. Lincoln walked slowly to the main entrance and passed in, saying to me as he did so, "Follow me, my son."

Very deliberately Mr. Lincoln mounted the stairway, and as he gained the hallway above looked around to see if I had accompanied him. Then, opening a door to his right, we went into an office where was seated John Hay, secretary to Mr. Lincoln, before a large open fire, writing busily. Mr. Lincoln said, "Take a seat, my son; I will be back in a few moments"; and picking up a small package of mail from the desk near him, opened a door to the adjoining office and went out, leaving me to the companionship of Mr. Hay, who soon retired as if on important business.

I occupied myself during Mr. Lincoln's brief absence in trying to collect my thoughts and prepare a set speech to pour into his sympathetic ears. Suddenly the door opened, and the tall form of the President, six feet four inches in height, towered above me. Closing the door quietly behind him, he drew the largest of the easy-chairs to one side of the glowing log fire, and sitting down, leaned his elbow on the arm toward me, and said, "Now, my son, what can I do for you?" You will note that all through my interviews with Mr. Lincoln he never addressed me without using the words—very kindly they sounded, too—"my son." Where now was my set speech? That I never knew. All I saw before me was a kind, sorrowful face, ready to listen to my story. I was not in the least embarrassed, as I supposed I should be, and at once began to tell Mr. Lincoln what I had come to ask of him. I said: "Mr. President, I have come to ask you to parole my brother, Lieutenant Waller R. Bullock, from Johnson's Island, where he is sick and wounded. He is extremely ill, and I want you to release him so that he may be brought home to die." I knew what he would ask me the first thing, and my heart sank as I heard the fateful question put.

"Will your brother take the oath?" said Mr. Lincoln.

"No, sir; he will not," I replied.

"He will have to die in prison if that is the only alternative. I cannot parole him," said the President. "I should like to do so; but it is impossible unless he will take the oath."

I replied: "Mr. Lincoln, my brother is very ill, and cannot live long in his present condition; and it would be a great comfort to our invalid mother to have him brought home so that he can be tenderly nursed until he dies."

"My son," said Mr. Lincoln, "I should like to grant your request, but I cannot do it. You don't know what pressure is brought to bear upon me in such matters. Why, there are senators and members of Congress who would be glad to have their relatives and friends paroled on such terms as you ask, and cannot accomplish it." (The same words used by Mr. Blair.)

Though somewhat disheartened, I again repeated the story of my brother's extreme illness, and the comfort it would be to my mother to have him with her in his dying condition. I said, "Mr. Lincoln, this is a case of life and death. If my brother remains much longer in prison on that bleak, dreary island, exposed to all the severity of an exceptionally cold winter, he cannot last very much longer. You are the only person in the United States who can do absolutely as you please in such matters; and you can release him if you desire to do so, no matter what people say or think."

Mr. Lincoln had so often said that it was impossible for him to parole Waller that I felt my last chance to gain his consent to my petition was to appeal to him as the court of last resort, and throw the consequences of refusal upon him personally.

Finally Mr. Lincoln sank into a state of deep meditation. He sat with his elbows on his knees, his face in his hands, and gazed long and intently into the great wood fire. He was not a handsome man; neither was he a graceful one. His appearance when in repose was rather dull and listless. Indeed, I was struck with his awkwardness while receiving the guests at his levee, walking upstairs, and sitting in his chair. His hair was cut unevenly on the back of his head, his features were rugged, and he had evidently paid but little regard to his tailor. I noticed how large his hands and feet were, how loosely his black suit hung upon his immense frame. And then, too, as I have before remarked, he had that far-away look in his eyes so often spoken of by those who knew him intimately during those awful years of blood and carnage, when his great soul was wrung with the anguish of a nation at war with itself.

Suddenly, without warning, and when, from his long silence, I had concluded my cause was lost, Mr. Lincoln sprang to his feet, his whole being alert, his eyes no longer dull, but clear and strong with the light of intense feeling and power, all the awkwardness gone, his face not handsome, but full of strength and intelligence, making it a pleasant face to look upon—one a child would not refuse to caress. Straightening himself to his full height, he brought his clenched hand down upon the desk with a bang, and said, as he looked me full in the face, "I'll do it; I'll do it!"

Walking over to his desk, he picked up a small paper card-case which held visiting-cards such as ladies generally use. Mr. Lincoln held it between his first finger and thumb up to his ear, and shook it to see if there were any cards left. I could distinctly hear the rattle of a single card. Finding what he was looking for, the President sat down, and placing the card before him, wrote very slowly and deliberately. I supposed he was writing an order to some clerk, or to John Hay, to have the parole papers made out. Such was my ignorance of the forms necessary to liberate prisoners that I imagined I should see a large official document with signatures and counter-signatures, seals, etc. Therefore I was much surprised when Mr. Lincoln arose, and, holding the card between his forefinger and thumb, read it aloud to me as follows:

Allow Lieut. Waller R. Bullock to be paroled and go to
his parents in Baltimore, and remain there until well enough
to be exchanged.

A. Lincoln.

Mr. Lincoln then held out the card to me; and seeing that I was somewhat disappointed in the size of the document, and hesitated to accept it,
he said, as a smile played about the corners of his mouth; "That'll fetch
him; that'll fetch him."

I thanked the President with all the warmth of my being. I felt that
by the act of clemency he had just shown, my brother had a chance for
his life, and that it was to Mr. Lincoln's kindness of heart and love of humanity that I owed the success of my mission. After once more express-
ing my thanks to the President and assuring him of the gratitude of my
father and mother and of our entire family, I prepared to take my leave,
filled with joy.

After handing me the card, Mr. Lincoln drew up one of the easy-
chairs before the fire, and throwing himself into a comfortable position,
began to ask me several questions. Said he: "Do you ever hear from your
uncle, John C. Breckinridge?"

"Yes, sir," I replied; "we hear once in a while from prisoners coming
through on special exchange; and sometimes we have been enabled to
receive letters via City Point by flag of truce."

"Well," said Mr. Lincoln, "I was fond of John, and I was sorry to see
him take the course he did. Yes, I was fond of John, and regret that he
sided with the South. It was a mistake." And then he made some further remarks about my uncle which showed his kind feeling for him.
He also referred to his visit to Kentucky soon after his marriage, and the
pleasant recollection he had of that period. (He had spent a few weeks in
Fayette County at my grandfather Bullock's, whose second wife was an
aunt of Mrs. Lincoln.) Altogether he was very kind, and I left the White
House with my heart overflowing with gratitude to the President.

One incident took place during my visit that goes to show how true and genuine was Mr. Lincoln's feeling of kindness toward others. Just as he was in the act of writing my brother's order of release on that little card, his son Robert came in, full of enthusiasm over the good qualities of his recent purchase. He was leaning over the back of his father's chair, and talking rapidly about his horse, when, suddenly remembering something he had forgotten to communicate, he said: "Father, Governor Hicks is dying." Senator Hicks was an ex-governor of Maryland, and had been very ill for some days.

Mr. Lincoln paused in his writing for a moment, and said in very sympathetic tones, without looking up: "Poor Hicks! Poor Hicks! Robert, order the carriage; I must go and see Governor Hicks."

In my haste to carry the good news to my parents, I arose from my seat at the first pause in the conversation, and bowed myself out of Mr. Lincoln's presence. I found the doorkeeper still on guard at the main entrance; and as he unlocked and unbarred the door he said: "It was well the President was out on the portico buying that horse, or you would never have entered these doors."

The night I reached home, a number of gentlemen were collected in my father's study. The success of my mission was the theme of conversation, and it was decided unanimously that I was the proper person to convey that parole to Johnson's Island, and bring my brother home. Mr. Henry Garrett, a brother of John W. Garrett, president of the Baltimore and Ohio Railroad, was one of those present. He was a true friend of our family, and kindly gave me a letter of introduction, which was directed "To All Railroad Employees," and read as follows:

This will introduce to your favorable notice our young friend Mr. John M. Bullock, who is traveling with a sick brother. Any attention that you may show him will be highly appreciated by

ROBERT GARRETT AND SONS.

Had I known how to use that letter, I would have ridden free from Baltimore to Johnson's Island and returned, such was the power of the Garretts during the war; but, being young, I failed to appreciate the true import of the communication, so learned its value only when too late to be of service. I found that Mr. Lincoln's name was a power wherever I went. That little card was an "open sesame"; and wherever and whenever I showed the signature "A. Lincoln," that settled the matter, and all further discussion ceased. As I stepped upon the ice to cross from Sandusky to Johnson's Island, a guard standing nearby said, "Where are you going?"

I replied, "To Johnson's Island, to see Colonel Hill."

"You had better obtain a permit first," said he.

I handed him Mr. Lincoln's card. As soon as he saw the order signed by Mr. Lincoln, he very politely remarked that I was "free to go over to the island," and pointed out to me the shortest route across. The ice was from three and a half to four feet thick, and heavy army-wagons were hauling freight to and from the island. Upon my arrival at Colonel Hill's headquarters, I was introduced to him by a young lieutenant named Phillips, whom I had met while he was in charge of prisoners brought through Baltimore from Johnson's Island on special exchange. I handed the colonel Mr. Lincoln's card. He took it, glanced carelessly at the writing; but his indifference lasted only for a moment, for as soon as he saw and realized what the order was—the release of a Confederate officer on parole, no oath required of him, and limited to the city of Baltimore—he was a truly astonished man.

"Well," he said, "this is the first time such an order has been received at this prison since the war began. However, this is the President's handwriting—this is Mr. Lincoln's own signature, for I know it well. But, by Heaven! Sir, I can't understand it. It is unusual, sir, to parole a prisoner on such terms."

Just as we were leaving Colonel Hill's office, I asked him, as a favor, to give me the card on which President Lincoln had written the order for my brother's parole, so that I might keep it as a memento of my visit to Washington and its important results. Colonel Hill declined to accede to my unbusinesslike request, and said: "No, sir; I cannot part with this document, as it contains my authority for releasing your brother from prison, and will be retained and filed with all other papers relating to the affairs of this office." But the official papers, granting the parole, were gratefully received, and proved to be an inviolable protection.

It was indeed a race with death to get my brother home before disease overcame all that was left of a once healthy man, worn to a skeleton from the effects of wounds and, later, pleurisy and pneumonia. The trip from Sandusky to Baltimore in the depth of a severe winter was a truly trying one, and a week was required to accomplish it.

Upon our last night out, February 21, 1865, we stopped at Cumberland, Maryland; the trains of the Baltimore and Ohio not venturing to run at night, owing to the frequent attacks by Confederate rangers whenever they attempted it. There was a Union force of about five thousand men in and about Cumberland, commanded by Major-General Crook. General Kelley was also stationed at this point as second in command. General Crook's headquarters were at the Revere House, while General Kelley's were at the City Hotel, three or four doors below. Upon our arrival at Cumberland, my brother's Confederate uniform at once attracted attention, and it was not long before several Union officers called upon us, and asked to see by what authority a Confederate officer was traveling free over the country. As always, when they found that his parole was given by authority of that magic name "A. Lincoln," they bowed themselves out of the room.

Much has been said and written in regard to Mr. Lincoln's character for kindness, his disposition to be merciful, his gentleness toward those in trouble, his leniency to those in distress, his clemency, and desire, when possible, to pardon those who were condemned to death. All this is no doubt true. The testimony of those who knew him best confirms all that can be said in his praise as to the noble nature of the man. I wish, however, to bear witness to one fact regarding Mr. Lincoln that impressed me, boy as I was, in a marked degree during my interviews with him. Before approaching the President I felt a natural diffidence, not to say awe, of the man who was Chief Executive of the nation, commander-in-chief of the Army and Navy, as well as the man who held the life of my brother in his keeping. To a boy of fifteen this feeling was only natural. The closer I approached the great man, however, the less I feared him, the higher my courage rose; and before the interview was over I was as much at my ease with President Lincoln as if talking to my own father. The reasons for this are to be found in just the qualities of heart with which he is accredited, and rightly so, by all the world.

No sooner had he laid his hand upon my shoulder and said, "My son," than I felt drawn to him, and dreaded less and less the interview he had granted me; and each successive question he asked put me more at my ease, until, when I was alone with him in his private office, all my embarrassment vanished, and I saw before me the countenance of a man I could trust, one which invited confidence. And thus it was that I saw this man at the head of a great nation engaged in the most stupendous war in the history of the world. All of his hours were spent in labor. His time was priceless. Senators, representatives in Congress, ambassadors of foreign courts, officers of the Army and Navy, were anxious and pressing for an interview, however brief; members of the Cabinet were debarred, according to the testimony of the doorkeeper. And yet, at such a time, this man of the people, this man among men, with the burden of a nation at war upon his shoulders, his mind bowed down by such responsibilities as no man ever bore alone since the world began—not even Napoleon at the height of his fame—left all these mighty questions and affairs of state long enough to enter into the pleasure of his soldier boy; long enough to give ear to the petition of a young lad praying for a brother's life—and that brother, in his eyes, an enemy of the state; long enough to leave his home to go and pay respect to a dying friend in his last hours. Such was Abraham Lincoln as I saw him in 1865.

Mr. Lincoln was slain by a madman. No section should be held responsible for such a deed. The South mourned as truly for his death as did the North. The assassination of Mr. Lincoln deprived that portion of our country of a protector both able and willing to stand their friend during all those days of struggling poverty and misery consequent to four years of war.

None more truly felt genuine sorrow for the death of Mr. Lincoln than my father and his family. To each one of us it came as a personal loss. And when, as one man, the nation bowed its head in the presence of death, and with mournful hearts and kindly hands draped its homes with the trappings of woe, no heart in all the land beat with truer sympathy, and no hands touched with greater reverence the funereal emblems that gave utterance to our respect for the nation's dead, than his to whom Abraham Lincoln had granted liberty and life.

A woodcut of Lincoln and Charles Sumner
reviewing Union troops in Richmond, Virginia.

TENDERNESS IN A RUINED CITY

Louis B. Reynolds

The Civil War was all but over, and Richmond, the Confederate capital, was in flames. Against the strong advice of his security forces, Lincoln, with very little protection, walked the streets of the ruined city. One of the very last acts of his life was this short but deeply moving visit to a rebel general's home. Pickett's legendary charge at Gettysburg was one of the bloodiest charges in American history.

N o more beautiful story of Lincoln was ever told than that related by Mrs. Pickett in her introduction to the remarkable book, *The Heart of a Soldier*, in which she gave to the world the love letters of the gallant Confederate general who was her husband. She writes:

"I was in Richmond when my Soldier fought the awful battle of Five Forks. Richmond surrendered, and the surging sea of fire swept the city. News of the fate of Five Forks had reached us, and the city was full of rumors that General Pickett was killed. I did not believe them. I knew he would come back; he had told me so. But they were very anxious hours. The day after the fire there was a sharp rap at the door. The servants had all run away. The city was full of Northern troops, and my environment had not taught me to love them. The fate of other cities had awakened my fears for Richmond. With my baby on my arm, I answered the knock, opened the door and looked up at a tall, gaunt, sad-faced man in ill-fitting clothes, who, with the accent of the North, asked:

" 'Is this George Pickett's place?'

" 'Yes, sir,' I answered, 'but he is not here.'

" 'I know that, ma'am,' he replied, 'but I just wanted to see the place. I am Abraham Lincoln.'

" 'The President!' I gasped.

"The stranger shook his head and said:

" 'No, ma'am; no, ma'am; just Abraham Lincoln, George's old friend.' "

" 'I am George Pickett's wife and this is his baby,' was all I could say. I had never seen Mr. Lincoln but remembered the intense love and reverence with which my Soldier always spoke of him.

"My baby pushed away from me and reached out his hand to Mr. Lincoln, who took him in his arms. As he did so, an expression of rapt, almost divine, tenderness and love lighted up the sad face. It was a look that I have never seen on any other face. My baby opened his mouth wide and insisted upon giving his father's friend a dewy infantile kiss. As Mr. Lincoln gave the little one back to me, shaking his finger at him playfully, he said:

" 'Tell your father, the rascal, that I forgive him for the sake of that kiss and those bright eyes.' "

*Illustration of John Wilkes Booth entering the Presidential Box
in Ford's Theatre, by Harriet Putnam.*

MEMORY OF LINCOLN

CARLA BROWN

What would it have been like to be a little boy living in an isolated little Illinois town on Easter Sunday, 1865?

One such boy never forgot. Let's listen to his story.

C harley Brown was not a happy boy as he went to his trundle bed in the twilight on that memorable night of Saturday, April 15, 1865. He had never been completely happy since his strapping young father, David, had joined the Army and gone off to fight. That was three years before. After tearful farewells, he and his mother had come to live with Uncle Abner and Aunt Martha on their farm twenty miles from town.

But tonight he was filled with a very special unhappiness, a sadness and an apprehension, different from anything that he had ever experienced before.

That same sadness and apprehension spread over the whole countryside. Every house, every home, every family lay under that shadow. For Abraham Lincoln, the President, had been shot in Ford's Theater in Washington. A neighbor, returning on horseback from the county seat, where there was a telegraph office, had brought the news that very day. Lincoln's condition was serious. The assassin had escaped, but the people out on the Illinois farms were not worrying much about that. Their minds were centered on the dreadful thought—would their beloved President die?

To them Lincoln had always been the "Man from Illinois." Even though he had been born in Kentucky and had attained his majority in Indiana, his neighbors in the prairie state always thought of him as one of their own. This was because he had grown up with the state, and had been identified with its development from the pioneer stage.

And so, when the news of Lincoln's injury gradually trickled out through the countryside, the farmers and the villagers were as stunned as if one of their own family had been stricken. Northern Illinois was still sparsely settled, and news was slow in reaching the remote villages, because only the county seats and a few large towns had telegraphic communication.

Charley's uncle lived in a big house near a crossroads. There were three other houses almost within stone's throw, and in the little square, where the roads met, there was a church that served the farms for two or three miles around.

Tomorrow would be Easter Sunday, and the church had been planning a very special and joyous Easter service. Charley was to have been the leader of the pageant of rejoicing. But with the sudden news that had arrived on Saturday, all that would be changed. It would be a service of prayer and intercession for one very near and dear to them all.

That night, when Charley went to bed, his mother knelt beside him and said, "Pray, Charley, pray. Your father loved Lincoln and trusted him. That's why he went away from us to fight. Pray that God will spare the President to his wife, and to his sons, and to the world."

And Charley, falteringly, did as he was bid. He repeated the words after her, not understanding exactly what they meant, but with tears coming into his eyes as they did into hers.

It was hardly dawn when he awoke suddenly. There was a faint mist, gray and shadowy, outside the windows. He sat up and reached across to touch his mother, who slept in a big four-poster close to his small one. But she was not there. The covers were thrown back. She had left the room.

And just then the sound that had awakened him was repeated, the long solemn reverberation of a bell breaking the dead stillness of the night. There was only one bell in all the countryside, the bell that rang on Sundays from the white church at the crossroads.

• • • •

It was an eerie sound in the solemn silence, and he trembled as he turned again to his mother's empty bed. Ordinarily the church bell was happy and cheerful as it pealed to summon him to Sunday school, or as it rang later in the morning while his mother walked to church. Now it had only a single low, deep note, which struck against his nerves and brought the tears to his eyes without his knowing why. Even as he struggled with his confused emotions, it came again.

This time the bell roused him to action. He jumped up and ran downstairs to the sitting room, to seek his mother's comforting presence. What he saw there stopped him on the thresh-old. His uncle, with trousers drawn hurriedly over his nightshirt, was sitting in his fireside chair, holding the big family Bible. His mother and his aunt, with shawls thrown around their shoulders, were clinging to each other, sobbing. Then his uncle's deep voice began pronouncing slowly the words out of the Book.

"The Lord gave, and the Lord hath taken away; blessed be the name of the Lord."

His mother saw him, even as another note sounded from the bell, and she held out her arms. He hurried to her.

"Don't be frightened, dear," she said. "Our beloved President is dead, and they are tolling the bell for him."

"Tolling?" questioned Charley.

"Tolling the years of his life, one by one," his mother explained. "Listen—that is eight. Once he was a little boy, like you."

Uncle Abner had turned a few pages, and was reading the Twenty-third Psalm, but Charley counted the strikes on the bell, hardly conscious of the voice of the reader.

At the twenty-sixth note, Charley remembered that his father was twenty-six. His mother laid her hand on her heart, and Charley knew that she had been counting too, and that she had had the same thought as he.

"Let us pray," said Uncle Abner.

They all knelt, four of them around the fireside, as Uncle Abner slowly and deliberately took their great sorrow to God and laid it on the altar of the Almighty Father. Charley kept close to his mother, and at each stroke of the bell he could feel her quiver with an odd little tremor.

"How long will it last?" he whispered as they rose from their knees.

"A long time yet," his mother told him. "Lincoln was fifty-six."

She went to the door and opened it to the sweet gray light of spring. The church windows were bright with candlelight.

"There will be a service," she said. "We must go. Get dressed, Charley."

His aunt protested. "Now, Fanny, you are not going to take that child out into this damp air," she said decisively. "And you should not go either. You'd much better stay warm in your bed and avoid taking cold."

Uncle Abner, who rarely went against his wife's wishes, interrupted: "I think we should all go," he said, gravely.

Charley's mother was always soft and gentle, but she had a will of her own. She had made no remonstrance when her husband had told her that he was going to war, but she had clung to him when he left, almost as if she feared that she would never see him again.

Charley remembered her on that day. He had never known her to look so pretty, and she stood and held his hand and waved and smiled until the train had rounded the bend, taking Charley's father away. It was only when the train had completely vanished and Charley looked up at her that he saw the tears streaming down her cheeks, straight through the corners of that brave, desperate smile.

All this went through Charley's mind as he stood there and counted the fortieth and then the forty-first stroke of the bell.

His mother was not weeping now, and there was no color in her cheeks. "Charley and I will have to go to the church," she said very softly and very gently to Aunt Martha.

They went upstairs and dressed quickly. Nine more strokes of the bell had tolled when Charley opened the door for her. Along the four roads, little knots of people were moving toward the church. And always the sound of that inexorable bell bade them walk slowly.

As Charley and his mother entered, the fifty-sixth note sounded, and after it, the silence seemed deeper and more impressive than the sound had been before.

The minister stood gravely in the doorway, greeting his people as they assembled. From him they learned that Lincoln had died on Saturday morning at half-past seven. The news had reached him by messenger at five o'clock Sunday morning. "We will have a brief prayer service now," he said, "and I will get a sermon ready for the regular service later in the morning."

• • • •

Presently he stood in the pulpit, and after a reading from the Scripture, he prayed, long and earnestly. Some of the congregation knelt, some stood— according to the practice of their various denominations. They were in a mood for a long prayer, and they got it, such a prayer as they had never heard before. It was a soul-shaking prayer, and when it was finished, the minister came down from the pulpit and spoke briefly and informally in a voice tense with emotion, of the great man who had just died—of his goodness, his wisdom, his brotherly kindness. Finally he dismissed them with a benediction which seemed to belong personally to each worshiper.

Charley was silent all the way home, but when he was alone with his mother in the quiet of their room, his unaccustomed thoughts broke into speech. "How do you get to be a great man like Lincoln?" he asked, and then determinedly he added: "I'd like to be like Lincoln when I grow up."

"Oh, Charley," his mother smiled. "That's a very big ambition for a boy just eight years old!"

"But he was eight, once," persisted Charley. "What did he do then?"

"I'll tell you what he did then," said his mother, fired by her son's spirit.

"He began when he was a little boy—perhaps even younger than you. You may never be a great man such as he was. Tonight, grieving for his untimely death, I almost hope not." She drew Charley close to her for a moment. "But you can always be as kind as he was. You can be as honest as he was—you know everybody all his life called him 'Honest Abe'! You can be as gentle as he was. You can be as good as he was. And if you are all that, you need never worry—you can just leave to God what comes of it all."

"I'm going to be just like him!" declared Charley, with firm resolve.

• • • •

That was more than seventy-five years ago. Charley never forgot that April night. He never forgot his mother's words. He never forgot his firm resolve to be like Lincoln, in kindness, in honesty, in gentleness, in goodness.

I know just how he looked when he was no more than ten. For I have a painting of him which was made on his tenth birthday. He was a handsome boy, with dark crisp-waving hair, and fine brown eyes.

Like Lincoln, he early lost his young mother, who loved him so dearly. Like Lincoln's father, David, Charley's father, married again, a worthy woman who gave Charley brothers and sisters. Unlike Lincoln, Charley married his first love, the sweetest and prettiest girl in the county. And then, forsaking the Lincoln profession but never the Lincoln character, he went into the ministry, and lived a long life of usefulness, goodness, and gentleness.

I think I am as grateful for him as I am for Lincoln.

You see, he was my grandfather.

PART FOUR

TO LIVE ON IN HEARTS IS NOT TO DIE

*One of the plaster-cast models for the Lincoln
Memorial made by sculptor Daniel Chester French.*

Famed poet Walt Whitman (1819–1892) spent most of the war cheering and caring for both Union and Confederate soldiers. Living between the White House and the Soldiers' Home, where Lincoln retreated to to escape Washington's heat, Whitman would often see the President. Though they daily exchanged cordial bows, they never spoke to each other. After Lincoln was assassinated, Whitman, like the rest of the nation, was shocked—so much so that he couldn't even eat. In the fever of the moment, he poured out his soul into the lines of this poem. It would be later on that he would pen the much longer paean to Lincoln, the elegiac, "When Lilacs Last in the Door-yard Bloom'd."

"O CAPTAIN! MY CAPTAIN!"

WALT WHITMAN APRIL 14, 1865

O Captain! my Captain! our fearful trip is done,
The ship has weathered every rack, the prize we sought is won.
The port is near, the bells I hear, the people all exulting,
While follow eyes the steady keel, the vessel grim and daring;
But O heart! heart! heart!
O the bleeding drops of red,
Where on the deck my Captain lies,
Fallen cold and dead.

O Captain! my Captain! rise up and hear the bells;
Rise up—for you the flag is flung—for you the bugle trills,
For you bouquets and ribboned wreaths—
for you the shores a-crowding.
For you they call, the swaying mass, their eager faces turning:
Here Captain! dear father!
This arm beneath your head!
It is some dream that on the deck
You've fallen cold and dead.

My Captain does not answer, his lips are pale and still,
My father does not feel my arm, he has no pulse nor will,

The ship is anchored safe and sound, its voyage closed and done,
From fearful trip the victor ship comes in with object won:
Exult O shores, and ring O bells!
But I with mournful tread.
Walk the deck my Captain lies,
Fallen cold and dead.

THE LIVING MYTH

JOSEPH LEININGER WHEELER

*America does not realize how much she owes to the fact that Lincoln is still
a living presence on Capitol Hill, unavoidable even if it is not sought.*
—ERNEST DIMNET (FROM *THE ART OF THINKING*)

Have you ever wondered—as I have—if Lincoln, had he served out
his second term and died a natural death, would be the world-
wide myth he is today? I think not. First and foremost, inevitably
he would have been vilified by all those who forced the horrors of the
Reconstruction on the southern people after the war. A myth, more often
than not, is based on the premise that the individual in question died at
just the right psychological time—often young. Think Marilyn Monroe,
John F. Kennedy, James Dean, or earlier, Shelley, Mozart, Alexander the
Great, and even Jesus Himself. Lincoln died just as he was completing
his mission, and as I point out in *Abraham Lincoln: A Man of Faith and
Courage*, that long epic train trip back to Illinois, when his embalmed
body was seen personally by up to a third of the nation, accelerated the
creation of the myth.

As is true with all myths, it takes time to create one. At his death, it
was way too soon for people to think much about myth or legacy—they
were in a state of shock. Too many were sorrowing for the more than six

hundred thousand who died—not counting the maimed. For ten years, southerners were treated as a defeated enemy. It was a terrible time to live through.

Over time, however, as life gradually returned to normal, and historians began to sort things out, there evolved a perception that only one man—Lincoln—had saved the nation from total destruction. Stories, very much alive in the memories of Lincoln's contemporaries, began to surface, first and foremost in the oral tradition, later in written form, and still later in printed form, all this reaching its fuller flowering during the period beginning in 1880, and not ebbing until the 1960s; however, by then, cinema and television took Lincoln into new dimensions.

Most Americans are unaware that the Lincoln myth is not merely a national one, but in fact global. He is, abroad, the only universally revered American, far more so even than Washington. People from all over the world make pilgrimages to the Lincoln Memorial. And they are awed. And they cry.

Lincoln is unique in that he has never gone out of vogue. Both political parties claim him and continually invoke him. Secularists have done their utmost to strip him of his spirituality, not realizing that without it, Lincoln would not be Lincoln. Advertisers have discovered they can sell *anything* if they can bring Lincoln into the equation. The same is true for filmmakers.

What is also unique about Lincoln is revealed in the stories selected for our last section: they continue to be written, he continues to be contemporized; in a way, each generation reinvents him in order to keep him relevant. In truth, he is as vibrantly alive—in ways even more so—today than when he walked the streets of Washington. He has become woven into the very fiber of the nation—our DNA, if you will. Indeed, for the world as a whole.

I am convicted that in America today, there is a growing hunger for something far, far deeper than the thousand channels of vapid meaningless chatter on cable and on our electronic gadgetry. Our current epidemic of suicides among the young is the proverbial canary in the coal mine: a signal that something is very wrong in our contemporary value system. People of all ages are searching for some sort of ethical and spiritual bedrock on which to construct a life worth living. I submit that they can find it in these Lincoln stories.

What I can't help but notice in these stories is that we learn far more from what Lincoln *was* than what he said. In these days of imperial presidencies, how jarring it is to read about a president who, like Christ, felt that humble service to all, young or old, rich or poor, regardless of race or religion, was what life was all about.

We have recently celebrated the two hundredth anniversary of Lincoln's birth, and now the 150th anniversary of the Civil War. But looming in the mists is 2059, the 250th anniversary of his birth, most likely dwarfing any Lincoln celebration that has gone before.

I feel that one of the key reasons I was born was to shepherd all these vanishing and ever so precious stories into the pages of this book so that they are not lost with me. It is my hope that they will endure on and on into the future, an integral part of American family life, and are reread during family story hours by generations still unborn.

I would love to hear from you. May you, too, come to love the *real* Lincoln as much as I do, after having spent a lifetime laughing and crying through these stories.

Osborne H. Oldroyd at the age of twelve.

A BOY WHO LOVED LINCOLN

KATHLEEN READ COONTZ

This is a very different Lincoln story from any other I have ever read. It all started with a thirteen-year-old boy—in 1857—and it ended almost seventy years later. Had Osborne Oldroyd not set out on his quest when he did, much of what he left for posterity would have either been lost forever or undocumentable.

His life, too . . . was not lived in vain.

O n a summer's evening in 1926, in the house where Abraham Lincoln died, sat an old man holding in his trembling hands a little piece of paper.

He did not have to glance at the check to know that it bore the signature of the Treasurer of the United States, that it was made out to himself—Osborne H. Oldroyd—and that it called for the payment of $50,000! A great deal of money! More than the old man had ever had even a passing acquaintance with in all of his eighty-four years. The worn, neatly brushed coat, and the carefully mended socks peeping above the low shoes were mute witnesses to the fact that funds were welcome— really needed—here.

Yet it was not of the amount of the check that Captain Oldroyd was dreaming of this quiet August evening. Something far more wonderful than anything that dollars can buy had just happened to this veteran—a dream which he had held in his heart for sixty-five years had at last come true. *Think of it! Wanting something with all your soul and might, living for it, working and sometimes going hungry for it—and then—suddenly one day to have it happen!*

• • • •

It all started back there in 1857, when the old man was a boy of thirteen. His long name, Osborne Hamiline Ingham Oldroyd, was a little bunglesome to write at the end of his compositions at school yet he was proud of it, for did not the initials spell the name of his beloved State— O-H-I-O—a State to which he longed to bring honor someday?

Osborne's father kept a little drugstore on the corner in the little village of Mt. Vernon, and Osborne was allowed to run a newsstand in one side. Every week the Pittsburg News Company shipped a package of books and magazines to their young agent in Mt. Vernon. One day he found in the weekly budget a little paper-covered book containing a speech of a certain lawyer in Springfield, Illinois, by the name of Abraham Lincoln. Always curious as to the contents of his periodicals, Osborne opened the little pamphlet and glanced over it. There was something in the forceful yet simply worded lines that caught and held the boy's interest. He turned to the back of the book and there found a brief summary of the life of the speaker. This man Lincoln had been born in a cabin in Kentucky, had attended school only a few days in his whole life, and had educated himself by reading and by studying law. He was now practicing law in Springfield.

How could anybody write like that who had never been to school! Osborne turned back and read the speech all over again. His father, coming up behind him, had to call him twice to supper before the boy heard, so engrossed was he in the words of this Kentucky rail-splitter. It was then—and only then—that Osborne Oldroyd met Abraham Lincoln, but between the boy and his hero there sprang up an association that was to last all of his life and become the moving spirit in his career.

Osborne was by nature a collector. He was all the time collecting something—marbles when he was a little boy, stamps and pressed flowers when he grew older. His resolution to collect Lincoln mementoes, however, was the beginning of a collection which was to last a life-time.

He wrote to the news company and asked them to send him everything that came their way about this man Lincoln. It was not long before he had other speeches and news items about him. He was thrilled later to receive a Springfield newspaper containing a picture of his hero and another lawyer by the name of Stephen Douglas, who had debated upon the subject of slavery.

Great things were beginning to happen in the nation at this time. Osborne, better, perhaps, than many of the men tucked away in this little Ohio village, was able to keep up with the happenings because of the information brought him through the Springfield paper he received.

Then came Lincoln's election as President of the United States, and the boy's heart thrilled with pride and admiration. Close upon the inauguration came the cry of "War! War!" and soon the quiet streets of the village were echoing to the tramp of marching regiments of soldiers.

Osborne was strangely restless to join them, but the elders said, "Wait, you are too young now; your time will come." But the boy was not content to wait long. The patient, worried man in the White House at Washington needed many soldiers in the field. So one night when the moon was rising over the little drugstore, Osborne, not yet eighteen, slipped away to join the boys in blue.

Before he went, however, he tied up all of his Lincoln mementoes, wrapped around them a little flag which had flown from a recruiting station near by, and laid them reverently in the drawer of the old highboy up in his little room.

Many times in camp or on the battlefield he thought of his treasures and of the man for whose sake they were collected. Through all of the horror and suffering of those long months, one desire burned in the breast of the young soldier—to look upon the face of Abraham Lincoln!

Once this almost happened. Toward the close of the war, his company was passing through Washington. Someone cried, "There goes Lincoln!" The young captain looked up with fast-beating heart, but a great wagon loaded with army paraphernalia rolled in front of him just then, and when it had passed, Lincoln was gone. Two weeks later, while his company was celebrating the end of the war, in Memphis, Tennessee, the adjutant rode up and in a loud voice read the notice of the President's assassination.

The world reeled for Osborne Oldroyd—the gallant young captain who had faced shot and shell undaunted! He crept off by himself, where he might hold communion with the great, gentle soul that had passed. Oh, that he might do something—something great for this man who had laid down his life for suffering humanity! There flashed through his memory the modest Lincoln collection reposing in the old highboy drawer up in his little room at home.

Captain Oldroyd remembers even now that he said aloud, "I shall go home and give my life toward collecting everything in the land to do with this friend of mankind—I shall raise to him a great memorial!"

The years that followed found him true to his resolution. While he was earning a livelihood in his Ohio town, he spent all of his spare time acquiring new Lincoln relics. Every editorial, every memorial service, every account of those last sad days was zealously gathered up by the young collector. With a burning desire to walk and live where Lincoln had walked and lived, Captain Oldroyd moved to Springfield, Illinois. Here, with a Springfield girl for his wife, one who had seen Lincoln many times and who was in hearty sympathy with his ambition, Osborne rented the Lincoln homestead and opened up a modest Lincoln museum.

There was not a great deal of interest in his undertaking, however, and many people thought the young man rather queer to give up so much of his time to collecting old worn-out furniture and other articles—even though they had belonged to Abraham Lincoln. They did not then dream that someday a great nation would rise up and bless the man for his sacrificial work. For each addition to the collection meant a real sacrifice to the young couple starting life together on limited funds. But nothing seemed too hard for the ardent hero-worshiper. When money was not forthcoming for railroad fare, he made his pilgrimages of collecting on foot. Many a dress for the devoted wife and a smoke for her husband went into some addition for the collection.

It was at this time that Collector Oldroyd acquired the furniture from the Lincoln homestead: the cradle that had rocked the Lincoln children, the cook-stove over which Mrs. Lincoln had baked cookies for little Tad and Willie before they went to the White House, the precious old office chair in which the young lawyer sat when he wrestled with intricate terms in law and later wrote the speeches that Oldroyd knew almost by heart.

A collector of anything must know his subject thoroughly. Although Captain Oldroyd was never permitted to look upon the face of "Father Abraham," he nevertheless knew Lincoln better than many people who had been so privileged.

In the long winter evenings he read and reread every line that the martyred President had ever written. He tramped for miles around the town, visiting homes that had known Lincoln and listening to the narratives of the inmates. From the many favorite jokes repeated to him, he gained his knowledge of Lincoln's famous sense of humor; from Lincoln's son Robert, and others who had come in intimate contact with him, he learned of Lincoln's likes and dislikes—in food, dress, and personal characteristics. In other words, Oldroyd the collector became intimate with Lincoln the man who had long ago entered his life.

A collection is valuable only when it is undeniably genuine. Realizing this, Captain Oldroyd determined that every article added to his collection must undergo a rigid test. Accordingly, he sifted all evidence carefully, and traced every new acquisition back to its place in Lincoln history before he added it permanently to his museum.

He was besieged with offers of "Lincoln walking-canes," but always met the fakers with, "My dear sir, Abraham Lincoln never carried a walking-cane in his life!"

By this time, interest was aroused in Captain Oldroyd's Lincoln memorial. The great man had been dead for twenty years, and people frequently dropped into the little museum, and paid the small admittance fee, to look upon the personal belongings of the man who appeared to grow greater as time passed. But the fees were not enough to keep the wolf from the door where Lincoln himself had once scrimped and saved.

With necessity pressing him hard, Captain Oldroyd went one day to the state officials and proposed to present the museum to the State, in return for a salary which would permit him to enlarge the collection without such severe deprivation to his family, which now included a little daughter. But the State was busy with more important things and was not interested in his proposition. Some enterprising easterner who had seen the collection offered the captain five hundred dollars for it. Five hundred looked mighty big to Captain Oldroyd, and he might have taken it had not the prospective buyer announced his intention of taking the collection to some other state. The collector felt that this would be like selling his birthright for a mess of pottage. Lincoln's things belonged here, in his adopted State or—there it was again, that old resolution about a national museum—at the capital of the United States.

Accordingly, in 1893, the determined man packed up his treasures, and, together with his wife and daughter, made his way to Washington. Here he met many who were interested in his enterprise and soon he had his museum established in what to him was the most hallowed spot of the capital city—the house opposite Ford's Theater, where Lincoln was carried the night he was shot and where he died on April 15, 1864. The whole city was pregnant with memories to the man who had clasped Lincoln's hand by means of that little paper-covered book, before his name was on every tongue.

Here was the great White House, with its portico under which the carriage had driven that last fatal night; the box at the theater, over which the flag Oldroyd had just bought had been draped; the little toy-shop out on Pennsylvania Avenue where the same woman who had sold little Tad and his father leaden soldiers wept as she told of his wondrous sympathy. In the sanctuary of the house where Lincoln had quietly breathed his last, Captain Oldroyd was permitted to live.

Spurred on by these new intimate reminders of the life of his hero, the collector rapidly added to his accumulation of relics. The exhibit, that first required one room, soon spread to two, later taking up the entire lower floor of the house; for the museum became popular with tourists and the growing fees enabled the owner of the exhibit to buy extensively.

Many articles, too, were donated from time to time.

One day a woman visitor stopped before going out of the museum and said to Captain Oldroyd, "You have many beloved things; but I have something of Lincoln's which is dearer than any of these."

"And what may that be?" inquired the old captain, jealous of this unknown treasure.

"The old plaid shawl that he wore," quietly answered the woman.

The shawl! Here it was nearly within his grasp, and he had searched all over the country for it! He offered the woman a price. She refused. He pleaded with her for the shawl, but she only shook her head. "I cannot part with it. It has meant so much to me, this big, homely shawl that he wore around his stooped shoulders. You see, my mother was a friend of Mrs. Lincoln's. When Mrs. Lincoln came back, after the President's death, she asked my mother to name something of Lincoln's that she would like to possess. My mother always thought of him in the plaid shawl, and she reluctantly asked if Mrs. Lincoln would part with it. The shawl was sent her a few weeks later, and I have always loved it. I have had sorrow in my life and disappointments, but somehow that old plaid shawl just seemed to breathe patience and to stand for all of the goodness and charity in the world. It may come to you some day; but I couldn't live without it now."

Realizing that here was a kindred spirit, in her love and admiration for Lincoln, the old collector refrained from urging the lady to part with her keepsake. Two years afterward he received a registered package from Chicago, and, opening it, found the plaid shawl and this little note:

"My mother died and in her will left her beloved Lincoln shawl to your museum."

So also came to Captain Oldroyd other Lincoln relics which had been precious keepsakes in a family and made valuable additions to his collection.

The last bit of Lincoln's writing he bought from the White House guard who had preserved it, but not before dire poverty drove the family to part with it. The guard, too, had memories connected with his treasure. Broken in health and spirit, he loved to tell of the night when President Lincoln wrote that last line.

"He was all ready for the theater. Mrs. Lincoln was in the carriage, impatient for him to join her. A soldier outside requested a pass, and I took the request to the President. Always considerate of others, he sat down and wrote that line—the last he ever wrote:

" 'No pass is necessary to authorize any one to go or return from Richmond. People go and return just as they did before the war.' "

Down in Kentucky one of the Hanks family, hearing of the Oldroyd collection, was instrumental in sending an interesting souvenir of his great cousin. It was a rough black locust rail taken from the fence which Lincoln built, with his father, around the log cabin on Goose Neck Prairie, Illinois, in 1830.

Captain Oldroyd hung it from the ceiling in the museum, where the eyes of all the young Americans who visited there might fall upon it the first thing—a reminder of the toil and frugality of the boyhood days of the great Lincoln.

Every nine-year-old boy enjoyed in the museum a certain privilege which was denied to others. He was allowed to hold in his hands the big Bible from which the child Abraham Lincoln learned to read, and to trace with his finger the scrawl in the front: "Abraham Lincoln, February 1818"—the proud announcement of a nine-year-old birthday boy who never knew a birthday cake!

The worn old Bible had had a long, roundabout journey before it finally fell into the hands of Captain Oldroyd. The old man liked to tell about it to the interested boys and girls who came to him.

"Some of my friends gave me the trip to Chicago to the World's Fair in 1893. I had seen all there was to be seen—so I thought—and was getting ready to go home when I came across the greatest treasure in the whole exposition—the old Lincoln family Bible. It was brought to the exposition by some Kentucky men and was being exhibited in a tent outside of the grounds. This was one of the Lincoln relics that I had long wanted to obtain. I began to bargain for the Bible, but they wanted $150.00 for it and I hadn't that much money in the world. But I couldn't go home without the Bible. I wired to one of my friends and asked to borrow the money. It came, and I went back the happiest man in the land, carrying the beloved and long-sought-for Bible safe in my bag."

The old collector loved to tell his stories about the relics, and found happiness, as always, in his work; but as the years began to go by an ache in his heart deepened. He was getting to be an old man and still the dream of his boyhood was unrealized—the dream of a national museum for Lincoln, one owned by, and cared for by, the Government.

Each year some senator or congressman introduced a bill in Congress providing for the purchase of the collection, and each year brought some disheartening delay in its passage. If the old collector had been in comfortable circumstances, he might have presented his museum to the Government; but, he argued, if they appreciate the worth of the collection, they will be willing to buy it. Then too Captain Oldroyd could ill afford to part with his life-work collection without pay.

Many times he might have sold the collection had the main motive been a mercenary one. The collection had become famous, and offers from all over the United States came to him. Illinois, finally awake to the fact of its loss, offered $50,000 for the Lincoln relics to add to their museum in Springfield. "Lincoln no longer belongs to Illinois, he belongs to the ages—and to the American people. The capital must have this museum," was the answer the collector sent back. A New York museum offered $100,000 for the collection, a little later, but received the same answer: "The collection must stay in Washington."

Following that came an offer from Henry Ford, as well as individual offers for certain articles, that would have kept the old man in luxury. But it was not money that he wanted.

When President Harding dedicated the magnificent structure of white stone known as the Lincoln Memorial, the old captain, standing near, looked out across the beautiful Potomac River whose misty shadows form a strangely fitting background for the building, and, shaking his white head, murmured to himself: "A wonderful memorial, a costly and beautiful thing; but I am offering them a more precious one—a thing that is a part of Lincoln himself!"

The collector had almost lost hope that he would ever live to see the fruits of his labor recognized by his Government, when one wonderful day in April there came the news that Congress had passed the bill for the purchase of the Oldroyd Lincoln-Memorial Collection. There then followed the August day which introduced Captain Osborne Oldroyd to our readers at the beginning of the story. Do you wonder that he sat like one in a trance? Can you picture now some of the things that went through his head—some of the memories that crowded upon one another as he looked around at the three thousand odd Lincoln relics he had accumulated?

The Oldroyd Lincoln-Memorial Collection, which has recently come into the possession of the United States, is the largest collection, devoted to a single individual, in the world. It is all the more remarkable when we consider that it was not made by committees with large funds behind them, but by one man over a period of seventy years of patient, unselfish search.

Had one born in Shakespeare's time gathered into one collection such an assortment of articles pertaining to the poet, he would have rightfully won the gratitude of all generations. This work of love is what Osborne Hamiline Ingham Oldroyd has done for his boyhood idol, Abraham Lincoln.

This Healy portrait was painted about 1871 from sketches made at City Point, Virginia, early in 1865, just before the close of the war. The original was owned by Robert T. Lincoln. The halftone plate was engraved by H. Davidson.

The museum contains a library of more than a thousand volumes, all relating to Lincoln; there are invaluable magazine and newspaper files; five thousand clippings; hundreds of sermons delivered throughout the nation at the time of the funeral; 253 portraits; 25 busts and life-masks; 171 memorial medals struck in honor of the martyred President; and countless letters addressed to or written by the man who in his great-heartedness never turned a deaf ear to sorrowing humanity. There are also the many personal articles that lead the visitor step by step along this career from its humble origin to the White house.

You may think of the old collector as happily spending the remainder of his life among his treasures as their custodian. Sometimes he glances up at a little worn brown-paper-covered pamphlet in a frame above his desk; sometimes he reads a bit from the volume containing every poem that was ever written about Lincoln—the last contribution of Captain Oldroyd to his memorial museum.

When you go to Washington you will want to look him up and hear from his own lips other stories of his adventures in collecting. He will tell you that the collection is a memorial to the hero of his boyhood and man-hood, but, as he talks, you will feel—I did—that it is also a memorial to the unswerving loyalty of a thirteen-year-old boy sixty-nine years ago.

A DECISION THAT TOOK COURAGE

John L. Roberts

The terrible Depression of the 1930s was raging, and the boy could find no one who would hire him for a job. Almost, he was ready to give up in despair—when he chanced to look down. There on the sidewalk was an expensive-looking wallet!

What he found inside brought both jubilation and temptation.

That night, he couldn't sleep.

Abe shoved the billfold deeper into the pocket of his patched but clean corduroys.

"It's nobody's business," he whispered to himself; "besides, I guess I found it."

Abraham O'Conner's father had moved west the previous year with his family, settling on a small farm near Spokane, Washington. His investment, though entailing no more expense than payment of delinquent taxes, had absorbed all of the meager savings which had been garnered during the years he had been employed in the iron foundry in Detroit, Michigan.

The family arrived at their new home in time to do the spring plow-ing. They then put in a garden which was to feed them for the coming year, and they hoped bring in a little revenue to help inflate the empty family wallet. They had also hoped that Abe, aged seventeen, would be able to pick up a few odd jobs here and there during the off season on the farm.

It was on one such job-hunting itinerary that Abe came to the city in his search for employment. He had just crossed Riverside Avenue and was approaching the *Evening Leader* Building to try to arrange for a paper route when he spied the billfold lying on the sidewalk. He picked it up quickly and slipped it into his pocket, then swung a rapid glance around to see if anyone had witnessed his action. Apparently not.

He buttoned the flap on his pocket and continued his way into the newspaper building. As usual, he was informed that at present there were no vacancies, but "if you will leave your name and address, you will be notified of any opening."

Jamming his hands into his pockets, he slouched out of the office. Then he remembered the billfold and began to wonder what was in it. He had put it into his pocket so quickly that he had not even given it a glancing appraisal. Seeking a secluded corner, he now examined his newly found possession.

It was a steerhide billfold of excellent quality. He opened it and saw in gold-engraved letters, the words, "Honesty is more valuable than gold. Trustworthiness is to be more highly considered than silver. Please return to Amos T. Woulds." Abe laughed. *Probably some country hick*, he thought. *Who is Amos Woulds, anyway, that he should presume his name is known by everyone?*

With this he explored further. He found no other identification, but he did find money. There was one ten, two twenties, and a one-hundred dollar bill [a great deal of money at that time]. The realization of this wealth frightened the boy. Whoever the owner was, he must be important to be able to carry so much money in his pocket. Abe started to walk rapidly as if to escape from an accusing conscience. After hours, it seemed, he arrived at the edge of town. He was tired, and it was already late in the afternoon. His thoughts returned to finding shelter for the night. He would not use any money from the purse—not yet!

Going into an auto camp, he asked if he could work for his supper and a bed.

"Sure, I need some work done. I'll give you a good supper and a bed to sleep in if you'll do it," George Hamilton, the proprietor, answered Abe's question. "That rick of wood needs splitting, and if you get through before supper, you can rake up the yard."

As they left the table, Mr. Hamilton handed the boy a book, and excused himself with, "I'm sorry I can't stay and visit with you, but I have to attend a meeting of my church board. Make yourself at home."

After he had gone, Abe looked at the book. It was *The Life of Abraham Lincoln*, by Ida M. Tarbell. Having nothing else to do, he decided to read until bedtime. However, he became so interested that he did not retire until he had finished the story of this great American from his Kentucky childhood to Ford's Theater.

That night in his dreams, Abe shared the experiences of this other Abraham. He was with him when he split rails, when he read by the firelight, when he walked the three miles out into the country to give the poor widow the six and one-half cents which he had short-changed her by mistake during the day. At this point he awakened with a start. His mind centered on the long walk Lincoln had taken merely to pay the widow a few pennies. Here he was, with $150 which did not belong to him, and he had not even made an effort to find the owner! *But I don't know who this man is,* he argued with himself. *Anyway, he probably doesn't need the money, and I do. Maybe God meant me to find it.* Then came the disturbing thought that perhaps the man was for some reason carrying all the money he had.

Abe's memory went back to the time when his father was out of work, and had spent almost his last cent for a sack of potatoes. Walking along the street, after an unsuccessful job hunt, he found two ten-dollar gold certificates lying on the sidewalk. He brought them home and put them carefully away. The next day he placed notices in all the newspapers, advertising the fact that he had found money. There were many answers, but none presented satisfactory proof of ownership. So after several weeks of waiting and inquiring, he used the money. The boy tried to reconcile his actions with those of his father. But the thought persisted that he had not even tried to find the owner of the billfold in his pocket! And he even knew the name of the person it belonged to, so there was a good chance he could return it. But would he?

Abe tried to go to sleep again, but in vain. He rolled from one side of his bed to the other, and then back again. He twisted and he squirmed. What should he do? He *wanted* that money. He *needed* the money—but it wasn't his! He began to think of Lincoln again—wondering what he would do under such circumstances, and fell into uneasy, dream-laden slumber, in which he had gone down town and spent the money for some new clothes and a second-hand car. But wherever he went, the money followed him, and when he stopped to rest, immediately each bill took in hand a drill and began to bore out his vitals. He awoke, chilled, and wet with sweat.

Again he slept. This time he saw Lincoln, the great man, whom people called "honest," walking toward him. As he came near, Abe could feel the force of his eyes as they rested accusingly upon him. Lincoln said nothing, but the boy thought of the long walk again. After this, sleep left him entirely. And despite all his efforts to the contrary, his mind reverted again and again to the great effort this man had put forth to return only six and a half cents.

What should he do? *I don't know how to find Mr. Woulds*, he told himself. *Anyway, it's his own fault he lost his money. He shouldn't have been so careless.*

But again came the thought of Lincoln, his accusing look, and his long walk. Even in the dark, with his eyes closed, he could see the words engraved on the billfold. "Honesty is more valuable than gold. Trustworthiness is to be more highly considered than silver."

At first break of dawn, Abe heard the camp proprietor stirring, so hurriedly arose, dressed, and joined him outside, welcoming a diversion from his troublesome thoughts. Mr. Hamilton, with a cheery greeting, handed him the morning paper. As he was paging through it, he came to the "classified ad" section. This he carefully perused, thinking that he might thus be able to locate a job. On the same page his eye caught the heading, "Lost and Found." He looked down the column, but there was nothing there about the billfold.

Now I can keep it, he assured himself. *If Mr. Woulds isn't interested enough to advertise for the money, he doesn't deserve to get it back.* Again Lincoln crossed the vision of his mind's eye, walking slowly, and this time he seemed to say, *But the money isn't yours, Abe.*

Thanking Mr. Hamilton for his kindness, Abe started for town. When he had walked a few blocks, his courage mounted again. He thought less of the money in his pocket and more of finding a job. He *must* find work today or go home. He could not continue wandering around indefinitely. Thus he walked and thought block after block, until he reached the center of the city and again unexpectedly found himself opposite the *Evening Leader* building. He stopped to consider.

Why have I come here? He asked himself. *I applied here for work yesterday and there was none.* He looked across the street. There, printed in gold and black on a window was the inscription: "*Leader* Want Ads." Abe speedily turned his eyes elsewhere and started back down the street. Then he stopped abruptly, wheeled about, retraced his steps, crossed the street, and entered the building.

Walking up to the counter, he was greeted by an efficient feminine voice, "Do you wish to place a want ad?"

The boy gulped, and stammered out that he did, then he handed the billfold to the girl, and informed her that he wished to advertise for the owner.

Opening it, she saw the gold-engraved words ending with, "Please return to Amos T. Woulds." She looked up at him with a smile and queried, "You don't know this town very well, do you?"

Abe, undecided whether to be angry or ashamed, blurted out, "Why?"

"Follow me and you will see," she answered him.

She came out from behind the counter and led him down the hall. At the end, he saw a glass door with the words, "Woulds Publishing Company," and below the name, "Amos T. Woulds."

His guide tapped on the door, opened it when so bidden, and introduced Abe to the man behind the inlaid mahogany desk, saying, "Mr. Woulds, this young man has found a billfold with your name engraved on it," and handed it to him.

Mr. Woulds took the billfold and laid it down on the desk, unopened; then he keenly surveyed Abe from well-polished shoes to neatly combed hair.

Reaching for a pencil, he wrote a few words on a sheet of paper, and handed it to the boy standing before him with: "Will you take this to the office for me, please? Wait for a reply."

After reading the note which Abe delivered, a clerk walked over to the other side of the room, took a sheet of paper from a file, brought it back and handed it to him with the explanation, "This was intended to go into the evening paper."

In surprise he read on it: "Lost: one steerhide billfold, engraved with the name Amos T. Woulds. Contains $150 in currency. Liberal reward offered to finder."

Abe took the intended want ad back to Mr. Woulds, who handed him a twenty-dollar bill with the words, "In fulfillment of my promise," and then queried: "Did you apply for a job in the circulation department yesterday?"

"Yes," was the reply.

"I chanced to be in that office at the time. Have you found a job yet?"

"No, sir, I have not," Abe answered and started for the door.

"Wait a minute, young man. Your search for work is ended right now. My office boy is leaving. The Woulds Publishing Company is honored to add to its ranks of employees a young man who really knows that 'Honesty is more valuable than gold,' and that 'Trustworthiness is to be more highly considered than silver.' Please fill out this card."

Abe carefully filled in the blanks on the card and handed it back to Mr. Woulds. The latter looked at his name, printed in full, then stepping around the desk and turning the boy to face the portrait of the Great Emancipator hanging on the wall, he said smilingly, "You have lived up to the reputation of your namesake, Abraham Lincoln O'Conner."

Drawn by Victor C. Anderson for Scribner's Magazine *in 1911.*

CAPTAIN, MY CAPTAIN

Elizabeth Frazer

*The river rat of a boy was hopeless—so said Officer Kelly. And Miss
Life was his last resort: if she refused to take the little terror—well, he
had no other alternatives left.*

I t was Friday afternoon, and half-past one to the tick by the placid,
round-faced clock above the blackboard. Forty pairs of blue and
gray and dusky eyes marked the downward-pointing black finger,
and straightway forty fond little hopes of the nation sprang to "position"
in their primary seats, folded forty pairs of grubby paws neatly behind
their backs, and trained their bright gaze toward Teacher's desk. Behind
it, focusing all these ardent beams, stood Miss Life, smiling a winged
smile out of her eyes—"Laughin' on her insides," Joe Cady called it—
and holding in her hand a small package.

Miss Life was not her real name. It had come to her in the dawn of
her career as a public school teacher in the purlieus of Abingdon Square,
when, one day, in a fit of black despair, she flung overboard the stereo-
typed course of Nature-study, root and branch and bugs, designed another better adapted to the little citizens of Jane Street, and enclosed it,
with a spirited defense, to the powers that sit in light in Fifty-ninth Street.

Something in the tone of this home-rule letter, crackling with defiance, touched a responsive chord in an Irishman on the Board, and moved him to save the brave young writer from the wrath that waits upon initiative.

"Let that Miss Life alone," he said, coining the name which made her famous. "And if by any means she can put the mystery and beauty and sacredness of life into those little waterfront rats, and longshoremen's kids, in God's name, give her a free hand, gentlemen, and I'll take off my hat to the lady!"

Which he did the very next day, invading Jane Street, and Public School Number Nine for the purpose. And from that one visit—but this is not the Irishman's story.

It was the hour marked on the program as Nature-study, and Miss Life had elected to instruct her charges in the gentle art of gardening.

"Today, children," she began, then halted, and threw a puzzled, questioning glance toward the door. From behind it proceeded strange sounds of muffled strife, of scratchings and scufflings, attended by heavy footsteps and an irate voice, as if an animal were being dragged, protesting, across the floor.

"It's that dog!" said Miss Life. "Hennie, you *must* tie him up better! Run out now and help the janitor."

"Hennie," a tiny boy, with a voice like a silver lute, a face finely powdered over with freckles like a quail's egg, and surmounted by an impenetrable jungle of inky hair, bounded from his seat. But before he could reach the door, it was torn open from the outside, and stalwart Officer Kelly, who each morning saluted Miss Life with extreme *savoir faire* at the corner of the block, and who was known throughout the district as the sworn adversary of truants, burst violently into the room.

The gallant copper looked flushed and disheveled. His helmet was askew, good red blood dribbled from a trinity of scratches which clove their ragged, crimson way down the line of his resolute jaw, and his Celtic eyes blazed with rage. More terrible than ever, in his disarray, he looked to the awe-stricken ranks of his Lilliputian foes like the veritable bright god of destruction, and they quaked in their dusty little boots.

Behind him pressed the Principal, with a worried countenance, and between them, at the extreme end of the strong arm of the Law, and firmly grasped by the Law's huge fist, hung a panting, wild-eyed atom of a boy.

"Why, Officer!" exclaimed Miss Life. "You are—wounded! What is it?"

"What is it?" stormed the wrathful guardian of the peace. "Well ye may ask what it is!" From his seventy-two inches he glowered down at his diminutive captive, who, from narrowed, blue-black eyes gave him back, balefully, glare for glare.

"'Tis a little divil out of Hades—a hot little spark out of h—" He stopped abruptly, realizing his gentle environment, and proceeded more judicially, though a groundswell of Celtic r's still marked the depth of his resentment.

"Thrree times today has he played hooky. The last time, I caught him red-handed, as it were, by the slack of his pants, just as he was skedaddlin' over the back fence. And, as I hauled him down, the young daymon whirled on me like a wildcat, and clawed a piece of me face off!"

Officer Kelly lifted the imprisoned member of offence, and regarded with strong disgust the black-rimmed nails, beneath which resided fragments of his own fair epidermis.

"But, Officer," protested Miss Life in bewilderment, "I'm sorry about your face—but that boy is not *mine*! I'm full. Look here." She swept a hand over her densely populated kingdom. Every small seat was indeed occupied by a passionately interested spectator.

The Principal beckoned her aside.

"I wish you would take him," he urged. "He is a new boy, and a bad one, I'm afraid. What Kelly says is true. I've tried him in three rooms today, and each time he has 'hooked it,' as he would say. This morning Miss Lacy attempted to restrain him, and he wrapped himself round her like a cuttlefish and bit a hole in her knee."

"He seems of a spirited disposition," murmured Miss Life. She stole a glance at the officer's lacerated jowl and her face bubbled.

"That's one name for it," remarked the Principal dryly. "His mother, who has just moved into the district, is like the old woman who lived in a shoe. The father—" Here followed the chronicle of one whose road was so beset with pitfall and with gin that a long-suffering community had been forced to sequester him in a country-house on the Hudson.

"It's good American stock," he concluded, "but just—petered-out! The boy is headed for the same place as his father, I suppose, but if we could get him interested—"

"I'll take him," said Miss Life briefly.

The Principal breathed a sigh of relief. "Good! The main thing is to give him the school-habit. He can read," he added encouragingly, "—if he wants to! And he writes like copperplate."

He turned back, laughing, at the door.

"Ask him what his name is!"

Miss Life, thus left in charge of her own quarter-deck, quietly took command.

"Release him, Officer," she ordered. She dropped into a low chair, the better to study her latest acquisition.

He was a slender wisp of a child, with a thin, dark, hard face, blue-gray eyes that had a trick of gazing steadily, and a crest of tar-black hair finer than spun silk. His clothes were foul with mud and in wild disorder. One coat-sleeve had been torn bodily from its socket, and hung, dismembered, by a drab lining; a precarious suspender had permitted the escape in the rear of a small rakish shirttail; and battered and rent stockings exhibited a pair of red bruised knees. But despite these signs of dirt and bloody war, there was something about him which Miss Life approved, a look of race, of stamina.

"Come here," she commanded gently.

He backed, sidling off like a hermit-crab, bright, hostile eyes fronting the foe.

"Naw, ye don't!" he muttered between immobile lips.

Miss Life's throat constricted. "Poor babe! He thinks I am going to beat him."

The officer looked at her with pitying contempt.

"Babe nothin'!" he scoffed. "Look at them saffron-tipped fingers. He's a cigarette fiend already."

For the first time, the boy opened his mouth and hurled a word like a rock at his adversary.

"Youreadamnliar!"

At this patently unjust charge, Officer Kelly made a swift lunge, plainly bent upon annihilation, when Miss Life intervened.

"What is your name?" she asked.

The sweet belltones of Teacher's voice and the soft beams of Teacher's eye had been known to pierce the joints of the armor of more seasoned, though not more fiery warriors, but it was a full minute, during which the new boy stared at her from under piratical, black brows, before he gave up the answer.

"Cappin."

"Cabin?" questioned the amazed, incredulous teacher.

"Cap'n!"

"Oh—Captain!" exclaimed Miss Life, beginning to "laugh on her insides." "I see!"

"That's the hell of a Christian name now, ain't it?" demanded Kelly— who himself bore the title of an archangel—speaking the simple thought of his mind. (Fifteen minutes later, over a foaming stein of beer, to the gallant officer's credit be it said, he remembered that slip of the tongue and drank deep of remorse.)

"It is a splendid name!" affirmed Miss Life warmly. "There was once a wonderful man called that." She quoted softly:

O Captain! my Captain! Our fearful trip is done,
The ship has weather'd every rack, the prize we sought is won,
The port is near, the bells I hear, the people all exulting,
While follow eyes the steady keel, the vessel grim and daring;
But O heart! heart! heart!
O the bleeding drops of red,

Where on the deck my Captain lies,
Fallen cold and dead.

Slowly, lured by the magical spell of words and voice, the young commander drew nearer, until one hand rested lightly on Teacher's knee, and his wide, deep eyes were fastened on Teacher's face.

"Did your Cap'n t'row a fit on his ferry-boat?" he demanded. "An' 'fall down cold an' dead'?"

Miss Life laughed, albeit unsteadily and with a bright mist in her eyes. Never was she able to repeat those matchless lines with composure.

"No, dear. He wasn't captain of a ferry-boat. He was the Big Captain of our country, and saved it from shipwreck. He was very fond of little boys, too! Monday I'll bring you his picture."

She stood up. "And now, Captain, my Captain," she said blithely, "choose the man you'd like to sit with today, and next week I'll fix you up regularly."

Captain ranged a judicial eye over his forty hosts, some of whom, in their passion for hospitality, had vacated their seats, and were sitting invitingly in the air beside them. His eye fell upon the diminutive boy with the marvelous kinks and freckles—and there rested.

"Him!" he pronounced, pointing imperially.

"Hennie" sprang to the extreme outer edge of his seat, his soft dark eyes shining with delight.

The Captain sat down.

Miss Life's smile was a pleasant thing to see.

"I think the Big Captain would like that!"

She turned to the officer. "Thank you so much!" she said sweetly. "I think we needn't detain you any longer from your duty. And, Mr. Kelly," she added in a low voice at the door, "don't go after Captain if he should take another notion to run away. Let him run. He'll come back to me."

"Who could help it?" murmured the gallant officer. He closed the door and opened it again.

"Will I leave you my club?" he inquired grimly.

"You may leave it with the Captain!" she allowed, smiling.

The enemy withdrew, discomfited, and she returned to her belated Nature lesson.

But the afternoon was not destined to pass in uneventfulness. Glancing at the clock, Miss Life saw that she must abridge the talk on seeds if the children were to plant them in the window-boxes prepared for the purpose. So, with a few explanatory words, she delivered the package of seeds to the monitors for distribution.

"Three to each one, boys," she said, "and be careful. For if you should drop one of those little spots of life on the floor without noticing, it would die and lose its chance to become a radish."

Due precautions were observed, each moist and grimy palm received its proper quota, and the mystical ceremony began. The monitors marshaled their respective hosts past the miniature garden-plot, the seeds were separated with some difficulty from sticky fists, and buried with lingering solicitude. Teacher, standing by in the role of sexton, marked each spot with a neat stick whereon were inscribed the date and the owner's name.

Last of all came "Hennie," proud leader of his line. Suddenly his decorous band broke rank, scattered like leaves before the first rude rattle of the gale, and in the open space thus cleared was revealed the Captain, down upon all fours, rushing about like a demented young quadruped, and pawing wildly at the floor.

"Git out o' the road!" he howled in fierce, anguished tones, uprooting in his path sundry pairs of shoes so that their owners toppled over backward. "Maybe you're trompin' on the top of it now!"

Miss Life reached the storm center swiftly.

"Why, Captain—dear lad! She exclaimed, bending over him in deep concern, "whatever is the matter?"

Captain pushed back a straggling elf-lock, wiped his nose upon a swarthy wristband, and lifted a hot, quivering face.

"I—I lost one of them little s-spots o' life," he faltered.

"Oh, well, dear," soothed Teacher, "I'll give you another this time."

Captain sat back on his haunches and looked at her long and piercingly from under frowning brows.

"Won't it die if it's lost," he demanded, "an' never git no chanct to grow up into a reddish?"

"Why—ye-es," admitted Miss Life weakly; "I'm afraid it would."

Captain began grubbing at the floor again.

Feeling the falseness of her position, Miss Life dropped down beside him to assist in the search. She had a vision of herself hunting madly throughout the night, scanning feverishly each speck of dirt by the dim light of a candle, in order to sustain her reputation as an idealist. By rare good fortune the lost seed was found, resting serenely between Captain's third and little fingers, and, together with its two fellows, hastily entombed.

One would like to record that from that day henceforth, never again was our hero guilty of "hooking it" from scholastic halls; but that he took prizes in deportment and cleanliness, and the bright yellow hue faded from his finger-tips, to be seen no more; that he graduated at the head of his class, grew into an honored and upright citizen, and, eventually, such is the privilege of our great democracy, became himself a President. And, in later years, looking back across the past, he was wont to ascribe all his success to the potent influences of Miss Life, and the Big Captain, whose dark brown face, worn and tired, with its expression of goodness, and tenderness, and deep latent sadness, looked down on him daily from the wall where Miss Life had placed it one memorable Monday morning—but such was not the road our Captain took.

In one particular only is the above history true. On Monday, according to her plighted word, Miss Life brought the picture of Lincoln. Captain was conspicuous by his absence. In the middle of the morning, however, when Teacher was inducting her B-2 Class into the mystery of "carrying" in addition, the door-knob was softly turned, the door softly opened the width of a crack, and Captain stood fearfully upon the threshold, holding his path of escape clear, and poised for rapid flight. But Teacher's back, at that psychological moment, was elaborately turned, and Teacher's attention, though there straightway arose a forest of wildly waving palms, eager to apprise her of the stranger's advent, remained stubbornly engrossed, and so, after an uncertain pause, the Captain slipped quietly into haven beside "Hennie."

Miss Life breathed a sigh of thankfulness, and, turning presently, threw him a warm, radiant smile.

Captain's response was instant, deep answering unto deep.

"Where's my picture?" he demanded. "The Big Cap'n what fell down that day onto the deck?"

"Here it is," replied Teacher, "just waiting to be unwrapped." She lifted from behind her desk a large, flat, brown-paper parcel. "Come on, Captain, and help me undo it."

Thus bidden, the Captain stepped forward and, bending over, unfastened the knots and tore away the coverings, until the picture stood revealed. It was a beautiful, clear print, simply framed.

Miss Life lifted it upon the desk in view of all the children. At that moment a shaft of pale morning sunshine illumined the room and caught within its radiance the two commanders—the small Captain, his hands thrust deep into his pockets and with lifted chin gazing steadily, and the Big Captain, upon whose rugged face, beneath its furrows of vast responsibility, of deep demands of life and death, there appeared to lurk an expression of quizzical tenderness.

"Do you like him?" questioned Miss Life softly.

The Captain tore his reluctant gaze away. "Is he mine?" he answered.

"All yours, my Captain, and for keeps. But wouldn't you like me to hang him on the wall, where we all may see him—just as a loan, you understand? I'll write your name underneath."

"*I* kin write it," retorted the Captain. And with Teacher's pencil, and bending above Teacher's desk, in clear though childish script, he signed himself. After which proprietary rite the picture was hung, but distinctly understood as a loan exhibition.

The rest of the morning, though not so specified upon the calendar, became a Lincoln's Day. Teacher told simply the story of the great Commoner's life and death; a blackboard lesson upon the subject won hearty approbation; "The Star Spangled Banner" was chanted lustily, after which the exercises concluded with the Captain's poem, which Miss Life repeated by request.

Throughout the following weeks, Teacher strove valiantly to attach the Captain as a permanent satellite to her pleasant system. But, although he listened with unflagging interest to her stories, and spurred her on for more, she had presently to acknowledge her inability to hold him. He was as erratic as a wandering star, visible one day in his place, vanished the next. Which only meant, Miss Life argued rather acutely, that her rowdy little star revolved about another centre. Something else attracted him more strongly. She wondered. . . . But a heavy program, and the presence of another satellite which threatened to demolish her system, diverted her attention from the runaway, and the days passed.

Came March, turbulent and wild-browed, with mud underfoot, passionate scuds of rain above, and all Jane Street blew its nose on mangy little hankies and snuffled. April brought a warm, radiant lull, and suddenly, almost overnight, as at the touch of a mystical wand, the world burgeoned. But not the Jane Street world. Across the wide, shining reaches of the river, on the Palisades, the earth wore a filmy, translucent robe of green which grew brighter with the days. Violets, white or faintly blue, breathed forth their fragile incense; the pale pink of arbutus gleamed shyly along dim, leafy trails; maidenhair hung its feathery fronds over hidden springs; the dogwood flung its starry white branches to the soft embracing air; a talking wind moved gently among the boughs of pines and maples; and above all arched the far clear sky, with one smoky segment veiling the spot where lay, battened down with steel and stone and mortar, the next-to-the-biggest town on earth.

Every Saturday Miss Life was afield, usually with some of her small constituency, and scientific research was pursued with a fine ardor. All Nature was looted for Jane Street.

Occasionally, however, she gathered her specimens in the company of a certain Irish Member of the Board, in whom the proximity of Spring and Miss Life had evoked such a dire, compressed, and trussed-up feeling, such a poignant aching of all the senses, as threatened speedily to burst all bonds. It has been said, wisely, that a little Irishman is a dangerous thing. Consider, then, how much greater the danger if the Irishman is big. It was, indeed, like walking abroad with a tall stick of dynamite stalking at one's right side which might explode at the lightest touch—say, for example, if Miss Life should stub her toe and stretch forth a lovely hand for aid. (At such sweet catastrophe, one might well imagine the distraught Irishman crying, "Havoc!" and letting loose the dogs of war!) So that at every moment Miss Life stood in imminent danger of being blown bodily out of the unmarried state—one which being unknown, she feared. Therefore, she went softly, with a faint smile in her eyes like that in the eyes of Raphael's Cardinello madonna, and wished for an eternal *status quo*—as if one could stop the advance of summer!

One morning, with an intuition that it was going to be warm, she arrayed herself in a cool dimity dress, sprigged all over with forget-me-nots. And then, feeling particularly gay of heart, and because the month was May, she finished off with a pair of open-work silk stockings and black pumps strapped across neat ankles.

"Who cares?" she murmured defiantly to her unpedagogic reflection. "The kiddies like it."

The day proved hot beyond expectation, thick, blowsy, and oppressive. The children were pallid and cross. To complete her distress, the Principal dropped in after lunch, to announce that the monthly reports must be in that afternoon. It was a loathsome task at any time, and, with wrath in her heart, she prepared some desk-work.

Papers and pencils were languidly distributed, and then Teacher inquired guilefully:

"How many of you have little baby brothers or sisters?"

Something like thirty-nine hands testified to the fact that the human race was not becoming extinct.

"I'se got twins!" announced "Hennie" with shy satisfaction.

"That's nice," replied Teacher hastily, "but don't tell me anymore! You see, I want you to write me a letter about the baby. Tell me his name and the color of his eyes and if he can talk or walk—a nice long letter all about the baby."

Pencils were eagerly gripped and the epistolary labors begun. Miss Life turned wearily to her roll-book. Since the Captain's advent in their midst the average of daily attendance had tumbled from excelsior heights of perfection down to the dead level of mediocrity. Opposite his name ran an almost uninterrupted line of sinister black checks. Which meant that the Captain had been absent or tardy or both nearly every day in the month. Miss Life frowned and hardened her heart. Something really must be done.

"Captain," she asked severely, "why were you absent this morning?"

The Captain, who was screwed up in his desk, composing furiously, raised his black crest, and bent an absent eye upon her.

"You gimme leave," he replied vaguely.

"Gave you leave to stay away from school? Nonsense!"

"You gimme leave yestidday in the middle of the afternoon to 'Scuse me please!'" he explained patiently, "an' I saved some of the leave over for this mornin'."

Teacher looked at him helplessly, and then her face bubbled.

"I think we'd better talk that over, my Captain. Can you spare a minute after school?"

He nodded. His glance rested dreamily upon Teacher, lifted for a second to the picture above her head of the immortal Madonna standing with the Babe upon trailing clouds, and dropped again to his earthly Lady. What were his thoughts? His look traveled from her face where the smile still lingered, down the pleasant, flowered dress, down below the hem, until there swam into his awareness the neatly shod feet, incased in lacy stockings.

The Captain's eyes brightened. He leaned far out of his desk, staring fixedly. Then he sat back, reached briskly for his pencil, and added another line.

Ten minutes later, when the letters were collected and Teacher tapped the bell for dismissal, she found him gazing pensive-eyed at the face of the Big Captain.

After school, with Captain leaning lightly against her desk, Miss Life sorted her epistles, stopping occasionally to read a line or gasp at some astonishing statement.

"That's mine," said the Captain suddenly. He laid a restraining hand over hers. "Read him."

And Miss Life read:

> Dear teacher the culler of his eys they are purpl. His name is QT and you got to be very careful of one thing about a baby on the top of its head that is its skul for if you was to press that dinge it would die in an ours time they must not walk befor they are so old or they will get bolleged. When I am 21 I will have lots of children, hoping you will do the same.
>
> CAPTAIN.
Privut dear teacher I like them
ventalated stokins
your
CAPTAIN.

Controlling a wild desire to laugh, for the young author's blue-gray eyes were fastened absorbingly upon her face, Teacher turned up her palm and squeezed the grubby paw lovingly.

"It's a beautiful letter," she assured him, "and I shall take it home to read aloud. What is Cutie's other name?"

"Jeff—an' his eyes are purple."

"But, dear," remonstrated Teacher, "children don't have purple eyes—not really purple, you know."

"Yes'm, Cutie he has," insisted Captain. Through narrowed lids he was blinking at a jewel upon Miss Life's left hand which flashed dazzling, rosy lights into his eyes. "He ain't got any sights, either," he added meditatively.

"Of course he has. Everybody has sights."

"Cutie hain't," returned Captain absently. He laid his head on one shoulder to catch the elusive pink glow of the gem, and this time it was green.

"But Cutie couldn't see if he didn't have sights!" cried Teacher, almost cross with her beloved black sheep.

"He don't," said Captain, simply. "He's blind. But he's awful cute!"

"Why—why!" gasped Miss Life. "Are you sure he is blind?"

The Captain nodded. "Yep—out o' both of his eyes he's blind. But he c'n hear all right. An' when Mamma goes off an' leaves hin all by hisself, he gits lonesome, an' that makes him mad, an' he kicks an' hollers. It's fierce—"

"Does Mamma leave him alone all day?" interrupted Teacher very gently.

"If she gits an all-day job, she does. An' Cutie he bangs on the door with his fists an' yells '*Ca'a! Ca'a!*' that's me," he explained, "he wants to play horse with."

"I see," said Teacher. Her eyes fell upon his card and the condemnatory black line of demerits. Suddenly illumination flashed upon her. She drew him close within the warm circle of her arm.

"And is that what makes you run away—to play with lonely little Cutie?"

"Um-hm!" The Captain stirred restively and disengaged himself. It disturbed him to be handled.

"He likes me," he confided, 'best of all! I'm learnin' him to turn a handspring."

Miss Life stared out of the window with unseeing eyes. Her mobile lips quivered. She had a vision of little Brother "Cutie," enraged (as who is not?) by loneliness, toddling blindly to the door, beating puny fists against the panels, and, with brief listening spaces in between, "hollering" ardently. And, at the same time, she saw the Captain in his seat at school, begin on a sudden to fidget, to stare vacantly and give offhand replies, and finally, raising a signal of distress, mumble, " 'Scuse me, please!"—and bolt.

The grand secret was out!

Miss Life turned back to him with shining eyes.

"You—*lamb*!" she murmured unsteadily.

The Captain took ruthless advantage of this sign of weakness. "Tell me that story 'bout the Big Captain," he commanded, "an' his little boy named Tad."

Drawn by Sears Gallagher for
Youth's Companion *in 1902.*

ABRAHAM LINCOLN'S ROSE

Isabel Nagel

A rose for Joy—and certainly no one would know the difference if he jumped over the railing and grabbed one.

J oy Alison turned restlessly in her narrow bed as she whispered, "I wish they hadn't named me Joy!" To her mother and brother she would show a cheerful face, but the faded wall of her slant-roofed bedroom knew the entire truth. Suddenly she laughed out loud. "If I don't get well," she cried, "if I never walk again, what a funny name it will be!"

"Joy Alison!" a boy's voice cried. "For shame! If you don't get well!"

She looked affectionately up at the tall, overgrown boy in his shabby clothes. "Home so soon, Dick? Why—did they give you a holiday after all?"

Richard Alison frowned, then quickly changed the subject by pulling a card from his pocket. "Miss Rand, the new cashier, sent you this, Joy. She painted it for you herself. Water colors!"

Joy looked at the dainty card. Upon it was painted in softly glowing colors a beautiful pink rose. Underneath, in hand-worked letters of gold, were the words:

TO JOY ALISON.
LINCOLN'S BIRTHDAY.

"Isn't it pretty!" said Joy. "And wasn't it good of Miss Rand to remember me?" Her eyes were wistful. "One can almost smell its perfume!"

"I knew you'd be pleased with it," was Dick's reply.

Joy attempted to smile, but instead a tear began coursing down her cheek, and, turning her face to the wall, she wept without restraint. Dick had never seen her weep. In all that dreary year since the girl had severely injured her spine by a fall on a flight of icy steps, she had shown ever a cheerful face. Bravely and smilingly she had borne all suffering—until today.

Dick felt his world crumbling about him. For that day he had broken the plate glass of a showcase in the confectionery store where he worked. His month's salary had been withheld from him to repay the loss, and he had been given his discharge without reference. On his return home he had found his mother broken-hearted over a two month's rent bill and the scorching of a fine waist she had been laundering for her most particular customer. And now here was Joy weeping as if her heart was broken.

Gradually the sobs died away, the rain of tears ceased. Joy raised a shamed and tear-stained face. "Such a goose I am, Dick," she said. "You and Mother toiling away to take care of me and help me get well, and I not even trying to help myself! I am so ashamed!" Joy tried to laugh, but could give only a ghost of a smile.

"Look here," said Dick, "don't you try to laugh if you don't feel like it. What is the trouble in particular, Joy?"

It was a long story, and Dick learned that, because it was Lincoln's birthday, Joy had been thinking about the school party the year before and the fun they had had. She had remembered how freely she could run about and play games with the rest . . . and then the coming home in the twilight and those slippery steps down which she had fallen.

Dick's hands were tightly clenched as he listened. When Joy paused for breath, he asked her if that was all that was troubling her.

"No," said Joy. "I read in the paper today about a celebrated foreign surgeon, Dr. Emil Fleishman, who had arrived here. It seems that he performs miracles, as it were, in hip and spinal diseases. He came to the United States especially to operate upon a rich girl's spine, and everyone thinks the girl will recover under his treatment."

Joy hesitated a moment, then looked straight up into her brother's eyes. "I felt very unhappy when I read that. I wished I was that rich girl—I was so hungry to walk. I just hated the world and everybody in it because I couldn't. Then when you gave me that pictured rose— that seemed to sum everything up. I didn't cry about my back, or about our poverty, or anything important. I cried because I didn't have a real rose."

At these words Dick straightened up and came to a sudden decision. He couldn't come up with thousands of dollars to pay that famous surgeon to cure Joy's lameness, but he could seek out a real rose. And although his sister protested that a rose in February would make a big hole in his tiny salary, he merely said, "I'll be back with that rose in a short time," and was gone.

Things seemed hopeless for Richard Alison as he made his way through the gathering twilight in search of a rose for his sick sister. Resolutely he crushed down all the forebodings about rent, doctor bills, and food. *Something will happen!* his passionate heart assured him, *Something that will take us out of this slough of worry. I'll pin my faith on that.*

It was a cold night, still and clear. As he moved uptown, Dick kept his eyes open for florist shops. Finding one, finally, he entered and timidly asked the prices of pink roses.

The clerk drew out a pot of long-stemmed beauties from the ice-box. "Nice and fresh," he said, "ten dollars a dozen."

Dick's heart sank. "How much for one?" he asked falteringly.

"Oh, about a dollar or a dollar and a half," said the clerk. He then thrust the roses back into the box, as if he knew Dick would not buy. And he was right, for Dick felt he would have no right to pay that much for a single rose, even if he had possessed that much money.

Each florist shop on the way uptown was the same—either no roses at all, or high prices. He wandered on until he found himself on Fifth Avenue. He could not bear to go home without the promised flower, and yet—what could he do? It was then that he decided to go back downtown on the east side of the city. Prices were not so high there. Surely there was some florist who would sell him one rose, just one!

Alas, the east side proved as fruitless as had the west! Heartsick at his repeated failures and wondering which way now to turn, Dick stumbled into Union Square. It was getting late. His mother would begin to worry. He moved on, involuntarily turning his steps towards the home where a sick girl was eagerly awaiting his return. "I must get it somehow," he murmured. "I can't—" He stopped short in utter amazement, his eyes upon a thick, large wreath of the desired flowers. As in a dream, the boy gazed on upward at the large statue of Lincoln which dominated the square. The wreath of pink roses had been placed at his feet in honor of the day.

Lincoln's kindly face smiled down at Richard Alison as if the great man could feel the turmoil in the boy's heart, as if he alone, out of the whole city, understood.

I'm sure Lincoln wouldn't mind my taking a rose, said the boy to himself. He lightly vaulted the railing that surrounded the statue, and, detaching a rose from the wreath, jumped back to the street again. He didn't notice the tall figure of a man who, standing slightly behind the statue, had watched his act with interest. Dick drew a long breath of dewy fragrance as he moved away. "Won't Joy be happy!" he cried. "Won't she—" He stopped short. He doubtfully regarded the rose which someone had given Lincoln on his birthday. "Why, I'm a thief! I've stolen this rose!"

Regretfully, Dick retraced his steps, vaulted the railing again, replaced the rose and regained the street. As he stood a moment looking first at the wreath of roses and then at Lincoln, the tall man drew near. "Why did you wish a rose?" he asked. He spoke with a strong foreign accent.

Reserve crept into Dick's face. "Thank you for your interest, sir," he said. "I'd rather not tell."

"You would tell *him*," replied the stranger, indicating the noble face above him.

Dick, glancing up at the kindly face of the great man whose birthday it was, felt sick all over. The understanding face, those deep keen eyes, the smile which seemed somehow to envelop, to enclose, to help the entire world, made the boy give up for a moment. His figure, so sturdily drawn up in reserve a moment since, dropped pathetically. Then, in a flash, he snatched off his cap. "Good night, sir," he said.

"Look here!" said the stranger. "Suppose I tell you that I have a special interest in boys. Suppose I tell you that boys are as dear to me as young brothers, that boys have given me some of the greatest pleasures in my life. And since I have accepted so much from boys, why can't just one boy, in their name, accept something from me. You yourself gave me much when you proved your honesty just now. To me honesty is one of the most admirable qualities in a boy. You can't imagine what pleasure it gave me to see you put that rose back. So you see, I am in your debt. Are you in trouble? You want something greatly, don't you? And it's more than a rose."

Dick looked up. There was something in the stranger's face—why, it gave Dick the same confidence that Lincoln's face gave. Something he wanted! "I want Joy to get well!" he blurted out.

"Is it so bad?" the stranger asked gently.

"Curvature of the spine. She can't ever walk again, the doctors say."

"It isn't so bad, then," declared the stranger briskly, "because—why, perhaps you have heard of me. Will you look at my card?"

Dick looked down at the card in his hand in almost stupid wonder. It was Dr. Fleishman who broke the silence, "I have an hour or two. I may be able to make Joy walk. Won't you take me to her? We will purchase the largest, sweetest rose we can find on the way—of course, it was for her you wanted the rose." Dick's eyes were so wildly happy that the doctor laughed softly.

The wistful, beautiful smile of the bronze Lincoln followed the eminent surgeon and the poverty-stricken boy. And presently, in the isolation of the square, the noble figure of the great man was left alone, his birth-day wreath of roses at his feet. Slightly apart from the others was the rose that Richard Alison had plucked for his sick sister. Probably to Lincoln, had he known, that one rose, twice given, would have been dearer than any flower he had ever received—a rose, indeed of honesty.

• • • •

One year from that night, on another Lincoln's birthday, a boy and a girl might have been seen coming uptown to Union Square. The two chatted and laughed merrily as they advanced, and it might have been noticed that the girl carefully carried a large box. As they came in sight of the statue of Lincoln they quickened their steps.

There were tears in the girl's eyes as she set the box down carefully, her eyes on the kindly face above her. "To think of last year and this!"

Dick's gaze followed hers. There was the same serene and lovable smile, the same gentle, unassuming dignity. "And to think," he said softly, "the whole thing grew, as it were, from Abraham Lincoln's rose." Then he added, in a burst of admiration, "Joy, America has many great men, but here, it seems to me is our greatest."

"There are many great and noble men in the world," replied Joy, softly, thinking of the doctor who had befriended them so well. "A noble heart like Lincoln's must find an echo, I suppose."

As Joy talked she opened her box. Inside was a beautiful wreath of pink roses, dewy and fresh. Dick vaulted the railing, took the roses Joy handed to him and reverently placed them at his hero's feet. And Lincoln smiled, as ever, on his children, that tender smile that seemed somehow to envelop, to enclose, to help the entire world.

Pen portrait was made from photos by Wayne Eaton,
engraved by Timothy Cole in 1877.

HE KNEW LINCOLN

Ninde Harris

Only a cub reporter, yet they were giving him the chance to cover a big story—a senator, two college presidents, a great minister—what an opportunity!

But then, the valve stopper on his mother's washing machine blew out and left his one good suit a soggy wreck!

What was he to do?

The dull thud of the electric washing machine wakened Jerry about ten o'clock. He turned over in his bed, muttering maledictions on all washing machines. He saw it was still early for a man who worked at night to rise. As he started to close his eyes again, he glanced at the calendar and saw that it was February 12, and remembered that he was to cover the Lincoln Club's annual luncheon in honor of that great American.

With a leap he was out of bed, the covers thrown over its foot. He must bathe quickly, get dressed, and do some of his routine work at the *Star* office before he went to the luncheon. The speeches after it were sure to last until four o'clock. He wanted to hear all of them, and get a good story for his paper. The evening papers had to go to press at two o'clock, so their stories could hit only the high spots.

This was his first big assignment. *Not such a bad assignment for a fellow who's been a cub reporter for only three months*, he told himself while the tub filled: *A senator, two college presidents, and a great minister to be among the speakers. Big meeting! Looks as if I'm making good with the* Star.

He whistled while he splashed water until his mother, reading carelessness in the sounds, came to the door and warned him not to get the clean window curtains wet.

Back to his room he went to don his best suit and new tie. The occasion demanded his best clothes. It was his big chance, as he saw it, to write a story which would inspire hundreds of people in his town to a greater degree of patriotism. Jerry knew the city needed this. He hoped to arouse a civic pride that would demand the school board build some new school buildings in the poorer quarters of town rather than a million-dollar high school building on the east side where only the rich lived, and where only two hundred high school pupils would be enrolled.

He told his mother about his plans while he ate his breakfast in the kitchen. She turned the current off the electric washer so she could hear him better. Because he worked until 2 A.M., and ate his breakfast alone, she had fixed a special little table in the kitchen. That hour was their time of visiting together.

"You know, Mom," he began, "if I make good with this story and get the raise I want, I'm hoping to have one of the basement rooms fixed up for a laundry and hire Mahala again, just as you used to do before so many of us got into high school and college, and you had to begin doing without everything."

"Jerry," his mother came over and put her arms lovingly around his shoulders, "I'm not thinking of a laundry room and conveniences myself. I'm hoping this story of yours will move folks so they'll do what you want them to do about the schools in this town—replace those dilapidated ones on the west side and down by the river. We don't need that high school building to delight some rich real estate men who want it to make their subdivision grow. Perhaps you can help out by showing them how Lincoln rose from uneducated poor people."

She was going to tell him more about the school buildings when she noticed that in some mysterious way the valve stopper of her electric washer had dropped out, and a stream of soapy water was pouring onto the kitchen floor.

She started toward it to turn off the water, but Jerry was there before her. He picked up the stopper from the floor, started to force it into the valve, and then his feet slipped. The next minute he was lying flat on the floor, the stream of water from the washer pouring onto his right shoulder and running down the inside of his coat.

Back on his feet again, Jerry and his mother laughed together, just as the Irish will in the face of accidents. But when both had sobered, and they could see the damage done to his clothes, her arms went close around him. "O Jerry boy, I'm so sorry! Now you'll have to wear your old suit to the banquet."

"Bother—I—" Jerry started and then stopped. Just a hint of the fear in his mother's eyes stopped him. He had been going to say that he couldn't possibly go to the banquet in his old clothes. He was going to impress her again with the standing of the men to be there, and give way to his own disappointment. But that look in her eyes stopped him in time. He resolved never to let her know what this accident would cost him.

So back upstairs he went to dress again. If he'd been a girl he would have cried, he concluded. As it was, he shut his teeth tight together and held his chin high. He'd go to the luncheon in patched trousers before he'd ever let his mother know just how deep his disappointment was.

But Jerry McGabe discovered a few minutes after he arrived at the office that he wasn't to go to the banquet at all. The city editor gave him a keen, searching glance as he, wearing his everyday suit, entered the office. "Guess you forgot the Lincoln Club banquet," he began. "Never mind, Jerry, you won't have time now to go home and dress for it. I'll send Bill Hawton. He's already dressed up as usual. You can take part of his beat—the firehouses and libraries. You may pick up some small stuff on them. Bill seldom does."

The city editor frowned severely at Bill, who merely ignored the look and began fussing at his tie.

Banquets and dinners were Bill's delight. They gave him a chance to be dignified in appearance and impressive in bearing. He liked to sit close to the celebrities, and actually felt at times that he was one of them.

Jerry was bitterly disappointed. Why, this was worse than he had dreamed it would be. He had planned to go in his old clothes, take a back seat, and write the story anyway. He wanted to write it so that it would rouse all Lindendale's civic pride and sense of fairness in making improvements for the entire city, and not just a part of it.

He decided to make some suggestions to Bill Hawton. He crossed over to him. "Thought perhaps there might be something in those speeches which we could localize and make relevant to the school board's building program," he began.

Bill looked at Jerry, whom he dubbed "the cub," with evident amusement. "Brother," he said, "that meeting and these speakers are too big to even think of the problems of this little burg, Lindendale. It's all about national problems. It's—"

But Jerry didn't hear the rest of Bill's remark, for the city editor called him to answer the telephone. An undertaker was calling to give a death notice, and who but the cub reporter would take small stories like that?

He ate his lunch at the regular thirty-cent counter across the street, and came back to the office to await more assignments. The editor soon had one ready. "You might stir around to some of the branch libraries," he said. "Get a list of the books most in demand at each one. The boss plans to use a little story on that each Sunday. Don't think it amounts to much myself, but the school superintendent is anxious to have him do it. And if there's anything Bill hates to do, it's to get those lists. He hasn't had one now for three weeks, and the boss is cross!"

So Jerry slipped into his overcoat again. He was positively sullen now. To hide the disappointment in his heart, he kicked the snow as he walked. He looked neither to the right nor to the left. When some boys at the Garretson school pelted him with snowballs, he didn't even turn to toss a few back at them. They opened their eyes wide and stood still and stared at each other. Jerry McCabe was usually a good fellow. Now he didn't even notice them. "Is he stuck up, or has he lost some of his pep?" they asked each other.

Jerry took down the names of the most popular books at that school branch library and started to hurry from the building. But the principal of the school sighted him. There had been an assembly, with speeches in honor of the day, and she wanted Jerry to take the program and write a story about it. Jerry took the program, but was wary in promising much of a story. For he knew the city editor hated stories with lists of songs or titles of speeches in them.

The next school he visited was the Altoona, one of three he and his mother had decided needed rebuilding. It was close to the river and very dilapidated. "Do the children read many books here?" he asked the librarian, who was a vivid little creature, just a girl in fact. "You'd think they would be too discouraged by this old building to even to check out books," he continued.

"Do they read?" she returned. "They certainly do—every book that comes to these shelves. They attend my story hours, too, and we have mothers' reading clubs. They're not the rich children who can stop school when their buildings are not to their liking. They come here, even when they have to hold umbrellas above their desks on rainy days.

"But if you want to see children with real zeal about reading and a librarian who's the wonder of the town," she smiled brightly, "go to the Cromwell school. It's the poorest building in the city, yet the library has the largest circulation of any branch. We've tried to get reporters to write that one up, but they don't seem to think much of it." Her eyes brightened. "Oh, I believe you're a new reporter on this beat. I do hope you can get something in your paper about the libraries. That other fellow was so high and mighty, I was reluctant to tell him the best places to get stories or help him with anything."

So Jerry went on to the Cromwell school building, built back in 1861. It had funny little windows; many chimneys telegraphing the story that it was heated by stoves; and it had a crowded cindery school yard. He found that the library was in the basement of the dilapidated building, at the foot of a dark flight of stairs. Surprisingly, the room had cheerful curtains at the little windows, still more colorful posters on the wall, and a little librarian who was charged with energy and interest in the work, and the little children, who filled the room almost to the overflowing point.

He discovered that she was telling a Lincoln story, and that she was too absorbed in it even to see him. He stepped into the shadows and soon forgot everything—the city editor, the grief he had felt because he would not see his name on the front page of tomorrow's paper, and was intently listening to the story she was telling. He heard her end it, and then say, "Now comes our beautiful Lincoln picture. We shall give it to Leonard Tuller this year, because the committee thinks that his hauling all the crippled children to school on his sled last winter made him the most deserving of all of you."

The children clapped their dirty little hands. They stood on tiptoe as Leonard, a thin little fellow, pushed through the crowd to get the picture. They stamped their feet, and they jumped up and down when he had taken it in his hands. And when he turned back toward them, Jerry saw his face, his eyes alight with joy and his whole face beaming with happiness. And high above his head, the little fellow held an expensive print of Abraham Lincoln, framed in a beautiful walnut frame.

Jerry didn't think of a story then. He wanted to shake Leonard's hand and meet the little librarian.

"This is the tenth picture of Lincoln I have given to the Cromwell children," she told one of her women patrons. "Just think: I've been here for ten years. Grandfather bought the first three pictures for me. You see, Grandfather knew Lincoln, and he wanted me to inspire one boy each year to try to be as much like the great American as he could. He said that each boy so inspired, would leaven a whole bushel more."

Jerry knew right then that there in that room was a big Lincoln story—not about the grandfather who had known Lincoln, but about the librarian and the ten children who had learned about Lincoln from the prints given to them during those ten years. He wondered if the librarian had all their names, and if he could find out from her where they were now and what they were doing.

He asked her if she had them. She nodded smilingly, and gave him all the names and present addresses. Three had left town. But she knew all about them—the boy who was still recovering in a government hospital and who had won a French Cross in the war; the one who was assistant engineer for a construction company in South America; and the one who was a missionary in South Africa. They were the oldest of "her boys."

Jerry dropped in to see some of the others. Tom Morris, acting as assistant secretary to a boys' club while he went to high school, had hung his picture of Lincoln in the club gymnasium. "When I tell the boys of the wounded soldier whose proudest boast was that he knew Lincoln, they are fairer and squarer in their games," he said. "I think they feel they know him, too."

Tim McCarthy's picture of Lincoln hung in his sick mother's room. Tim was having a hard time going to school and acting as nurse for her. Of him it was said, "He gets these children to do their part of the work by telling them about Lincoln. It does seem that we all knew him, so naturally do we all talk about him now."

On and on Jerry visited the people who "had known Lincoln." And from the west side of town he finally went back to the office of the *Star*. There Bill Hawton, back from the banquet, was talking pompously of the celebrities he had met. But Jerry hardly heard him.

He dropped the finished story into the city editor's copy basket as he went out to cover his beat, and didn't have time to think much about it until he was back at the office writing more short news items. Then the city editor came over to his desk. "Sent out and got a photograph of that librarian in your story," he said. You weren't here, so I sent Miss Lilly."

Jerry's cheeks glowed. They sent out for photographs at the *Star* only when some story was particularly good. He was pleased, but he wasn't expecting the front-page spread that came in the first edition.

There was his story in the center of the front page, with his name signed in a very conspicuous way. On one side was a picture of Lincoln; on the other, one of the little teacher.

Later he thought to look for the story of the Lincoln Club luncheon. He looked a long time before he found it on an inside page, just three paragraphs long and placed in an inconspicuous corner.

He couldn't keep from walking up to the city editor, "I don't think I know the value of stories yet," he confessed. "I was bitterly disappointed to miss that Lincoln Club."

The man who had read stories and made up papers for ten years, and who had made many good feature writers in that time, shook his head. "That's not a real story at all," he explained. "Big stories are stories of accomplishment like this one. Why, son, this is the best story we've had this year! It's a real Lincoln story. That library teacher made those youngsters feel they really knew Lincoln. He's influencing that neighborhood as if he were alive. And you, with the heart throbs your story has in it, made me feel as if you had known him, too.

"The boss agrees. He's writing an editorial on the work done by those schools in the poorer parts of town, and demanding that the board give them new buildings instead of building that useless million-dollar high school."

Jerry carried a stack of papers home under his arm. He woke his mother to show them to her. "Mother," he began, "there will be a raise for me out of that story. You're to get every cent of it until you have that washroom fixed. Though I'm blessing that old washer for breaking when it did."

His mother sent him on to his room while she read the story and then the editorial, and quietly and thankfully she folded her hands. "With him writing that way and thinking of me first of all, when he gets a raise," she said softly, "it looks as if my boy was one of them that knew Lincoln."

Illustration created by an unknown artist for Harper's Magazine *in 1894.*

MR. LINCOLN, I LOVE YOU!

M. L. O'Harra

Morning after morning, the Englishman studied the President slowly walking back and forth on the White House grounds. The watcher would never afterward be the same.

During my pastorate of a church in Abingdon, Illinois, from 1904 to 1910, I had among my parishioners a couple, Mr. and Mrs. Joseph Hart. The latter was a woman of unusual intellectual culture and was personally acquainted with Abraham Lincoln from her early girlhood.

Her home was the Half Way House between Springfield and Bloomington, Illinois. When she was about ten years of age, Mr. Lincoln and another attorney stopped at her home to get a drink of water. She had placed her doll against the gate, which caused the men a little trouble to open. The attorney with Mr. Lincoln peevishly kicked the doll away, and it flew into the dust. But Lincoln picked it up, carefully wiped off the dust, and then handed it to her, and said, "There, little girl, your dolly is all right now."

But the story I especially like to tell is this:

Several years before I knew Mrs. Hart, she was in Springfield to attend a memorial service on the anniversary of Mr. Lincoln's death. This was held at the monument which had been erected to his memory.

The speaker on that occasion was a Mr. Affleck. In the course of his address he stated that he was an Englishman, and lived in Springfield until he was a grown man, at the time of the opening of our Civil War. He told his audience that the sympathy of England at first was with the South.

He described the sneering attitude of the English nobility toward Lincoln, the "despised rail splitter." They were amazed that the American people would elect such a "numskull" as President of the United States! "What could such a fellow as that do?" was their question, and they mockingly waited for a fiasco. But gradually they began to sit up and take notice.

Affleck decided to go to New York for the purpose of studying at close range this remarkable character. So great was the fame of Lincoln in New York that he decided to go to Washington and see for himself. He rented a house near the White House so that he might be near Lincoln.

It was Lincoln's custom to rise early in the morning and take a walk through the White House grounds. This was the only time he could be alone.

Mr. Affleck told how morning after morning he saw this tall, awkward-looking man walking slowly back and forth, head bowed and shoulders bent, as one carrying the burdens of a nation upon him. Affleck's heart kindled with great sympathy for this silent man, walking alone in the early morning hour.

"How many times," Affleck declared later, "I would have gone to him and put my arms about him, and told him how much I sympathized with him. But I hesitated."

One morning Affleck could not deny himself any longer, so he walked over to the grounds, unobserved by Lincoln, and reaching out his hand, touched him on the shoulder. Then, with a countenance full of sympathy, he said "Mr. Lincoln, I love you!" Mr. Lincoln received him cordially.

Mr. Affleck closed his address by saying, "My one great wish is that I might be buried near to Lincoln's grave, that in the Resurrection I might be permitted to see Abraham Lincoln rise to meet his God."

It had been raining all morning. People stood under umbrellas. The sun had been hidden all morning, but just as the speaker said these last words, the sun broke forth and shone upon the monument. It was covered with water, and seemed to be baptized with ten thousand dazzling diamonds. People simply went wild with fervor. They laughed and cried and shouted in an ecstasy of emotion. "It was," said Mrs. Hart, "the most remarkable scene I have ever witnessed."

EPILOGUE

PERSONAL MEMORIES OF ABRAHAM LINCOLN

Robert Brewster Stanton

Often, during all these years of studying our sixteenth president, I've wished I could have been the proverbial fly on the wall, at Lincoln's side all during the Civil War years, to observe him in all kinds of settings, in all levels of stress, in dialogue with all kinds of people—this way, I could arrive at my own unvarnished take on Abraham Lincoln. So you can imagine how serendipitous it was, at the very end of decades of Lincoln biographical scholarship and story accumulations, to stumble on just such a firsthand analysis, penned by someone who first observed Lincoln as a boy at his father's side, and later as a man, with a man's broad perspective. Naturally, I felt it was a must for this book.

I t is proper at the start to make clear how I, a comparatively young boy at the time, could know anything personally and intimately of so great a man as Abraham Lincoln.

My father, the Reverend Robert Livingston Stanton, D.D., a Connecticut Yankee, whose New England family dates back to 1635 and 1620, after his graduation from the College of Lane Seminary . . . My father graduated from the college, but only spent two years there in his theological studies, having spent six years under the tutelage of Doctor Lyman Beecher and with Henry Ward Beecher as a classmate, and going through that period of wild anti-slavery agitation there which nearly broke up the seminary and finally led to the splitting of the Presbyterian Church into its North and South branches—took up his first pastoral work, in 1839, in the little church of Pine Ridge, Adams County, Miss., and in 1841 removed to Woodville, Miss.—at which place I was born, in 1846, my mother being also from the North—and he lived in Woodville as pastor there and in New Orleans, and as president of Oakland College, Miss., until 1853.

During all my father's life in the South he was a true abolitionist. He knew the institution of slavery from the inside. He condemned the position of the South, particularly the position of the Southern church on slavery, but he knew the Southern people and he loved them too. He devoted all his efforts to furthering the aims of the American Colonization Society, of which he was an officer, and in which he earnestly labored up to the time when war finally swept away all possibility of its success.

When the dark days of '61 came my father recognized that perhaps God, in his inscrutable knowledge, knew a better way, and he became a war parson and was one of the foremost in his calling to hold up the hands of the war President, and, unlike some other abolitionists of that day, he stayed by him to the end.

It has always been my belief that the reason why Abraham Lincoln and my father became such warm friends was because he brought to the President a certain inside knowledge of the South and its people, from an earnest and loyal follower, and Mr. Lincoln welcomed such direct information when they discussed together the perplexing problems of those days, as they so often did.

Thus it came about that I, even so young, going with my father, came to know Mr. Lincoln personally, and was able to sit with him for hours at a time, in his private office at the White House, and listen to those talks and discussions and observe him at close range, and study his every word and action at times when there was nothing to disturb, and when only one or two others were in the room.

The first time I saw Mr. Lincoln was in February, 1861, a few days before his inauguration, when, as President-elect, he was stopping at Willard's Hotel in Washington. A crowd was passing through his reception-room in a continual stream, so that I had only a few minutes to observe him but I lingered as long as I could. At that time his countenance seemed to betray anxiety, or was it weariness from those continued handshakings? I could not determine which it was in the first and few moments of seeing his face. But as some friend would accompany the grasp of his hand with a word of cheer, or a "God bless you," the warm grasp was returned, the hearty "Thank you" accompanied with that sweet, gentle smile of his; and at other times, when someone seemed to strike a tender chord by what was said, his eye became moist by what appeared to be a starting tear.

The first time I heard Mr. Lincoln speak was at his first inauguration. I was then fifteen years of age, but I stood near to him and drank in every word he said. My mind had been prepared by the discussion of possible events since the election of the previous November, and startled by the President-elect coming to Washington in disguise (though against his wish) to save him from threatening enemies, so that I was in a frame of mind full of excitement and expectation as I stood listening to those gentle, yet firm and earnest, utterances in that first inaugural, surrounded as I was, so close to the platform on which he stood, by that band of determined Northern and Western men who, known to but a few and unrecognizable to the crowd, were armed to the teeth to protect him and repel the threatened attack upon his person.

At this late day, I cannot recall a single sentence of that first address, nor shall I attempt to refresh my memory by reading it at this time. What impressed me then, and remains as clear today as ever, was the man and his character as they came to me not so much in what he said, but in the manner in which he spoke: gentle, loving, yet earnest, unafraid, determined, ready to take up any burden or any task and carry it through, as God gave him the strength.

Four years later, I stood on the same spot and listened to the President's second inaugural address.

During those four long, weary, suffering years, what burdens had he not borne? Burdens from the tragedies of the war itself, from the bickerings and slanders of those who should have been his staunchest friends, some almost within his own household, and from that deepest of personal sorrows when his beloved little son William died.

From the first time I met him, I saw gathering on his face, month by month, that sad, anxious, far-away expression that has so often been referred to and frequently been so exaggerated. Therefore, at that second inauguration, I think I was well fitted to understand the depth, the earnestness, and the sincerity of those immortal words: "With malice toward none, with charity for all."

But how came I, a boy so young, to understand at all the man of whom I speak, and the questions of those trying days?

The winter before, I had sat in the gallery of the Senate and the gallery of the House and heard those ominous, foreboding speeches, from both sides of the chambers; and later I listened to the orations of the great leaders, Charles Summer in the Senate and Thaddeus Stevens in the House, as well as many others; besides the vindictive utterances of the "fire-eaters" from the South. I saw delegation after delegation withdraw from the Congress as their several States seceded from the Union, and heard the defiant yet sorrowful and tearful farewells of those Southern men who really loved their country well, but loved their States and their beliefs better.

With this education in national affairs in those stirring times, and my father's instructive talks at home—we were chums during all of his life—together with my reading of the newspapers of the day, I felt that I was somewhat posted on the problems of the hour, and I longed to hear something of those same problems from the lips of the great man who was leading, and was destined to lead, the nation through the darkest and bitterest experiences of its life.

My opportunity came at last. My father took me to see the President when he called to discuss with him some of those problems of the country and the war. My father was his personal friend and I did not wonder at his reception. But is it possible that I ever can forget the way Abraham Lincoln received me—a mere boy? His cordial manner, the warm grasp of that large, kind, gentle hand, the fascinating though almost evasive smile, and the simple word or two of welcome, were so earnest and sincere that I thought he intended me to understand—and so I felt—that he received me not as a boy, but as a man, though very young. That first warm hand-clasp (though later I had many more) from that good and great man is one of the most cherished memories of my life.

Of course, I did not enter into the conversation. I simply listened in admiration, drinking in every word he said with reverence, for I was not one of those who ever doubted him for a moment. My unbounded, youthful admiration had not lessened, but had expanded, from the first day I heard him speak—March 4, 1861.

At that very first meeting I heard Mr. Lincoln discuss and explain some of his perplexing problems and how he solved them. One in particular. It will be recalled that all through the war of the Rebellion, certain critical friends, as well as enemies, charged that in many of his acts the President went beyond his Constitutional and legal rights and exercised a power almost dictatorial.

On that, to me, memorable evening he discussed with my father this very phase of his administration of national and State affairs, for undoubtedly he had overstepped State rights. He freely acknowledged that some things he had done, and decisions he had made, were possibly beyond his constitutional right to do. Yet he knew the necessity, and with his bold, unafraid determination, and his clear and marvelous insight into the true nature of things, he, in those emergencies, did what he felt to be right, as God gave him the vision to see the right.

How did he explain his actions? In these few simple, and even humorous, words: "I am like the Irishman, I have to do some things 'unbeknownst to myself.'"

He never sought nor desired the opportunity to exercise his power, as is so clearly shown by his long, patient, yet sorrowful consideration before he performed his greatest act. This, also, he at other times discussed with my father. The one object he always kept in view was to save the Union of the United States, and not simply to abolish slavery. And he continued unmoved by the howls of all abolitiondom and the arguments of those who thought they knew better than he; patiently waiting for the proper time to do the right thing. And when he found it, and not before, then it was that he used his power and put his name to the Emancipation Proclamation.

• • • •

I had seen Mr. Lincoln many times before I first met him, but this was the first time that I had had the privilege and honor of sitting close to him and studying him at leisure.

Through the whole of the campaign of 1860, while recognizing his ability, he had been characterized as "Old Abe," the long, lank, gawky rail-splitter. On coming to Washington he had been ridiculed for the manner in which he had entered the city, and spoken of as that rough, uncouth Westerner from the prairies of Illinois who had dared to come among the exclusive, high-born, generally Southern people of the capital. I, as a boy, knew many of the families of those old, exclusive, prewar Washingtonians, for I had lived there with my grandmother on my mother's side, an English woman who went to Washington about 1800, and I had heard, more particularly from the dames of society, those bitter, cutting remarks about Mr. Lincoln's uncouth mannerisms and uncivilized behavior.

What was my surprise, then, when I saw him and heard him at that first inauguration! There I saw a tall, square-shouldered man with long arms and legs, but, as he came down the east steps of the Capitol and onto the platform from which he spoke, he walked with such a dignified carriage and seeming perfect ease, that there was dispelled forever from my mind the idea that he was in any way uncouth or at a loss to know the proper thing to do or how to do it.

When he began to speak I was again surprised, on account of what I had heard of him. He spoke so naturally, without any attempted oratorical effect, but with such an earnest simplicity and firmness, that he seemed to me to have but one desire as shown in his manner of speaking—to draw that crowd close to him and talk to them as man to man.

His manner was that of perfect self-possession. He seemed to me to fully appreciate his new and unexpected surroundings, to understand perfectly the enormous responsibilities he was undertaking, but at the same time to have perfect confidence in himself that, with God's help, which he always invoked, he could and would carry them through to a successful conclusion.

As Colonel Henry Watterson has so clearly expressed his own impressions on hearing the same inaugural, "He delivered that inaugural address as if he had been delivering inaugural addresses all his life."

It was, however, when sitting close to him in his office, listening to those animated and earnest discussions, as well as on other occasions, that I learned to know him and understand, as I thought, his almost every movement.

When sitting in his chair in quiet repose, leaning back listening to others; when he was preparing to reply, as he straightened up and even leaned forward; or while pacing the floor listening or speaking, I never saw him once when, as was so often said, he seemed in the least at a loss to know what to do with his hands or how to carry his large feet. His every movement, his every gesture, seemed so natural, so simple, so unconscious, and yet so suited to the matter in hand and the circumstances at the time, that they impressed me as singularly graceful. Graceful may seem to some a rather strong word to use.

It is true that his figure was tall, lean, possibly lank, and in a sense "ungainly." Yet with all this he had that dignity of bearing, that purposeful, self-possessed, and natural pose which, to me, not only demanded admiration but inspired reverence on almost every occasion. In intimate association, the movements of his body and the gestures of his arms and hands were so pleasing that all impressions of ungainliness were swept away. So I say, Mr. Lincoln was singularly graceful.

Is it any wonder then that when some years ago I stood before that statue of some imagined Lincoln which Barnard had brought forth, and patiently studied it, the result was to produce in me a feeling of profound sorrow that such a grotesque caricature should ever have been made of the man whom I knew personally and loved so well?

Mr. Lincoln's hands and feet were large, but not unduly so in proportion to the size of his body. And many large things, even though not symmetrically beautiful in themselves, can be graceful both in repose and in the delicate curves and the sensitiveness of their movements.

Mr. Lincoln's walk, whether while quietly moving about his office, on the street, or on more stately occasions, was most dignified, easy, natural, and pleasing. His head was usually bent a trifle forward but not bowed, except on special occasions. There was, to me at least, no evidence of loose joints, jerky movement, or clumsiness. At one time I saw him under circumstances which, if any could bring out those reputed defects in his carriage, should have done so. It was at a meeting of the Houses of Congress, gathered in the House of Representatives to celebrate some victory of the war. The chamber was packed, and the galleries overflowed with men and women. I sat in a front-row seat. The door opened on the opposite side, and as the Marine Band played "Hail to the Chief," Mr. Lincoln entered. The whole audience rose and cheered. He glanced up at the throng and there appeared on his countenance a bright, beautiful, but gentle smile of thanks, nothing more. In a moment this was gone, and holding himself perfectly erect, with an expression of unconcern and self-possession, he walked across the hall up to the speaker's desk with a simple grandeur and profound dignity that would be difficult for anyone to surpass.

At another time I saw what at first surprised me greatly. It was at the great review of General McClellan's Army of the Potomac, that army that had been getting ready so long. Seventy-five thousand men of all arms were gathered on the Virginia plain, and a throng had come out from the capital to see them. In a little carriage my father, mother, and I were among the spectators. We were placed within twenty feet of where the President's carriage stood. The military spectacle was of course inspiring, but what interested me more was observing Mr. Lincoln's part in the grand review.

Only lately I was asked, here in New York, whether it was true that Mr. Lincoln went to that review dressed in an old, yellowish linen suit. It was not. He was dressed in his accustomed black broadcloth, long frock coat, and usual high silk hat, this time a new one.

I was close enough to him to clearly note his every movement and see the expression of his face. As the commander-in-chief of the Army and Navy of the United States rode down that long line, mounted on a magnificent charger, followed by the general and his staff, he sat and rode his horse as if it were the one thing in the world he knew how to do. He sat perfectly erect, not stiffly, but at perfect ease, and in all that throng of trained military men there was not a general who bore himself with more, no, not as much, dignity, and rode with more true military bearing than the President.

This was one time when I saw him, as he rode down the line, when his face seemed never to change. His eyes then were not listless, his whole countenance beamed with one expression—that of pride in the thoroughly organized Army that he believed would bring victory.

After the review was over the single road leading from where we were was filled with carriages bound for Washington. My father whipped his horse in line immediately behind the carriage of the President. It has always been a wonder to me that after that military pageant the commander-in-chief of the Army was not provided with a cavalry escort to clear the way and protect him from possible accident. His carriage was merely one in a long line of similar carriages hurrying home as best they could. John Hay sat on the back seat with the President. As the procession ahead slowed up or halted, Mr. Hay turned round and raised his hand in warning to us not to run over them.

I have said that Mr. Lincoln's movements were graceful. What is it that compels me to declare that his face, to me at least, was beautiful? Again, beautiful may be a strong word to use, but I do not mean "pretty." No! not anything so common.

I know his cheekbones were too prominent, his cheeks somewhat sunken, his mouth large and at times "ungainly," his chin, especially with the whiskers he wore, appeared too far out from his mouth, his whole face furrowed (but not nearly so deep as is generally supposed), and his eyes "half listless." This latter, however, not always so even when inactive, but only on special occasions.

I saw him when he was cheerful, gay, convulsed in hilarious laughter; saw him when he was being twitted by a friend, when he was humorously acknowledging the justice of that twitting; saw him when he was sad and sorrowful, sad from his own sorrows, sad for the sorrows of others, sad and at the same time cheerful for his sick and wounded boys in blue, sad and worried over the suffering of his country. I saw all these moods at various times; and each and every feature of his face exactly as it was, but there was a something that came out from behind them, and spoke not in words, but shone and spoke through them by means of them, and turned them all into real beauty. And in all these moods, first or last, that spirit of beauty which I saw spread over his whole countenance and drew one to him as by the power of magic.

It was when sitting perfectly quiet, listening to some important statement or argument, studying some complex problem, that those features which have been called ungainly showed more plainly. At such times the furrows of his face seemed deeper, the eyes more listless, and the large mouth looked larger and more poorly formed, but as he gathered the meaning of what was being said and seemed to be formulating his reply, the eyes began to open and you first saw the twinkle of stars, then the furrows in his cheeks almost disappeared, the mouth seemed to be completely re-formed, a light broke out spreading all over his face. In important cases of discussion his eyes flashed veritable fire as he spoke, and, as has been said by another, there came from that mouth "flashes of genius and burning words, revelations as it were from the unknown." Then it was that the beauty which I saw was sublime.

If the matter in hand was of a lighter vein, the same awakening came, but the brighter light of his face turned into that charming smile, gentle, evasive, or sparkling and humorous, which always appeared to me so bewitching. So, whenever I happened to be near him and at first saw that sorrowful, depressed, faraway expression we have heard so much about and which under the burdens he was bearing did darken his face frequently, I had only to wait, sometimes only moments, until the real spirit of the man, his hopefulness, his trustfulness, his cheerfulness, returned and each feature regained its share of that real beauty of soul that shone through them, which held me and everyone who knew him so firmly and drew me to him by some very natural yet magical power that swept away every impression and memory of his appearance except that of beauty.

I was once asked to examine a collection of more than one hundred original photographs of Mr. Lincoln and pick out the one I thought the best likeness of the man as I had known him. In many of them I could see a perfect picture of his face as I had seen him (*at times*), but none of these was my Lincoln nor was it the Lincoln as the other men of those days knew him.

The picture I was looking for was one that showed something of the spirit of the man as I have feebly attempted to describe it. At last I found it. It was the same one I had had in my collection—so unfortunately burned—and which I had cherished since 1861.

It is true that this photograph was taken before the burdens of the Civil War had pressed so heavily upon him, but all the earnestness of his character is there, some of the sadness, and much of the brightness and joyfulness of his spirit (although it does seem suppressed), and some little, also, of that light which I have spoken of as coming out through those rugged features. This picture comes nearer than any photograph of which I know in portraying something of that startling magical power

*Original negative taken by Mathew Brady
during the darkest days of the Civil War in 1863.*

which drew all men to him and held them enchanted when in his presence, even though the "beauty," which I saw, of sparkling eye and smile, may be lacking . . .

• • • •

It has been said that Mr. Lincoln was so depressed by the actuality of the war that he never really laughed outright. That is a mistake. I saw him and heard him laugh heartily and loudly more than once during those darkest days. To me he had three distinct smiles. The first was when speaking he seemed to wish to impress you with the interest he had in you. This smile was very faint, but beautiful and bewitching. The second was much more open and broad, and when listening to another speak. The laughter came when that other turned a humorous point, and particularly when that point was turned against the President. Of the third smile I shall speak in a moment.

It was not my pleasure to know Mrs. Lincoln personally, but I saw her many times under varied circumstances. She was a much maligned and misunderstood woman.

For many months, during the war, I acted as a volunteer visiting day nurse in the hospitals in Washington and Georgetown. I assisted the regular nurses, and occasionally helped the surgeons, and did my little bit to cheer the sick and wounded. So that I saw some things that the public could not see. Many times I saw Mrs. Lincoln come to those hospitals, go through the wards distributing flowers, little gifts, kind words, smiles, and sympathy to the suffering heroes. And these little acts were done in a manner that, it would seem to me, they could not have been done except by one whose whole heart was in the cause and in the same way as that of her husband, and whose love and active help were given freely and sincerely to those suffering boys in blue.

It was on similar occasions that I was enabled to note that third smile on Mr. Lincoln's face, of which I have spoken. He also came to the hospitals frequently, sometimes with his wife, but usually alone, when I saw him.

As he alighted from his carriage and entered the building, particularly toward the end of the war, I was impressed by the sadness of his countenance. It seemed as though all the suffering in that hospital had come out to meet him and had entered into his face. As he went along the rows of cots, pausing here and there and leaning over some especially suffering lad to speak a kind word or two, the sadness of his face did not entirely disappear, but over it came a light and such a bright, cheering, though gentle smile that his whole countenance was illumined by something more than human interest, as sympathy and love came out to the boy, from his very soul. Those were some of the times when I felt that no one could see in that charming face anything except beauty.

• • • •

On the night of April 14, 1865, I was nowhere near Ford's Theatre. We were living then in the old home on North B Street, Capitol Hill. Everything was so quiet there that we did not hear of the tragedy of the night until the next morning. As soon as possible I went down to the neighborhood of the theatre. What surprised me most was the smallness of the crowd gathered there at that time. I had no difficulty in moving about close to the steps of the house opposite, where the remains of the President still lay. I stood very close to those steps until finally there came out that little band of mourners and gently placed the body of the murdered President in the hearse.

What surprised me most, as I think of that day, was the small number of followers that accompanied that sad little procession. There were so few people that followed, I was able to walk close to the carriages and at times I was so near that I could have laid my hand on the wheel of the hearse. I followed all the way to the White House grounds. Nor did the crowd increase to any great proportions, as we neared the end.

At the east gate of the White House, there were soldiers and no one was admitted to the grounds. I had gone a little ahead and stood on the pavement close to the gate. This absence of a great crowd on such an occasion was not due to any want of interest or sympathy, but was rather caused, as it seemed to me, by the terrible shock that had passed over the city, and because every one was so depressed that but few had the desire to rush forward to form or join a crowd. Those on the sidewalks stopped and with bowed and uncovered heads stood still in silence and grief. That there were so few gathered at the gate of the White House grounds, this little incident will show.

I had pushed forward and taken my place on the sidewalk close to the carriageway, and turning to look at the little funeral cortège approaching, I saw an old negro woman, a typical Southern cook, her head wrapped in a red-and-yellow bandanna, and her large blue-and-white kitchen apron still on, come running across the street. She passed in front of the hearse and had no difficulty in taking her place beside me within two feet of where it would pass.

Even at that early hour the negroes of the capital had been stunned, then driven to almost frenzy, by the rumor that now Mr. Lincoln was dead they would all be put back into slavery.

As the little procession passed in, great tears rolled down the cheeks of that old negress, and she gathered her big apron over her face and sobbed aloud. Then there seemed to come to her soul a great light and a great courage. She dropped her apron and said in a firm though broken voice: "They needn't to crow yet. God ain't dead!"

NOTES

INTRODUCTION

"Lincoln, the Man of the People," by Edwin Markham. Published in
Poems of American History, by Burton Egbert-Stevenson (Boston:
Houghton Mifflin, 1908), p. 349. Illustration: Photo (Grant Anniversary). *Century Magazine*, February 1909, p. 495. Original texts owned
by Joe Wheeler.

"It Took Over 150 Years," by Joseph Leininger Wheeler © 2012.

PART ONE: THE FRONTIER YEARS

"Once to Every Man and Nation," by James Russell Lowell. Published
in the December 11, 1844, *Boston Courier* as "Verses Suggested by the
Present Crisis"; in 1845 it was published in a pamphlet as *The Present
Crisis*. Reprinted by Thomas Bird Mosher in Portland, Maine, 1918.
Illustration: October 7, 1858, photo taken after Galesburg, Illinois,
debate. *Century*, 1909, p. 481. Original texts owned by Joe Wheeler.

"Countdown to the Civil War," by Joseph Leininger Wheeler © 2012.

"How Lincoln Paid for His First Book," by Earle H. James. Published
in *The Youth's Instructor*, February 12, 1924. Reprinted by permission

of Joe Wheeler (P.O. Box 1246, Conifer, CO 80433) and Review and.
Herald Publishing, Hagerstown, MD 21740. Illustration: *The Life of
Abraham Lincoln for Young People*, by Harriet Putnam (New York:
McLoughlin Bros., 1905), frontispiece. Original text owned by Joe
Wheeler.

"Childhood in Lincoln's Town," by Octavia Roberts Corneau. Published
in *The Youth's Companion*, February 5, 1925. Illustration: *Century
Magazine*, January 1887, p. 388. Original texts owned by Joe Wheeler.

"He Loved Me Truly," by Bernadine Bailey and Dorothy Walworth.
Reprinted with permission from *Reader's Digest*. Copyright © 1945
by the Reader's Digest Association, Inc. Illustration: *Our Young Folks*,
February 1873, p. 150. Original text owned by Joe Wheeler.

PART TWO: CIVIL WAR—THE EARLY YEARS
"Three Hundred Thousand More," by James Sloan Gibbons. Included
in Stevenson, *Poems of American History*, p. 440. Illustration: Paint-
ing, "Drafting the Emancipation Proclamation," by F. Walter
Taylor. *Scribner's*, February 1916, p. 132. Original texts owned by Joe
Wheeler.

"Stalemate," by Joseph Leininger Wheeler © 2012.

"When Lincoln Passed," by Mabel McKee. Published in *The Youth's
Instructor*, February 4, 1930. Reprinted by permission of Joe Wheeler
(P.O. Box 1246, Conifer, CO 80433), Review and Herald Publishing, Hagerstown, MD 21740, and Fleming H. Revell, a division of
Baker Book House. Illustration: *The True Story of Abraham Lincoln*,
by Eldridge S. Brooks (Boston: Lothrop, 1896), p. 157. Original text
owned by Joe Wheeler.

"The Strength Conquered," by T. Morris Longstreth. Published in *St. Nicholas*, February 1924. Illustration, p. 351. Original text owned by Joe Wheeler.

"More than His Share," Author Unknown. If anyone knows the author, original source and date, or author's next of kin, please send to Joe Wheeler (P.O. Box 1246, Conifer, CO 80433). Illustration: Brooks, *The True Story of Abraham Lincoln,* p. 229. Original text owned by Joe Wheeler.

"Boys in the White House," by Ruth Painter Randall and Joseph Leininger Wheeler. I am deeply indebted to the late Ruth Painter Randall, for had she not written her insightful book, *Lincoln's Sons* (Boston: Little, Brown, 1955), pp. 44, 71–87, this chapter would not have been possible. Included in Joe Wheeler's *Abraham Lincoln: A Man of Faith and Courage* (New York: Howard/Simon & Schuster, 2008). Illustration: Brooks, *The True Story of Abraham Lincoln*, p. 157. Original texts owned by Joe Wheeler.

"The Tall Stranger," by Arthur Somerset. If anyone knows the original source and date of this old story, or author's next of kin, please send to Joe Wheeler (P.O. Box 1246, Conifer, CO 80433).

"The Missionary Money," by Olive Vincent Marsh. Published in *St. Nicholas*, February 1918. Illustration: p. 303. Original text owned by Joe Wheeler.

"Just Folks," by Mary Wells. Published in *Youth's Companion*, February 3, 1921. Illustration: p. 67. Original text owned by Joe Wheeler.

"The Sleeping Sentinel," by L. E. Chittenden. Published in Chittenden's *Recollections of President Lincoln and His Administration* (New York:

Harper & Brothers, 1891), pp. 40–46. Illustration: *Youth's Companion,* February 4, 1892, p. 59. Original texts owned by Joe Wheeler.

"Lincoln and the Little Drummer Boy," by Roe L. Hendrick. Published in *Youth's Companion,* February 7, 1901. Illustration: Brooks, *The True Story of Abraham Lincoln,* p. 226. Original texts owned by Joe Wheeler.

"Only a Mother," Author Unknown. Published in *The Review and Herald,* n.d. Reprinted by permission of Joe Wheeler (P.O. Box 1246, Conifer, CO 80433) and Review and Herald Publishing Association, Hagerstown, MD 21740. Illustration: *Century Magazine,* January 1887, p. 370. Original text owned by Joe Wheeler.

"A Schoolboy's Interview with Abraham Lincoln," by William Agnew Paton. Published in *Scribner's Magazine,* December 1913. Illustration: *Century Magazine,* June 1897, p. 185. Statue of Abraham Lincoln in Lincoln Park, Chicago. Engraved by J. H. E. Whitney. Original texts owned by Joe Wheeler.

PART THREE: CIVIL WAR—THE LATER YEARS
"Battle-Hymn of the Republic," by Julia Ward Howe. Stevenson, *Poems of American History,* p. 384. Illustration: Gardner Civil War photograph. *Century Magazine,* June 1900, p. 274. Original texts owned by Joe Wheeler.

"High Tide at Gettysburg," by Joseph Leininger Wheeler © 2012.

"Across the Great Plains Just to See Lincoln," by Caroline B. Parker. Published in *St. Nicholas,* February 1926. Illustration: from *Outing Magazine,* 1906, in Joe Wheeler collection. Original text owned by Joe Wheeler.

"A Lesson in Forgiveness," by T. Morris Longstreth. Published in *St. Nicholas*, February 1923. Illustration: p. 338. Original text owned by Joe Wheeler.

"Ransom's Papers," by Mary Wells. Published in *Youth's Companion*, May 25, 1911. Illustration: *Great Stories Remembered III*, by Joe Wheeler (Wheaton, IL: Focus on the Family/Tyndale House, 2000), p. 78. Original texts owned by Joe Wheeler.

"Tad Lincoln," by Wayne Whipple. Published in *The Youth's Instructor*, February 8, 1927. Reprinted by permission of Joe Wheeler (P.O. Box 1246, Conifer, CO 80433) and Review and Herald Publishing Association, Hagerstown, MD 21740. Illustration: Alexander K. McClure, *"Abe" Lincoln's Yarns and Stories* (Chicago: Thompson & Tomas, 1901), p. 136. Original text owned by Joe Wheeler.

"The Heart of Lincoln," by Louis B. Reynolds. Published in *The Youth's Instructor*, November 20, 1956. Reprinted by permission of Joe Wheeler (P.O. Box 1246, Conifer, CO 80433) and Review and Herald Publishing Association, Hagerstown, MD 21740. Illustration: *Century Magazine*, 1886–87, p. 249. Original text owned by Joe Wheeler.

"The Perfect Tribute," by Mary Raymond Shipman Andrews. Published in *Scribner's*, July 1906. Illustration: p. 1a. Original text owned by Joe Wheeler.

"Mary Bowman, of Gettysburg," by Elsie Singmaster. Published in *Harper's Magazine,* October 1912. Illustration: p. 709. Original text owned by Joe Wheeler.

"Tad Lincoln's Goat," by Seth Harmon. Published in *Young People's Weekly*, February 8, 1948. Reprinted by permission of Joe Wheeler (P.O. Box 1246, Conifer, CO 80433) and David C. Cook, Colorado

Springs, CO 80918. Illustration: *Century*, November 1890, p. 1. Original texts owned by Joe Wheeler.

"President Lincoln's Visiting Card," by John M. Bullock. Published in *Century Magazine*, February 1898. Illustration: *Century Magazine*, September 1897, p. 736. Original texts owned by Joe Wheeler.

"Tenderness in a Ruined City," by Louis B. Reynolds. Published in *The Youth's Instructor*, September 20, 1956. Reprinted by permission of Joe Wheeler (P.O. Box 1246, Conifer, CO 80433) and Review and Herald Publishing Association, Hagerstown, MD 21740. Illustration: William A. Stoddard, *Abraham Lincoln* (New York: Fords, Howard & Hulbert, 1876) p. 453. Original text owned by Joe Wheeler.

"Memory of Lincoln," by Carla Brown. Published in *The Young People's Weekly*, February 7, 1943. Reprinted by permission of Joe Wheeler (P.O. Box 1246, Conifer, CO 80433) and David C. Cook, Colorado Springs, CO 80918. Illustration: Putnam, *The Life of Abraham Lincoln for Young People*, p. 128a. Original texts owned by Joe Wheeler.

PART FOUR: TO LIVE ON IN HEARTS IS NOT TO DIE
"O Captain! My Captain!" by Walt Whitman. Stevenson, *Poems of American History*, p. 537. Illustration: *Scribner's*, October 1919, p. 424. Original texts owned by Joe Wheeler.

"The Living Myth," by Joseph Leininger Wheeler © 2012.

"A Boy Who Loved Lincoln," by Kathleen Read Coontz. Published in *St. Nicholas*, February 1927. Illustration: p. 257. Original text owned by Joe Wheeler.

"A Decision That Took Courage," by John L. Roberts. Published in *Youth's Instructor*, July 3, 1934. Reprinted by permission of Joe

Wheeler (P.O. Box 1246, Conifer, CO 80433) and Review and
Herald Publishing Association, Hagerstown, MD 21740. Illustration:
Century, February 1909, p. 501. Healy portrait was painted from
sketches made at City Point early in 1865. Original text owned by
Joe Wheeler.

"Captain, My Captain," by Elizabeth Frazer. Published in *Scribner's*,
February 1912. Illustration: p. 23. Original text owned by Joe
Wheeler.

"Abraham Lincoln's Rose," by Isabel Nagel. If anyone can provide
information about the original source, date, and author's next of kin,
please send to Joe Wheeler (P.O. Box 1246, Conifer, CO 80433). Illustration: *Youth's Companion*, February 12, 1903, p. 74. Original text
owned by Joe Wheeler.

"He Knew Lincoln," by Ninde Harris. Published in *Youth's Instructor*,
February 1, 1931. Reprinted by permission of Joe Wheeler (P.O. Box
1246, Conifer, CO 80433) and Review and Herald Publishing, Hagerstown, MD 21740. Illustration: pen portrait made from photos by
Wyatt Eaton, engraved by Timothy Cole, in 1877, *Century*, February
1909, p. 492.

"Mr. Lincoln, I Love You," by M. L. O'Hara. Published in *Sunshine
Magazine*, February 1963. Reprinted by permission of Garth Hen-
richs and Sunshine Press. Illustration: *Harper's*, July 1894, p. 197.
Original texts owned by Joe Wheeler.

EPILOGUE

"Personal Memories of Abraham Lincoln," by Robert Brewster Stanton. Published in *Scribner's Magazine*, July 1920, p. A-1. Illustration:
frontispiece for July 1920 issue of the magazine. Original text owned
by Joe Wheeler.